THE WISDOM OF ANTS

Shankar Jaganathan is passionate about economic history, sustainability practices and corporate governance. A chartered accountant and law graduate, he has varied experience in corporate, academic and social sectors in a career spanning twenty-five years. A select list of the entities and institutions he is/was associated with includes Wipro, Azim Premji Foundation, Indian Institute of Science, Union Bank of India, Oxfam India and Narsee Monjee Institute of Management Studies. He currently divides his time between corporate consulting for rapidly growing entities, teaching, research and writing. He is also an independent director on the boards of Indian corporates and NGOs, and teaches at leading management schools.

Shankar is the author of *Corporate Disclosures: 1553-2007: The Origin of Financial and Business Reports*, published by Routledge in 2008. This book was selected by the Indian Society of Training and Development, New Delhi for commendation in 2010 and was awarded a cash prize.

THE WISDOM OF ANTS

A Short History of Economics

SHANKAR JAGANATHAN

First published by Tranquebar, an imprint of westland ltd, in 2012

Published by Westland Business, an imprint of Westland Books, a division of Nasadiya Technologies Private Limited, in 2024

No. 269/2B, First Floor, 'Irai Arul', Vimalraj Street, Nethaji Nagar, Alapakkam Main Road, Maduravoyal, Chennai 600095

Westland, the Westland logo, Westland Business and the Westland Business logo are the trademarks of Nasadiya Technologies Private Limited, or its affiliates.

ISBN: 9789360456702

10 9 8 7 6 5 4 3 2

Typeset by Ram Das Lal, New Delhi
Printed at Saurabh Printers Pvt. Ltd

Dedicated to

Mr Azim Premji,
The Visionary Philanthropist.

Actions speak louder than words.

Contents

Foreword

Critics of the capitalist model have long been concerned about economics dominating all aspects of our lives and crowding out other important considerations, be they social, political or ethical in nature. This extreme economic focus is seen to reduce the humane connect between individuals in a society and make them less responsible to each other. The widening income and wealth disparity, coupled with a deep social divide, has only heightened the anxiety of these critics. On the other hand, there are people who have been blind supporters of the capitalist, free-market model, believing it to be the path to all kinds of well-being.

The 2008 financial crisis has certainly prompted many to re-examine the basic premises of the prevailing economic models. Even people in the extremities of the two camps have been engaged in debate and exploration.

As an interested observer not belonging to either of these groups, I have often wondered if economics is a subject that should be left to the specialists. Economics no longer deals with technical issues that touch the periphery of our lives, and that can be left to the sole care of specialists. By impacting human life in multiple ways and at multiple points, I think economics has come into the popular domain uninvited. Given its entry, I believe every individual has an obligation to think for themselves and contribute to setting a basic economic agenda for their society.

The choice between alternative economic paths is quite sharp and has a significant influence on most important issues in society. In addition, the alternatives are built on very distinct foundations. At the core, the choices revolve around finding the balance between a few key issues: for example, promoting self-interest vs. altruistic behaviour as the primary driver in society; creating a competitive vs. cooperative environment; choosing between the social good and individual good; and using economics with the definiteness of a physical science vs. the tentativeness of a social science. As is apparent, these are difficult and complex choices.

There is certainly helpful reading material available for any 'non-economist' to think through these issues, but not much of this material has the historical sweep of Shankar Jagnathan's book, *The Wisdom of Ants: A Short History of Economics*.

The Wisdom of Ants is a book on the 'philosophy' of economics, which is panoramic in view, historical in approach and conceptual in nature. By looking at a long time-span of three millennia, and across all major civilizations, cutting across diverse ideologies and relating them to the challenges of the twenty-first century, this book fills a critical gap in our popular discourse. While this book may not provide any new or definite answers, and each one of us may have different views on the issues, it does raise a set of relevant questions and captures alternative approaches in answering them. I liked in particular the narration of historical episodes: resolving the value paradox, the three contests between the demand-side economists and their supply-side counterparts spread over two centuries, and the birth of the Nordic economic model. The simplicity of these narrations, rich in detail and strong on emotions makes them memorable and conceptually vivid.

I commend this book to all interested citizens who want to form their own views on economic issues rather than borrow the views of others (despite the fame or renown of their proponents). I think forming our own views, and not borrowing those of others is at the core of creating a thinking society, which in turn is at the core of creating a better society. So, even on economic issues, we must take up this responsibility of thinking and forming our own views, and not 'outsource' it to the professional economists. This is not to say that amateurs (like me) should be deciding the mechanics of the economic system or driving it. But as interested and affected parties we definitely have the right, if not the duty to set the charter for the economics professionals.

The charter that I personally subscribe to is the development of a just, equitable, humane and sustainable society and I hope that the economists (and everyone else) consider this seriously.

Azim Premji
Bangalore

Introduction

'It is the story that matters, not just the ending.'

— Paul Lockhart

A strange paradox is at play. Contrary to the expectations of many who view the emergence of economics as an answer to the problems of scarcity, this discipline rather than decreasing in importance with the wealth at our command, has increased. Not only has its prominence grown, but economics is also invading other spheres of human life. Garry Becker, the Nobel laureate, said, '"Economic imperialism" is probably a good description of what I do.' This comment was in the context of his work on examining issues like marriage and the decision to have children using an economic lens. By equating the decision to have children with buying consumer durables, he imperialistically expanded the domain of economics by shrinking the scope of other social sciences.

The increasing influence of economics in many spheres of human life is not a fringe phenomenon, and has slowly but surely influenced mainstream thinking. Stemming from this is the widespread support for ideas that place the market as the primary decision-making apparatus in society. Given this increased importance accorded to the economic lens in viewing human life, it is worth examining the factors that have led to this situation. *The Wisdom of Ants* attempts to trace the journey of economics from relative obscurity to its current dominant role in human history.

The evolution of *Homo economicus* as we travel back in time is fascinating. We see that many concepts which are widely accepted today, were previously ignored, criticized, discouraged and scorned. Similarly, the importance given today to economic issues such as promoting personal wealth creation, was absent in the past as multiple other ethical, religious and social considerations clamoured for mindshare. The rise of economic issues above the maze of ethical, religious and conceptual hurdles over the last three millennia is captured in the first part of the book. The three main concepts – private property, social sanction for self-centred individualism and a materialistic outlook – are marked as the key features that elevated economics to its current dominant status.

The notion of private property emerged in spite of the ethical obligation to share without receiving anything in kind. Further, unlike the animal kingdom where only possession is recognized, the idea of titles to property surfaced in human society. The title holders derived benefits even in the absence of possession, providing an incentive for enterprising individuals to exert more in order to gain property and have a comfortable life. This was perhaps the birth of entrepreneurship.

As some individuals accumulated wealth, religious mandates laid a duty of charity on them, to share their surplus wealth with their less-resourceful brethren. Lending and borrowing would have been an acceptable alternative to charity, as they would have protected vulnerable human life without making unilateral transfers. However, prevailing religious practices often prohibited receiving interest on loans, thereby limiting lending. Interest was seen as usury, a sin that represented uncharitable behaviour by the lender.

Nevertheless, human beings are innovative. In the middle of the second millennium, human ingenuity came up with logic to justify interest payments, marking a prominent way in which self-centred behaviour became socially sanctioned.

Concurrently, this diluted the religious mandate to support brethren. Permitting interest payments further accelerated wealth generation. Greater wealth translated to an increase in demand for the quality, quantity and variety of goods and services. By itself this may not have led to anything significant, but for the emergence of a new philosophy that quantified happiness and equated it to the utility of the goods and services consumed. This propelled economics to the centre stage of social debates.

How can a single book encompass all the ideas and history of a discipline as diverse as economics? It may not be possible, yet a brief, multi-faceted canvassing of this discipline's history can help us understand some of the most important ideas in economics and economic thinking. More importantly, it can provide the backdrop to the evolution of economic ideas over the course of human history, something which is dealt with extensively in the second part of this book.

Initially, economics began to come into its own as a realm of ideas in related disciplines like ethics and public administration. As we examine the period 400 BCE to 1500 CE for economic ideas, we discover that private property was accepted, but social consent for self-centred individualistic behaviour was not yet conceded. The diversity of ideas that confront us is staggering. In the four prominent civilizations — Greek, Indian, Chinese and Islamic — where economics never emerged as a distinct discipline, economic issues were closely examined. Economics was more philosophy, as ideas about exchange of goods, happiness, wealth, inequity and statehood dominated this thinking. The writings nearest in nature to economics by one prominent thinker from each civilization are taken as representative of its prevailing economic ideas. While Aristotle, the philosopher, and Ibn Khaldun, the historian, examined the life of an individual, Kautilya and Lord Shang, both political advisors, were engaged in identifying the principles for managing a kingdom. In these writings the seeds of economic ideas are visible, developing later in a more nourishing environment where the social sanction for a self-centred individual was provided. Within these writings themselves, where self-centred behaviour was considered, economic ideas become more distinct.

Despite the absence of what we today see as hardcore economics, these writings are extremely important as they debate the more ignored issues in economics today: human happiness, unequal wealth distribution and the social safety net. These debates were not just confined to these four civilizations; they were widespread and prevailed in other parts of the world too.

In the five-hundred-year-long period starting in the tenth century, material prosperity in Europe accelerated, leaving the rest of the world behind. In a unique trend, European GDP for the first time grew much faster than the population growth. A probable source for this acceleration lies in the beginning of royal sanction for monopolies, which were earlier viewed as unethical as they were held to be socially unfair. This marked a major shift, as monopolies gained social respectability with the royal sanction. As the right to grant monopolies in England moved from the monarch to the parliament, pamphlets mobilizing support to monopolies mushroomed, flourishing not just in England, but across Europe. There were the first writings that are predominantly economic in nature. Clothed in national interest, self-centred behaviour took an acceptable, patriotic form. Adam Smith, with the comprehensive effort of 25 years of toil, collated the main economic arguments prevailing across major European countries to present a cohesive doctrine which allowed the pursuit of self-interest, giving birth to economics as a formal discipline. Many would argue that capitalism began then, an idea that this book explores in detail.

As trade in communities and economic exchange between nations increased in Europe it became the epicentre of novel economic ideas. From 1776 to 1929, Adam Smith's doctrine of self-interest shook the foundation of Utopian ideas that had prized altruism for thousands of years. In an interesting twist, Smith himself attributed success in the marketplace to sympathy, an emotion akin to altruism. He noted that in trade – which represents voluntary exchange among participants – success is achieved only by stepping into the shoes of the other party and valuing their needs. In showing the benefits of voluntary exchanges, Smith brought markets to the centre-stage. With markets came the idea of price, and accompanying this was the interesting paradox of the disconnect between price and value. The concept of utility that emerged in explaining this paradox placed economics on a firm footing as a subject worthy of study in the universities.

The centre of gravity shifted from Europe to North America in the twentieth century. At the same time, the focus too shifted from the study of individual market players to the behaviour of the market itself. The trigger for this change was the collapse of economic activity in the 1930s triggered by the New York stock market crash in 1929. This crisis reignited a century-old debate between two opposing schools of thought: the demand-side economists and the supply-side economists. Impelled by the presence of large pockets of poverty flourishing in the midst of the unprecedented prosperity generated by the Industrial Revolution, Simon de Sismonde, the nineteenth-century French economist, questioned the ability of markets to resolve this challenge and suggested active government intervention.

However, he was up against his compatriot, Jean Baptiste Say, who argued that the market was the only path to economic prosperity. This debate continued in the twentieth century with Keynes and Hayek representing the opposing sides and developing the logic proposed by their predecessors. In the twenty-first century too, this unresolved debate continues as the opposing schools slug it out while developing a plan to revive the US economy in the aftermath of the 'Great Recession' of 2008. This hat-trick over the three centuries of debates forms the fifth chapter of the book.

An important point to consider is how the market economy managed to assert its dominance in such a short period. The process by which free-market advocates from the supply-side economics school achieved comprehensive victory in the last three decades of the twentieth century has hinged around the institution of the 'Nobel' Prize for Economics. It can be seen that, over the last four decades, economic theories advocating free markets were rewarded and reinforced by the 'Nobel' Prize awards. As markets assumed importance, the most active of all markets, the financial market, and its fastest growing segment, the derivatives market, were then given a prophetic status as the barometer of future economic outlook in directing economic initiatives across the globe. A corollary to this development was the neglect of alternate thoughts and ideas that could have provided some restraint to this unfettered run of market economics, which came to a crashing halt with the 'Great Recession' of 2008. The cachet of winning the 'Nobel' prize appears to have subtly overshadowed the importance of looking at empirical evidence in substantiating individual viewpoints about how economic matters could be handled.

For the first time in the beginning of the nineteenth century, due to many factors such as a radical shift in the English Poor Law, labour began to be priced in the market based on its demand and supply, which decided the wages in urban centres. Prior to this, human subsistence was not directly related to wages, as families lived in rural settings with free access to many natural resources like land, water and forests that provided them with many essential goods for life. Increased urbanization witnessed greater freedom for the masses, along with a dilution of social bonds and safety nets, which on many occasions turned out to be 'iron' cages. A visible impact of this change was in factories that employed young children and women for long hours in often inhuman conditions. A few individuals sensitive to these changes questioned the ability of markets and private property to erase these social problems, leading to Socialism, a new school of thought. With socialism as the leitmotif, many ideas mushroomed in response to large-scale human misery. Socialism soon turned into a broad term with several interpretations linking it to Communism at one end and Gandhian socialism at the other. What all these schools had in common was a belief that private property, self-centred behaviour and a materialistic outlook needed to be curbed, if not totally eliminated. At the birth of the twenty-first century, it looked as if Socialism was a failed idea, as the Soviet Union had collapsed and China was increasingly adopting a capitalistic path, leaving no options for Socialism's supporters. However, the economic crisis of 2008 has revived the hopes of many socialists. This book discusses the relevance of Socialism in current times and tries to explore its potential manifestations.

The idea that any historical analysis is entirely objective is flawed. A writer is by no means free or without prejudice and an awareness of one's own preconceived notions is perhaps the first semblance of objectivity. Furthermore, the reader's ability to filter what is presented is another significant factor. It is with this belief that I seek to identify the three basic economic challenges of the twenty-first century, the circumstances under which they emerged and the attempts made to overcome them. The first of these challenges is the increasing disparity in income and wealth between different sections of the population. At its most basic level, this is visible in the fact of over a billion people starving with inadequate nutrition on one hand and another billion people fighting obesity, as a consequence of consuming excess calories; all this in a population of less than seven billion. The balance between individual responsibility and social duty for the wellbeing of the vulnerable sections of society, especially the children, the aged, the sick and the unemployed is the second challenge. The third and the final challenge is of finding a true indicator for measuring economic progress, as the choice of what and how we choose to measure reflects what we truly value. Though conceded by all as an inadequate measure, if not an inappropriate one, the computation of GDP, which only measures economic activity and not human welfare, continues to rule the roost. This is well illustrated in the current fight against an economic slump, where the primary focus seems to be reviving GDP growth, rather than looking at the human cost of the downturn. Between the two extremes of Communism, which negates private property, and capitalism, which celebrates it, there are other experiments we can learn from. It appears that the answers do not lie in extremes – they rarely do.

To conclude, if this book succeeds in enhancing the reader's appreciation of the long journey of economics from much before it formally came to be called by that name, its under-currents and cross-currents, its relation to other disciplines, the personalities who shaped its thinking and the central role that it plays in our lives today, I would consider my job partially done. On the other hand, should a segment of readers review the current importance given to economics and the role of markets in resolving social issues, I would feel my efforts are more than adequately rewarded.

PART 1: The Origin

For a thorough understanding of economics, one needs to look at the basic prerequisites which led to its birth. The three basic ideas that laid the foundation for economics as a distinct discipline in the eighteenth century are: private property or individual ownership; social sanction for individuals to be self-centred and material acquisition being the measure of welfare. The first part of this book outlines the origin and evolution of these three critical ideas.

These three basic ideas are an inherent part of mainstream economic thought and tend to be taken for granted. However, they are by no means undisputed. They have been challenged repeatedly during periods of economic crisis because of the social costs involved in maintaining their ubiquity. As the economic crisis of the moment subsides, these debates decline in intensity and the challengers do not make any significant dent in the acceptability of these ideas, hence they continue to rule the economic world. Therefore, it is useful for any individual interested in understanding economics to specifically trace the evolution of these three ideas and the reasons for their enduring importance.

Chapter 1

Need Legs to Stand: The Basic Prerequisites

He who has not first laid his foundations may be able with great ability to lay them afterwards, but they will be laid with trouble to the architect and danger to the building.

– Niccolo Machiavelli in *The Prince*

Economics emerged as a distinct subject only in the last three hundred years, as a consequence of three distinct concepts gradually becoming socially acceptable: personal property, self-centred individualism and material consumption as the standard way to measure welfare. The origin and evolution of these concepts, which led to the development of economics as a distinct discipline, is examined here. Starting with the nexus between scarcity, private property and economics, we examine the absence of private property in hunter-gatherer societies. Thereafter, the link between agriculture and the advent of private property is outlined. While tracing the second prerequisite, that is, the growing social sanction for self-centredness amongst individuals, we need to also examine the link between religion and altruism. Here, by studying the religious injunction against usury and later, how usury was justified, we see that this led to the legitimization of profit-making in a way that patently sanctioned self-centred behaviour and latently approved human greed. The final prerequisite of measuring welfare by the amount of material consumption is seen via the phenomenon of urbanization, the advent of patents which contributed to mass-produced luxury goods and the development of a new philosophy, Utilitarianism, that provided a method to quantify and rank happiness.

The Land of No Winter

'We have been turned out of paradise. We have neither eternal life nor unlimited means of gratification'[1] Lionel Robbins, the British economist, remarked in 1932. He continued further in the same vein and defined economics as 'the science which studies human behaviour as a relationship between ends and scarce means which have alternative uses.'[2] This definition is often popularly shortened to the phrase 'limited means, unlimited wants'. Was there a time in human history when wants were limited, but the means to satisfy them were not? If yes, this era would be the time before the notion of economics was born.

Our search for the era of limited wants, but not limited means, can take us to two contrasting places. One is in Paradise, which is said to have no material constraints, and the other, on our Planet at a time when the wants were so little that the available means looked abundant. Here we follow Marshall Sahlins, who called hunter-gatherer economies 'The Original Affluent Societies'. He observed:

> The hunter, one is tempted to say, is "uneconomic man". At least as concerns non-subsistence goods, he is [the] reverse of that standard caricature immortalized in any General Principles of Economics, page one. His wants are scarce and his means (in relation) plentiful.[3]

By this definition, the hunter-gatherer era could be seen as the pre-economics era. This era would have begun with the appearance of humans at around 1 million BCE. From then, till the advent of agriculture, in around 10,000 BCE, humans lived as hunter-gatherers. This was the form of life for about 99 per cent of human existence on this planet.

Hunter-gatherers lived in communal groups with anywhere from 20 to 100 members. These groups were characterized by a basic division of labour between hunters and gatherers[a], free access to resources, simple tools, and the need to make limited efforts to meet their current requirements. Some view this lifestyle as idyllic. Unlike the grasshopper in Aesop's fable of 'The Ant and Grasshopper'[b], the hunter-gatherers lived in a land with no 'winter' and so could afford to live with no thought to meeting tomorrow's needs today. But what could have prompted humans to emulate the ant after following the grasshopper for over 990,000 years?

The Wisdom of the Ant

Two distinct traits marked hunter-gatherer societies: the absence of storage as a concept and regular food sharing within the group. To the modern economic mind, both these traits look like extremely foolish behaviour – a failure to realize the benefits from both storage and hoarding to the individual. Researchers in the twentieth century have tried to analyze

---

a   An influential conference held in Chicago in 1966 titled 'Man the Hunter', examined the division of labour in these societies. Their conclusion that the division of labour was based on a gender divide is now not unanimously accepted. The conference deliberations were later published as a book under the title *Man the Hunter* in 1968.

b   As the fable goes, in the summer, while the ant was busy gathering food for the barren winter, the grasshopper lived a carefree life. But when the winter came, the ant lived off its store while the grasshopper was left starving and lamented its absence of foresight.

hunter-gatherer societies by conducting observational studies, predominantly in Africa, Australia and South America. These studies range from observations spread over a few days/months to the Harvard-Kalahari Project covering a period of 27 years from 1963 to 1991.[4]

These studies have attributed regular food-sharing amongst hunter-gatherer groups to one of four causes, namely mutualism, nepotism, reciprocity and tolerated theft.[5] One view of the motive for mutualism is the need for cooperation in hunting-gathering pursuits – essentially a team activity. Food sharing promotes the sustained cooperation required for successful hunting-gathering. Likewise, nepotism in the sharing of food among mates and their offspring is seen as a genetic trait critical for their survival. Reciprocal sharing insures the giver against an unproductive hunt in the future. Tolerated theft, the fourth and the last cause, is seen as the result of a sub-conscious cost-benefit analysis of defending surplus food.

A rational analysis for the absence of storage among hunter-gatherers may throw up ideas ranging from ignorance of storage benefits to the absence of storage techniques. However, some observational studies have found Tanzanian hunter-gatherer groups like the Hadza knew how to preserve meat by drying it, but they did not choose to do so.[6] In addition they were also observed consuming meat incrementally over the period of a week, disproving the hypothesis that they had not thought of the benefits of consuming food over a period of time, that is, essentially holding on to it for later. It is important to explore whether these hunter-gatherers were driven purely by an altruistic motive or had an alternative rationale for their food-sharing practices.

Analyzing the hunter-gatherer economy using the lens of current economics can distort the picture, as the basic premise of limited means and unlimited wants that we take for granted today may not have held good, considering the limited needs of the people in this society. When this basic condition of scarcity is absent, as it was in the hunter-gatherer era, the viewing lens may also need a change. Since mobility is a primary asset in hunting and gathering, could the hunters, like jockeys in a horse race, be prioritizing light-footedness to enhance it? Could the hunter-gatherers be using the lens of mobility instead of scarcity for their decision making? The picture becomes clearer once we change our lens. Mobility is the prized quality, as scarcity does not present a challenge. Storage answers the scarcity challenge but hampers mobility. Not only does storage reduce mobility, it also requires committed resources to defend the store-house. On the other hand, sharing increases the mobility of the group by 'fueling' the entire team. Therefore in the hunter-gatherer economy storage could have been a liability and sharing a valued asset.

The rationale of mobility prevailed for almost 99 per cent of human history during which period hunting and gathering was the dominant lifestyle. It is also a matter of fact that for these 990,000 years, the standard of living remained more or less stagnant: the annual average individual consumption in this period increased by just one international dollar from $92 to $93 *(for a detailed computation see Box 1.1)*. The idyllic view of the hunter-gatherer lifestyle celebrates their egalitarian society, minimalist material needs, communal living and ecological balance in contrast to their stagnant standard of living.[7]

Box 1.1: Estimates of the Size of Global Economy & Annual Average Individual Consumption, 1 Million BCE to 2000 CE

Year	GDP International Dollar 1990 (Billion)	Annual Average Individual Consumption in International Dollars 1990	Population (Million)
1 Million BC	0.01	92	0.125
300,000 BC	0.09	92	1
25,000 BC	0.31	92	3.4
10,000 BC	0.37	93	4
1000 BC	6.35	127	50
1 AD	18.5	109	170
1000 AD	35.31	133	265
1500 AD	58.67	138	425
1600 AD	77.01	141	545
1700 AD	99.80	164	610
1800 AD	175.24	195	900
1900 AD	1,102.96	679	1,625
1950 AD	4,081.81	1,622	2,516
1960 AD	6,855.25	2,270	3,020
1970 AD	12,137.94	3,282	3,698
1980 AD	18,818.46	4,231	4,448
1990 AD	27,539.57	5,204	5,292
2000 AD	41,016.69	6,539	6,272

The table is a rough estimate of the size of the global economy and the average individual annual consumption over the human history made in 1998 by J. Bradford Delong, Professor in the Department of Economics, U.C. Berkeley. This estimate is in turn based on multiple other estimates, prominent among which are Kremer's population estimates, made in 1993, and Angus Maddison's GDP estimates made in 1995.

This computation starts with the global population as a given and the size of the economy derived thereafter. This is based on a positive correlation between population growth and increase in income levels, i.e. higher income translating to higher population growth rates due to affordability, as seen during the period from 1820 to 1950 CE. This correlation is applied to the beginning of human history. Population estimates for the earlier periods are computed by relating the pace of population growth to the population size.

These estimates are measured in international dollars, a hypothetical currency, which is based on what one US dollar could buy in different countries in 1990. The size of the economy in different years is estimated by computing the dollars required to buy the entirety of global consumption at the time.

The unabridged paper containing the estimates made by Prof. J. Bradford Delong, can be found in "Estimating World GDP, One Million BC," which is available at http://econ161.berkeley.edu/TCEH/1998_Draft/World_GDP/Estimating_World_GDP.html

Around 10,000 BCE, humans began to discover a new lifestyle – the agrarian way. At the heart of the agrarian lifestyle is the concept of storage – a part of the harvest from a prior crop is used to seed the next harvest and a granary is required to meet subsistence needs during the gestation period between seeding and harvesting. As a result, humans had to meet their daily requirements for survival not from the abundance of nature, which could usually provide for the limited needs of the hunter-gatherers, but from the limited store set aside in the granary.

The granary insured humans against starving on a futile hunt day. But in turn it demanded protection, not just by the might of its guards, but also by the social sanction of society. This social sanction gave birth to the concept of private property. Private property is chronologically the first of the three essential concepts that led to the development of economics as a distinct discipline. While the concept of private property arrived concurrently with the agrarian lifestyle, its rationale was articulated much later, when economics was being recognized as a distinct discipline.

The concept of property is different from possession. Tracing the need for this distinction could build a deeper understanding of economics. The logical point to start this journey is from its seed stage.

Seeding Private Property

Agriculture marks the birth of civilization and the break from savagery. Humans, who like other animals had lived off nature till then, began to influence their future through plant cultivation and animal husbandry. Did agriculture lead to the emergence of the concept of private property?[c] It seems so,

---

c   There is a school of thought that believes private property first emerged at the collective level of social groups like clans and family before it evolved to the level of individual ownership. This line of thinking however does not materially alter the sequence of how economics emerged as a distinct discipline.

as the concept of private property could not have held much relevance in the hunter-gatherer era for reasons which are quite apparent: they shared all their gains within the group without demanding an exchange in kind.

It is not that the hunters got their rewards without any effort. They had a wide variety of hunting techniques to obtain food. Their techniques varied with the environment and the choice of prey – but a common feature among different hunting techniques is the short time-lag between effort and reward. Hunting endeavours rarely extend beyond a day, in exceptional cases, a couple of days. It is only in the use of traps and nets that we see a larger time-lag between building the trap or net and gathering the prey. A key change from the hunter-gatherer lifestyle to the agricultural lifestyle is the time-lag between effort and reward. What was an exception in the hunter-gatherer lifestyle now became the rule in agrarian life.

The agrarian lifestyle requires tilling the soil, planting seeds, nourishing the crop and guarding the harvest before it can be reaped and consumed. This translates to a time-horizon ranging from a couple of weeks to a few months. An individual investing this effort needs to be assured that he or she will enjoy the fruits when the time comes. Or as John Ruskin, the famous English philosopher put it, 'that a man who works for a thing shall be allowed to get it, keep it and consume it in peace; and that he who does not eat his cake today shall be seen without grudging to have his cake tomorrow.'[8] This idea of an individual choosing their own time to eat the 'cake' embodies the concept of private property. Ungrudging consent to this is necessary for its acceptance by other members in the society.

The most logical explanation for private property was provided by John Locke, the seventeenth-century English philosopher. Locke traced the origin of private property to hunter-gatherer societies, building his reasoning from scratch: 'Though the earth and all inferior creatures be common to all men, yet every man has a property in his own person; this nobody has any right to but himself.'[9] From this base, Locke started with the individual, reasoning that the result of an individual's work is for his or her own benefit. Natural objects were common to all, but when invested with an individual's labour, they became that individual's private property. Using the analogy of a man eating an apple, Locke asked, 'when did they begin to be his?' He identified five moments of possible ownership: When the apple is digested in the man's stomach, when he ate it, when he boiled it, when he brought it home, when he picked it up. He then answers if picking it up does not make it his personal right, nothing else can. Elaborating further, Locke argues that though the apple is given in common to all of humanity, they are not each required to give consent to let the man make the apple his personal possession. Otherwise, people would starve with plenty around if this consent was essential.[10]

Locke used a different analogy to extend the concept of private property to the hunting sphere. Here he asked the question of whether a hare which is yet to be caught can be a private possession. Replying in the affirmative, he wrote '...being a beast that is still looked upon as common and no man's private possession, whoever has employed so much labour about any of that kind as to find and pursue her has thereby removed her from the state of nature wherein she was common, and has begun a property.'[11] This concept of private property as identified by Locke is validated by the practices followed for food-sharing among hunter-gatherer groups even in recent times. The 1990s observational study[12] among the Aka hunter-gatherers in North-eastern Congo showed that the onus to share the food is on the 'owner'. The 'owner' of a hunted prey was held to be the owner of the first spear that touched the animal even if it was not a fatal blow. The same principle was followed with traps and nets too. This 'owner' had the duty to share, following certain well-defined principles. The hunter who dealt the second blow was given the dorsal midriff. The hunter delivering the third blow was given the head. If the first blow was dealt with a borrowed spear, the borrower got the rump. The rest of the animal belonged to the 'owner' of the first spear with which the first blow was dealt. Based on this illustration, it looks as if the early justification for property was based on effort, and where many collaborated, a common agreement of the relative importance of their individual efforts gave rise to property rights.

Ownership in the Animal Kingdom

The concept of ownership is not uniquely restricted to humans but prevails amongst other species too. Studying ownership patterns in the animal kingdom can throw some light on the need for and the value of this distinct concept. The principle of ownership amongst several varieties of animals, birds and insects seems to be based on first occupancy. Occupancy can be seen as the first result of labour, as any further effort can be expended only after the place is occupied. This principle has been observed among animals and insects in the wild.

In an interesting piece of research involving wild horses living in their natural habitat in the Rachel Carson Estuarine Sanctuary in North Carolina, the ownership behaviour of these animals was observed in relation to water.[13] Water was scarce in this sanctuary. After heavy rainfall, fresh water would accumulate in pools, providing watering holes for horses. Bands of horses would stop at these pools to drink water. When one band occupied a pool, it would often be challenged by another band. Over 76 hours of observation involving 233 contests between bands were recorded. In these contests, 80 per cent of the time, the resident band prevailed. In the 20 per cent of the instances where the resident band lost, the raiders were larger in number. In the absence of might as a factor, occupancy seems to be the primary factor determining ownership. Similar contests were documented after studying butterflies and primates, and in all these observations, the incumbent prevailed. Multiple opinions exist as to why the incumbent prevails, but the most compelling logic is offered by the dove-hawk theory.[14]

The dove-hawk theory describes a contest between members of the same species exhibiting different behaviours. When two doves contest, both will posture a bit and each will have equal chance of success. When a dove and a hawk contest, the hawk will take the whole territory. But, when two hawks contest, the cost of the battle to the contestants will be more than the value of the territory in dispute. Maynard Smith, the proponent of this theory, showed that an evolutionarily stable strategy[d] is for all incumbents to behave like hawks and engage in a vicious battle, and all intruders to behave like doves. Subsequently, this theory was conclusively tested in a study involving butterflies in England.

The speckled wood butterfly is a species found near Oxford in England.[15] Male butterflies occupy shafts of sunlight under a tree canopy. At any time, only about 60 per cent of the male butterflies can find a sunny patch. Their presence in the sunlight increases their chance of finding a mate. Vacant spots are

---

d An evolutionarily stable strategy is one that ensures that the population of the species will grow. Possession of property at least cost will enable the species to grow and multiply. When two hawks contest, both pay a high price, impacting the ability of the species to grow and multiply.

immediately occupied. An incumbent of a sunny patch drives away intruders. In these instances, incumbents behaved like hawks and intruders like doves. However, when two butterflies were tricked into thinking they had each occupied the sunny patch first, the battle lasted on an average ten times longer than where a clear incumbent was recognized. Therefore, when two contestants believed they were the incumbent, it became a battle of hawks.

In the human world, unlike in the animal world, the right to property is not limited to possession alone. In addition to possession, there is the concept of title to property. A title to property entitles the beneficiary to the rewards of ownership even in the absence of possession. Such a concept seems to be absent in the animal kingdom. What could have led to this unique concept?

Let us look at a hypothetical situation in a village in approximately 5000 BCE. The village is inhabited by around fifty families. One day, there is news that a dangerous man-eating tiger is prowling around the village outskirts. The tiger has already destroyed cattle belonging to the villagers. One man in the village is renowned for his strength and fighting skills. But he, like the others, is working in his fields. The families affected by the tiger are not able to thwart it and continue to lose their cattle. It is a matter of time before the affected families come to the warrior requesting him to defend them. At this moment a major decision has to be taken by the villagers. If the warrior abandons his fields to fight the tiger, who will compensate him for the loss he will suffer in his fields? It is possible that our warrior gained the right to the property of his fields, even though he did not occupy or possess them, as he was engaged in 'social' duty. In return for the title to his property, he would pay wages to the individual who maintained his fields for him. Could this be the origin for the right to title or the right to property, as distinct from possession?

Box 1.2: The Right to Property

The Right to Property is different from the possession of property. Distinguishing between the two concepts of property and possession, P.J. Proudhon, the French economist, uses an illuminating analogy in his 1840 essay titled *What is Property? An Inquiry into the Principle of Right and of Government*. Looking at the relationship between two individuals engaged to be married, he noted that before marriage they only have a right to property, or a claim, on each other. It is only after marriage that they have both the claim and possession of each other.

While the right to property is universally recognized today, there is no consensus on its justification. About half a dozen theories have been advanced. Among the earliest and the most obvious justifications for private property is possession or occupancy. Cicero, the Roman philosopher, observed that the whole world is like a theatre. Anyone entering the theatre has the right to a seat. The sole condition is that they can only occupy a vacant seat, i.e. a seat not already occupied by another.

The second justification for private property, was advanced by Thomas Aquinas and is based on his observation of human nature. Aquinas saw in private property the primary motive for diligence and extra efforts in husbandry, innovation and care for wealth. This observation is reinforced by the fact that the absence of private property stalled material progress for 99 per cent of human history. It is only after the advent of private property that human civilization materially flourished.

The third justification that is more widely accepted today is the right of the labourer to the fruits of his or her labour. John Locke, the English philosopher, wrote that 'the earth and all inferior creatures are common to all men'. But every person has a property in their own person, which extends to the labour of their body and the work of their hands. An individual can remove what is common to all and make it his or her own by expending labour on that article, as discussed above.

The fourth justification, which forms the basis for the Universal Declaration of Human Rights by the United Nations, is that property is an inalienable right of human beings. This right is embedded in every human being and accrues to people just by virtue of being a human; it requires no other qualification. The right to live embeds within it the right to own the means of living.

In recent times, material progress depends more on intangible assets rather than tangible properties. For individuals to invest their time and effort in creating intangible assets requires protection through ideas like copyrights, patents and brands and their enforcement by law. Intellectual properties are titles without possession in the conventional sense, for there is nothing material to possess. The basis for their protection and enforcement is a result of legislation that is enacted by the peoples' representatives. Hence the fifth justification believes that property is a product of law.

Today there are multiple theories justifying private property (see Box 1.2). But the effect of private property on human welfare is a hotly-contested question. People who believe that efficiency can bring about welfare, support private property and want it defended. But others who see social welfare beyond the ambit of private property want curbs on it. This was a debate in which Locke, who provided the most logical justification for private property, had a specific viewpoint. For him, private property was not an unlimited right. It has well-defined limitations. He logically defined these limits using the analogy of fruits and nuts.

The Fruits and Nuts of Property

John Locke first gave a liberal definition of private property then sought to limit it. He asked the question: 'why has God given us the world in common?' – and answered it: 'to enjoy'. Continuing this line of reasoning, he identified the basis for the amount of property a man can own as: 'As much as anyone can make use of to any advantage of life before it **spoils**'[16].

Locke also identified that some goods were more enduring, such as nuts which last for a year, as compared to others, like fruits which rot within a week. Based on this identification, he laid down the limits of 'just property', that is, those things really useful to the life of a person. According to him, property is not to be measured by the amount of possession, but in its durability. Locke insightfully posited that all things really useful to humans and necessary for their subsistence are perishable. If only perishable materials existed, there would be no incentive to amass private property. However, by mutual consent, humans invented money, a medium to exchange perishable property for more enduring ones or also to accrete property. Locke remarked, 'Find out something that has use and value of money amongst his neighbours, you shall see the same man will begin presently to enlarge his possessions.'[17] Money led to the accumulation of property beyond subsistence needs, for in the absence of money there was no incentive to amass property.

Current capitalistic thinking is anchored in the right of the individual to own private property. John Locke, to a large extent, provided the justification for private property and thereby rationalized the capitalistic system. However, his last observation on private property has been more or less ignored, where he concluded, 'what portion a man carved to himself was easily seen and it was useless, as well as dishonest, to carve himself too much or take more than he needed.'[18] Locke may not have visualized the human appetite for amassing property nor the way this expanded with technological developments. In contrast, Lewis Henry Morgan in his epic 1877 book, *Ancient Society or the Researches in the Lines of Human Progress from Savagery through Barbarism to Civilization*, presciently identified the expanding nature of property as influenced by technology, saying 'The growth of property would thus keep pace with the progress of inventions and discoveries.'[19] The advent of money and the development of technology only provided an opportunity for the latent instinct in individuals to amass property. But what converted this potential into reality was the patent sanction of and admiration from society towards rich and wealthy people.

To summarize then, the advent of private property in society was the first prerequisite for the development of economics as a distinct discipline. Initially, the need for storing material goods in a society which faced scarcity gave birth to private property. In contrast to the limited ambit of material goods requiring storage, it was a contest in the spiritual domain that saw social sanction granted for the pursuit of a purely self-centred agenda, the second prerequisite for the development of economics. For many centuries, the choice before humans had been to either eat well or sleep well. The fear was that chasing temporal life on this earth to eat well would result in disturbed sleep, as eternal life could be at stake. It was a tough choice for the individual.

To Eat Well or To Sleep Well?

In most early human societies, concern for the afterlife was a primary motive. The guiding principle, as William Paley, the eighteenth-century philosopher, put it was, 'the hope of heaven and the fear of hell'.[20] Individuals were expected to willingly undergo hardship in their 'temporal life' on earth in return for the promise of everlasting salvation. Life on this earth was seen as an admission test to Paradise. Being born into a wealthy or a poor family was part of the divine plan: a wealthy individual was to live a pious life and use the wealth to further God's will by helping the poor, who were to bear the ordeal of their temporal life for rewards in the afterlife. This was the divine mandate, and an individual was supposed to do nothing to alter it. To eat well, or to pursue an economic agenda, was looked down upon, as it distracted from life's primary mission. Pursuit of the religious goal enabled the individual to sleep well, content in the belief of rewards in the afterlife. A high price was often paid by those people who opted to act at variance with the divine plan. The denial of the economic agenda was embodied in the prohibition on usury, which prevented individuals from taking interest on loans. All the three revealed religions – Judaism, Christianity and Islam – forbade usury.

The word usury comes from the Latin noun *usura* which means use. Usury was the price paid for the use of money. 'Where more is asked than what is given'[21] is one of the most concise definitions of usury. This was also the first time usury was defined by a state – that of Charlemagne's Christian Kingdom, in the ninth century. Prior to this, the ban against usury was purely a religious one. Usury was initially seen as the absence of charity. Later, it also implied profiting from the distress of brethren. This was not only considered an evil but also unjust. Over time, it was declared a sin, a form of robbery. The prohibition against usury was more rigorous than even that against murder. While killing under certain circumstances was sanctioned, usury had no such exception. The Second Lateran Council in 1139 CE even decided that the unrepentant usurer would not be buried in hallowed grounds.[22]

As the concept of universal brotherhood gained acceptance in the Christian world, the only option available, of lending to non-Christians who were not considered brethren, also evaporated. The commercial instinct in humans is tough to extinguish. When all the paths seem blocked, they discover a new avenue. It was a theological debate that diluted the religious sanction against usury in the Christian kingdom. A loss to the lenders was viewed differently from a gain made by them. While the etymology of usury was the Latin noun *usura* meaning use, the source word for interest was the Latin verb *intereo* which meant 'to be lost'[23]. Unlike usury, interest was not a profit made by the lender, but a compensation for the loss suffered by them. Dilution of usury was the first step in the construction of the 'rational' human mind oriented to 'eating well'. It blossomed in the Christian world.

Manufacturing a Rational Mind

Once a crack is found in the shield, it is a matter of time before the whole thing disintegrates. This was what happened with usury too. Initially the quantum of interest permitted was a compensation for time and effort spent in making loans – a wage for administering the loan. This was seen in the 1460s when the first public pawnshop in the form of a charitable institution called *mons pietatis,* was set up in Perugia, by its

Governor Barbarus.[24] Financed by charitable donations, it was run for the benefit of the poor. A fee of 6 per cent was charged to defray administrative expenses. This was in contrast to the 32.5 to 43 per cent interest permitted for private pawnshops, run by 'manifest usurers' or licensed lenders.[e]

Permitted interest, which initially consisted of administrative expenses only, gradually expanded. The loss incurred by the lender on the property sold to generate money for loans was included. A subsequent addition was the opportunity cost of lending. The opportunity cost was computed based on income from 'census', a form of state loan. At that time, interest on state loans was permitted as damages, and not as interest. The logic was that the lender would rather have his principal back than receive interest on the loan.[25] In all these elements of compensation, risk was not explicitly considered, as that had an element of usury i.e. profit for 'use' of time. Despite these changes, the pursuit of profit was still frowned upon. The change in attitude towards profit in the Christian world was triggered by new ideas emerging in Germany and France. Martin Luther and John Calvin led the challenge against the traditional church authorities in the sixteenth century. The trigger for this challenge were the hard-sell techniques used to market 'indulgences' to raise funds for building St. Peter's Church in Vatican City.[26]

But what are indulgences? What was the logic for the sale of indulgences by the Vatican? Christians believe that man is born in sin.[27] A life of repentance and penance would absolve them of their sins and provide them redemption. The church, as part of its

---

e   Licensed lenders in the Christian kingdom were members who did not belong to their faith and were mainly Jews, who had restricted access to other professions.

religious services, provided an avenue for repentance by defining penance that was usually public, harsh and humiliating. Over time this definition was diluted. It was commuted to private, less harsh and non-demeaning tasks like prayer, fasting, giving alms and contributing to the church funds.[28] The first Crusade in 1095, which had among its objectives reclaiming Jerusalem, led to the issue of a Papal bull, a Vatican directive in the nature of a *fatwa*[f]. The 'Bull of Crusade' provided redemption to the individuals who joined the crusade. Later, people financing the crusade were also assured of redemption. The redemption was conveyed in the form of indulgences, a document attesting to their redemption issued by the Church on the express authority of the Vatican. The sale of indulgences was formalized into a revenue stream by the church for their social and construction activities.

When the Papal authorities decided to rebuild St. Peter's Church in Vatican City, funding it through the sale of indulgences was a logical choice considering the enormous amount of money required. The construction took 120 years, from 1506 to 1626, as the Church was to house 60,000 devotees and be built across six acres. Resources for this construction were mobilized from the entire Christian world. Funds collected from the sale of indulgences were shared with the local province; only half the collection went to the Vatican construction.[29] Aggressive propaganda backed the sale of indulgences. The letter written by Martin Luther to the Archbishop of Mainz in 1517 highlights the practice:

> Papal indulgences for the building of St. Peter's are circulating under your most distinguished name, and as regards them, I do not bring accusations against the outcries of the preachers, which I have not heard, so much as I grieve over the wholly

---

f   Fatwa – a religious commandment or order issued in the Islamic world.

false impressions which the people have conceived for them;
to wit, the unhappy souls believe that if they have purchased
letters of indulgence they are sure of their salvation.[30]

As the sale of indulgences continued, Martin Luther protested
the practice on the grounds that the Church, as an intermediary,
was not required for a man to obtain salvation. He held that
salvation came from faith in God's infinite mercy and not by
redeeming sins with payments to the Church. Every individual
shaped their own future. This was a major shift that called each
individual to define their own values by their own reading of
the Bible, without an intermediary like the Church to interpret
it. Martin Luther's initiative shifted the focus from the Vatican's
explanations to individual interpretations, providing the
required space for changes in social practices and social outlook
for the first time in several centuries.

In all the revealed religions, interpretation makes a big
difference and interpretations depend on the prevailing
situation and the perspective of the viewer. Around this time,
John Calvin, the French reformer, differentiated between
biting usury and business loans. Calvin argued there is a major
difference between making a business loan and the profession
of usurious lending for private consumption. He argued it was
a merchant's own diligence that created a business profit and
diligence is a virtue. A diligent engagement in a profession
was seen as equivalent to dedication in religious life, as the
profession too was held to be a part of the divine plan. Hard
work engaged the mind and time spent away from work was
time spent not glorifying God. If work was worship, profit
and wealth were visible answers to one's prayer. More profit
and greater wealth showed that the individual was more
worthy in the eyes of God. With this new attitude to profits,
the view on usury too changed. Usury was now permitted if

it did not injure the brethren. In 1547, Calvin set 5 per cent interest as the maximum permitted rate.[31] Now, the pursuit of profit was justified and, with one caveat, wealth accumulation legitimized as well. The caveat was that the wealth achieved from business should not be used for personal indulgences and luxurious lifestyles. But wealth could be accumulated and used productively. The code of conduct for an ideal Christian was a life of thrift, diligence, sobriety and frugality: in short, an endorsement for the pursuit of profit.

The Birth of Economics

The endorsement of the idea that an individual should pursue profit, combined with the well-entrenched private property system in European society during the late Middle Ages, escalated the demand for a practical science to accelerate the human quest for material progress. The result was the birth of economics as a distinct discipline, in the eighteenth century.

The ideas initiated by Martin Luther and John Calvin were soon transformed into a practical science by Adam Smith. In 1776, he published his magnum opus *An Inquiry into the Nature and Causes of The Wealth of Nations*. In this advancement, the mandate for pursuit of profit was moved one step ahead, when he pinned down the prime factor in the relationship between individuals in a society to their self-love. He wrote:

> In almost every other race of animals each individual, when it is grown up to maturity, is entirely independent, and in its natural state has occasion for the assistance of no other living creature. But man has almost constant occasion for help of his brethren, and it is in vain for him to expect it from their benevolence only. He will be more likely to prevail if he can interest their **self-love** in his favour, and shew them that it is for their own advantage to do for him what he requires of them.[32]

Calvinism had indirectly aligned the economic agenda with the prevailing religious ethos by equating hard and unremitting work to a pious life. Profit was a reflection of individual virtue and no longer tainted with the exploitation of the weak. The frugal lifestyle that Calvinism prescribed took the sting out of any criticism that could be directed against the pursuit of a pure economic agenda. But Adam Smith converted this indirect economic agenda into a direct economic goal. The ingredients of diligence, sobriety, thrift and frugality, directly targeted at economic goals accelerated the pace of wealth accumulation.

Preceding Adam Smith, Bernard Mandeville described English society in 1706, when it was at the forefront of realizing material progress. In a poem titled *The Grumbling Hive or Knaves turn'd Honest* he captured the qualities essential for achieving material success. This poem was republished in 1714 under the title *The Fable of the Bees or, Private Vices, Public Benefits*. This book created a social uproar comparable to the effect of books like *The Prince, The Leviathan,* and *The Origin of Species*. In the preface, Mandeville explained his logic for penning the verses. His main idea was to illustrate the impossibility of enjoying both the material comforts of life and retaining the virtue and innocence of a Golden Age.[33] Ending a fourteen-page poem critically describing the English society in its every facet and profession, he concluded with the following words[34]:

> *Nay where the People would be great,*
> *As necessary to the State*
> *As Hunger is to make 'em eat,*
> *Bare Vertue can't make Nations live*
> *In Splendour; they, that would revive*
> *A Golden Age, must be as free,*
> *For Acorns, as for Honesty.*

Two centuries later in 1930, John Maynard Keynes, the twentieth-century economist, wrote an essay titled *Economic Possibilities for our Grandchildren*. In this essay he visualized a future when the economic problem of human survival would be solved or its solution will be within sight. To reach this stage he prescribed patience and in the interim advocated:

> For at least another hundred years we must pretend to ourselves and to everyone that fair is foul and foul is fair; for foul is useful and fair is not. Avarice and usury and precaution must be our gods for a little longer still. For only they can lead us out of the tunnel of economic necessity to daylight.[35]

Keynes only expressed in prose what Mandeville had earlier communicated in verse, with one difference: what Mandeville saw as a constant state, Keynes viewed as a temporary phase. The basic difference between the two was that Keynes segregated human needs into two classes – a finite absolute need, which is essential for survival and the unlimited relative needs that feed our vanity by making us feel superior to our fellows. But today, the biggest challenge that keeps economics on the centrestage is our ever expanding essential needs. What made the list of essential needs grow over time? How did luxuries turn into necessities? Did the availability of luxuries and their public display contribute to this?

Converting Luxuries into Necessities

The Great Exhibition of the Industries of All Nations opened to the public in Hyde Park, London on May 1, 1851. Two years earlier, while announcing plans for the Exhibition as the head of the Royal Commission, Prince Albert remarked,[36]

> Gentlemen, the Exhibition of 1851 is to give us a true test and a living picture of the point of development at which the

whole of mankind has arrived in this great task, and a new starting point from which all nations will be able to direct their further exertions.

The inspiration for this English event was the grand success of the French National Exposition of Industries and Agriculture, held in Paris in 1849. The Paris Exposition was itself a continuation of a series of expositions that began in 1798. The French government, smarting under the runaway industrial progress of the English, decided to counter it with a series of fairs to encourage French industry and entrepreneurship.[37] These expositions recognized innovative French businesses with rewards. The 1849 Exposition hosted in a venue covering 22,000 square metres, had an open courtyard with water fountains and orange and lemon trees for fragrance. The nine product sections[g] and one geographical section (for Algeria) displayed 4,494 exhibits in all.

The English event surpassed the French extravaganza. Organized with private funds, the event lasted for about six months, between May 1 and October 15. It generated a surplus of £186,000. The building that housed the event used 250,000 glass panes and was called The Crystal Palace. With a length of 1851 feet to signify the year, it was 108 feet tall at its highest point, large enough to accommodate about 60,000 visitors at once. Crowning the 14,000 exhibits displayed in the Crystal Palace was the 'Kohinoor' diamond from India. Among the other exhibits were fabrics and furnishings, sewing machines, electric clocks, musical instruments, machinery, farm equipment, and kitchen equipment such as knives and

---

g   Agriculture and Horticulture, Machines, Metals, Instruments of Precision, Chemical Arts, Ceramic Arts, Fabrics, Fine Arts and Diverse Arts.

gas stoves, among others. Six million visitors, i.e. about 25 per cent of the population at the time, saw the Great Exhibition. For the first time, luxuries only in the realm of a miniscule elite were marketed to a much larger group, laying the foundation for the birth of the middle class.

The Great Exhibition, which marked a critical point in the human quest for material progress was a result of the fusion of three distinct forces — social, technological and philosophical. The release of labour from agricultural operations which began in the fourteenth century, was the social force. The development of mass-manufacturing techniques which commenced in the eighteenth century was the technological force. Utilitarianism, the new philosophy, was the glue that held the first two forces together. They combined together for the first time in the United Kingdom to propel consumerism to the global centre-stage. The effect of this movement was to place economics, which was only one among the multiple social sciences, at the top of the pecking order. A century later, in 1969, this was formally acknowledged by the institution of a 'Nobel' Prize for economics, the only social science placed on par with the two physical sciences, physics and chemistry. But what were the factors that unleashed these forces?

The Urban Tilt

The right of the masses to visit the Great Exhibition in London was a newly-won freedom. Their position had changed significantly from the state of servitude at the beginning of the second millennium. In 1066, William the Conqueror ascended the English throne. Immediately thereafter he decreed that he alone owned all the land in his kingdom. However, in return for an oath of loyalty and commitment to knightly services,[h] the King granted a fixed tenure in portions of the land across his kingdom to his knights.

The knights in their role as landlords evolved the manorial system. On an oath of loyalty from serfs, the lords granted them the right to cultivate their land. The oath obligated the serfs to provide service to their landlord. One member from each family was required to work on the lord's own land for two to three days in a week, which was called the 'week work'. In addition, during the time of sowing and harvest, the entire family along with their draught animals was required to work on the lord's land. This obligation resulted in restricting the serfs' rights to sell their own oxen or to get their daughters married without their lord's consent.[38] In addition, the serfs were bound to their land. They could not leave their land without the lord's consent. This consent was available only on the payment of an agreed amount to compensate the lord for the loss of their service. Even in the case of the serf's death, the eldest son was granted the tenancy only on payment of an 'entry fine'.[39] In return for these stringent commitments, the lord was obligated to provide for the basic needs of his serfs and protect them. The rural economy was predominantly a self-sufficient system, with little or no interaction with the external world. But the rapidly growing urban life was distinctly different.

Where the serfs had a regulated life, town residents enjoyed their liberties. These came at a cost. They had to not only cater to their own needs, without a landlord to provide for them, but also pay for their liberties. In addition, towns could collect taxes and levies from their

---

h The knight's service was the obligation to fight for the King at his royal command.

residents in return for granting them the freedom to ply their trade. The residents had the right to hold fairs and markets in addition to regulating trade and electing their own town officials.[40] Their trades were regulated through merchant guilds.

Trade regulations in these towns covered the prices for products too. The price of any good was to be the fair price – fair to the buyer and to the seller. Neither the buyer nor the seller was to take advantage of the other's constraints. In addition, individual sellers were restrained by the guild when they had the opportunity to exploit a shortage situation. The price was the payment for an honest day's work.[41] Food was the largest market of that time. By 1202, the price of bread was fixed with reference to wheat prices and the ale price linked to barley.[42] The baker and the brewer would get a fair wage for their labour. But soon these principles would change. The catalyst was an epidemic of the Black Plague, which took a heavy toll on human life.

The Black Plague that swept through Europe through the 1340s tilted the power equation between the landlord and the serfs. The loss of human life due to plague[i] in the United Kingdom is estimated at 33 - 50 per cent[43] of the total population. The sudden reduction in labour availability forced landlords to hire outside labour to supplement their own. During harvest time, the shortage of labour resulted in significant wage increases to outside labour. This provided an opportunity for the labourers to live better, giving them a

---

i   Estimates of life lost vary between a low of 20 per cent and a high of 90 per cent. The lower rates are more recent estimates. Walsingham writing in the reign of Richard II (1377-1399), quoted the popular belief that the mortality rate was around 90 per cent.

glimpse of a better life ahead. Some started playing truant to escape work at the pre-plague wages. The landlords on their part began to think of their options too.

The initial response of the landlords was to force labourers to work. In June 1349, an ordinance was passed which was later enacted as the Statute of Labourers of 1351. It provided that every man or woman, able-bodied and not having their own land to live upon, nor being already engaged, was to accept work at the pre-plague rate of wages. Refusal to work resulted in imprisonment. Paying or accepting higher than the stipulated wage was punished by levying a monetary penalty. The statute covered not only agricultural labourers but also carpenters and construction workers. The adverse impact on labourers due to this wage freeze was partially mitigated by restraining price increases in essential food articles. While the statute provided some relief, the landlords did not depend only on the laws to bail them out. They found other uses for their land that needed less labour, coming up with not one but two alternatives.

The landlords resorted to sheep rearing and stock-and-land lease. Sheep rearing not only required less labour but also promised greater reward as the wool export markets were accessible. Stock-and-land lease was an effective way to transfer the responsibility of handling labour to the lessee. Landlords provided both the land and the stock required to cultivate it. The lessee used their family efforts more diligently for their own benefit and judiciously supplemented these with hiring outside labour where essential. As these practices proved profitable, the landlords willingly released labour engaged in agriculture. Over the next two centuries, the character of the rural economy changed. The dependence on serfs reduced and labour so released from the rural economy gradually moved into the towns and cities, providing the required inputs for mass manufacturing. They provided not just labour for the production process but more importantly, a large number of 'free' individuals who 'mined' their intellect to provide the technological fillip.

The Patent Spurt

Luxury goods were not new to human beings. Since the dawn of human civilization, every society has had an elite class and they have had their share of luxuries. The luxuries either made their personal lives pleasant or enhanced their social standing. The most visible enduring indulgences of the ancient societies were in their monuments. Two key features of these monuments stand out: the scale as seen in the Egyptian pyramids, or the intricate workmanship as reflected in the South Indian temples of Belur and Halebid in Karnataka.

The Great Pyramid of Cheops, located at Giza, was the largest pyramid built. Using 250,000 limestone blocks, each weighing 2.75 tonnes, it measures 481 feet tall and 756 square feet at the base. This was the tallest human construction until the Eiffel Tower was erected in 1889. The Greek historian Herodotus recorded that it took 100,000 men twenty years to build this structure[j]. The intricate sculptures in the Belur and Halebid temples were created over a period of 103 years, spanning the work life of three generations. A salient feature of these monuments is the humongous human effort required to build them. Similarly, the personal luxuries used by the elite of these periods also required intricate work or were exotic products procured from distant places, needing substantial human effort. But in the eighteenth century, a major change

---

j Current scholars estimate the effort required to build the pyramid at 20,000 men working for twenty years.

was in the offing. Machines were about to supplement human labour. Machines would multiply the luxury output beyond any scale hitherto conceived.

The movement of people from rural to urban areas unleashed a sea change. Urban residents had the freedom to choose their trade from an increasingly large pool. As Daniel Defoe in 1726 noted in his book, *The Complete English Tradesman,* 'An Estate's a pond, but trade's a spring.'[44] A spring it was, gushing out patents. In the 140-year period from 1711 to 1850, 13,023 patents were filed. For the first time, tools were being designed for use by other tradesmen. The design and manufacture of capital goods as we know it today became a distinct occupation. Earlier, artisans built their own tools, or if not, designed them themselves for others to build. But the concept of patents saw individuals devote their attention to building capital goods for use across industries.

The two major types of designs, for steam engines and production machinery, were used across multiple industries. Production machinery accounted for 27 per cent of patents issued during the period 1711-1850 and 7 per cent related to steam engines. The patents for machineries of general production were saws, lathes, drills, presses, bearings, lubricants, drive bands, axels, springs, hinges, steering and brakes. In the steam engine segment, boilers, furnaces, condensation, water supply, flues and vents, valves and gauges, stationary, rotary and oscillating engines for agricultural, railway and marine uses were patented.[45] This English development was in sharp contrast with the two dominant economies of that time – India and China, which relied on the skill and ingenuity of their artisans. One European traveler to India in 1782 noted 'Indian crafts look simple to us, because in general they employ fewer machines using only their hands and two or three tools to work with, where we would use over a hundred.'[46] The use of machinery eliminated human fatigue, and power from inanimate sources made mass production feasible. The cotton textiles industry was the first where mass production was used. In 1760, Britain imported 2.5 million pounds of raw cotton. The imports increased to 22 million pounds in 1787 and fifty years later it was over sixteen times higher at 366 million pounds.[47]

The gush of new technological inventions changed the world as never before. But this change was most profound in the social sphere. This dramatic social transformation is best captured by *The Penguin History of the World*, which notes, 'Within a fairly short time – a century and a half or so – societies of peasants and craftsmen turned into societies of machine tenders and bookkeepers.'[48] At the material plane, the result was amazing – The Great Exhibition of 1851, displayed 14,000 products. The initial gains made by the advent of technology did not dissipate. It has continued for another 160 years and is still going strong. This momentum is fueled by an ideology that could end all the other ideologies.

The Economists' Dogma

Every human culture has produced philosophers. Their quest has been to find the meaningful life – perhaps true happiness and a path to it. These explorations have resulted in different answers. The religious life prioritizes bliss in the afterlife in preference to the pursuit of earthly gains, using the yardstick of virtue. The moral life restrains individual instincts by placing their actions in the larger context of society. Both these lines of thinking require an individual to adapt to existing codes, which is the less strenuous option. But disruptions occur when individuals start thinking on a clean slate.

Starting with a clean slate, Jeremy Bentham wanted to design and implement a model prison, which he named the Panopticon. Developing the framework, he penned his thoughts in the book *An Introduction to the Principles of Morals and Legislation.* Writing in 1789, he captured the secular sentiments of the time, with the first two sentences in the book, 'Nature has placed mankind under the governance of two sovereign masters, *pain* and *pleasure.* It is for them alone to point out what we ought to do, as well as to determine what we shall do.' With this basic assumption, he went on to outline his framework for legislative decisions.

The happiness of a community is 'the sum of the interests of the several members who compose it.' Hence legislative decisions should be based on actions that maximize the happiness of the community or minimize its pain. To measure individual happiness he outlined seven[k] features of pleasure – intensity, duration, certainty, propinquity, fecundity, purity and extent. He then outlined a three-stage process to quantify the effect of a legislation or social action. In the first stage, he sums up the net pleasure score of the individual most affected by the act. In the second stage, he identifies the number of other individuals who will be affected by it. In the final stage, he measures the pleasure scores for the individuals affected by the act. These three stages give the required data for approving the act. The quantification process was subsequently called by different names – felicific calculus, utility calculus, hedonic calculus

---

k   While intensity, duration and certainty are self-explanatory, propinquity measures the time-lag between the action and result, fecundity measures decline in effect on repetition, extent measures the number of individuals touched, and purity measures the after-effects.

and the likes. The idea itself came to be called the greatest happiness principle. But this was only at the societal level.

John Stuart Mill extended the concept developed for evaluating social and legislative action to the individual sphere. He wrote 'The creed which accepts as the foundation of morals, Utility, or the Greatest Happiness Principle, holds the actions are right in proportion as they tend to promote happiness, wrong as they intended or produced reverse of happiness.'[49] With this, he equated morals with utility and put the pursuit of happiness as the primary aim of human life. But he was not the first to recognize it. Among the Greek philosophers, Epicurus had preceded him, saying: 'We maintain that pleasure is the beginning and end of a blessed life.' He however qualified this pursuit of pleasure. Chasing pleasure, if it resulted in long term pain was to be avoided and conversely, it was worthwhile to put up with pain if it meant long term pleasure. He elaborated by highlighting that the pursuit of pleasure is not an invitation to drinking and carousing, that results in a pleasant life, but a simple vegetarian diet, the company of a few friends and a modest garden would suffice where sobriety, honour, justice and wisdom prevailed. Mill too, on his part, distinguished between different qualities of happiness when he wrote 'It is better to be a human being dissatisfied than a pig satisfied;'[50]

With the passage of time, in an interesting twist, the concept of utility seems to have given way to physical output in measuring performance. Highlighting it, Joan Robinson the twentieth-century economist, writing in her book *Economic Philosophy*, noted that by focusing on maximizing physical output and defocusing utility, the issue of wealth distribution was almost ignored. She illustrated her observation by comparing a smaller quantity of physical goods equally distributed with a much larger quantity of goods unequally distributed.[51] Robinson highlighted the potency of this philosophy by remarking, 'This [Utilitarianism] is an ideology to end ideologies, for it has abolished the moral problem. It is only necessary for each individual to act egoistically for the good of all to be attained.'[52]

Thus by the end of the eighteenth century, all the three prerequisites required for Economics to flourish as a distinct discipline were in place. Private property was in existence for the longest period of time, with social sanction for a self-centered individual gaining acceptance by the fifteenth century and acquisition of goods equated to welfare gaining popular support in the eighteenth century. It can be seen that, parallel with these developments, economic thoughts too emerged in three distinct stages providing a roadmap for tracing their evolution — initially in discussions on ethics and administration, later underlying the trade and commerce debates before finally emerging as a distinct discipline in academic circles.

Endnotes

1   Robbins, Lionel, *An Essay on the Nature and Significance Of Economic Science*, Macmillan and Company Limited, 1945, Second Edition, Revised and Extended, p15

2   Ibid p16

3   Sahlins, Marshall, The Original Affluent Society, an extract from *Stone Age Economics*, Aldine, 1972

4   Hitchcock, R., M. Biesel and W. Babchuk, Environmental Anthropology n the Kalahari: Development, Resettlement, and Ecological Change Among the San of Southern Africa, *Explorations in Anthropology*, Vol.9, No.2, p173

5   Baker M.J., and K. Swope, *Sharing, Gift Giving and Optimal Resource Use Incentives in Hunter-Gatherer Society*, Department of Economics, United States Naval Academy, Annapolis October 2005, p5

6   Marlowe, Frank W., What Explains Hadza Food Sharing?, *Research in Economic Anthropology*, Volume 23, 69-88, p84

7   Foley, R., Hunting Down the Hunter Gatherers, *Evolutionary Anthropology: Issues, News and Reviews*, Volume 8, Issue 4, p115

8　Ruskin, John, *Munera Pulveris, Six Essays on the Elements of Political Economy,* Second Small Edition, George Allen, Sunnyside, Orpington, p74

9　Locke, J., *The Second Treatise of Government,* Forum book, The Liberal Arts Press, Inc., 1952, p17

10　Ibid p18

11　Ibid p19

12　Kitanishi, K., Food Sharing Among The Aka Hunter-gatherers in Northeastern Congo, *African Study Monographs,* Suppl., 25:3-32, March 1998, summarized from description in p10

13　Stevens, 1988, Rachel Carson Estuarine Sanctuary

14　Maynard Smith and Parker, 1976

15　Davies, 1978

16　Locke, J., *The Second Treatise of Government,* Forum book, The Liberal Arts Press, Inc., 1952, p19

17　Ibid p29

18　Ibid p30

19　Morgan, Lewis H., *Ancient Society or the Researches in the Lines of Human Progress from Savagery through Barbarism to Civilization,* transcribed for www.marxist.org by Ibne Hasan, p363

20　Mill, John Stuart, *Utilitarianism, On Liberty, Consideration on Representative Government,* Everyman's Library, 1972, xiii

21　Homer, Sidney, *A History of Interest Rates, 2000 BC to the Present,* Rutgers University Press, 1963, p70

22　Braudel, F., *The Wheels of Commerce, Civilization & Capitalism, 15th to 18th century, Volume 2,* A Phoenix Press Paperback, 2002, p560

23　Homer, Sidney, *A History of Interest Rates, 2000 BC to the Present,* Rutgers University Press, 1963, p73

24　Ibid p78

25　Ibid p78

26　Kiermayr, R. How Much Money was Actually in the Indulgence Chest?, *The Sixteenth Century Journal, The Journal of Early Modern Studies,* Vol.17, No.3 (Autumn 1986), p307

27　Rider, C., *An Introduction to Economic History,* South-Western College Publishing, 1995, p85

28　Rev. Covolo, Ed., *The Historical Origin of Indulgences,* Catholic Culture, Living the Catholic Life, http://The Historical Origin of Indulgences. htm

29　Kiermayr, R. How Much Money was Actually in the Indulgence Chest?,

The Sixteenth Century Journal, The Journal of Early Modern Studies, Vol.17, No.3 (Autumn 1986), p307

30 http://Medieval Sourcebook Martin Luther Letter to the Archbishop of Mainz, 1517. mht

31 Homer, Sidney, *A History of Interest Rates, 2000 BC to the Present,* Rutgers University Press, 1963, p80

32 Smith, A., *The Wealth of Nations,* Bantam Classic, 2003, p23

33 Mandeville, B., *The Fable of The Bees,* Penguin Classics, 1989, p54

34 Ibid p76

35 Keynes, J. M., *Essays in Persuasion,* W W Norton & Company, 1963, p 372

36 Reported in the *Illustrated London News,* October 11, 1849

37 Hafter, D. M., The Business of Invention in the Paris Industrial Exposition 1806, *The Business History Review,* Vol.58, No.3 (Autumn 1984), p317

38 Warner, G. T., *Landmarks In English Industrial History,* Blackie & Son Limited, 1930 edition, p34

39 Rider, C., *An Introduction to Economic History,* South-Western College Publishing, 1995, p33

40 Warner, G. T., *Landmarks In English Industrial History,* Blackie & Son Limited, 1930 edition, p42

41 Ibid p53

42 Ibid p66

43 Ibid p83

44 Quoted in Briggs, A., *The Age of Improvement 1783-1867,* Longman 1979, p38

45 Sullivan, R. J., The Revolution of Ideas: Widespread Patenting and Invention During the English Industrial Revolution, *The Journal Of Economic History,* Vol. 50, No.2, (June 1990), p361

46 Braudel, F., *The Wheels of Commerce, Civilization & Capitalism, 15th to 18th Century,* Volume 2, Phoenix Press, 1982, p303

47 Watson, P., *Ideas, A History From Fire to Freud,* Weidenfeld & Nicolson, 2005, p553

48 Roberts, J. M., *The Penguin History of the World,* Third Edition, 1997

49 Mill, J. S., *Utilitarianism, On Liberty, Considerations on Representative Government,* Everyman's Library, 1992, p7

50 Ibid p10

51 Robinson, J., *Economic Philosophy,* Penguin Books, 1968, p.55

52 Ibid p53

Part 11: A Short Biography of Economics

Economic ideas evolved with material progress. Over about a million years of human history, progress measured by annual average individual consumption[a] shows three distinct inflection points. The first inflection point occurred around 10,000 BCE and coincides with the advent of agriculture. Private property, the first prerequisite for economics as a distinct discipline also emerged around this time to support agriculture, a long-gestation project, where results are separated from efforts by a few weeks or months. The second impact is seen around the fourteenth century. This time, the acceleration seems to have been limited to Europe, but was so significant that, despite being confined to a limited geography which was not the most populated, its impact was seen in global per capita consumption numbers. Did the second prerequisite for economics – social sanction for a self-centred individual – also emerge during this period? The third shift can be seen in the second half of the nineteenth century, when the mass production of luxury goods promoted a materialistic outlook, which seems to have captured the human imagination.

By the twentieth century, all three prerequisites for economics to be shaped as a separate discipline were in place. The year 1969 marked the crowning of economics, when a prize for distinguished contribution in economics in the memory of Alfred Nobel was instituted by the Swedish central bank. This placed economics on par with physics, chemistry, literature, medicine and peace, as a vital subject for human development.

---

a   See Chapter 1 for details.

The second section of this book briefly explores the biography of economics as it evolved into a stand-alone subject. In the period from 400 BCE to 1500 CE, only private property, the first of the three prerequisites, was recognized. The economic ideas of this period were embedded in ethical discourses or political prescriptions. Though basic economic concepts like monopolistic markets and hoarding as a means to enlarging profits emerged, they were not socially accepted, as the idea of self-centred individuals pursuing materialistic goals was socially frowned upon. It is possible that these social concerns may have stopped further exploration that could have led to the emergence of economics as an independent discipline.

During the period from 1300 to 1776 CE, economic ideas gained momentum, breaking these social shackles. This period saw the idea of a self-centered individual gain social acceptance. Merchants, along with corporate shareholders and employees, were the dominant players who initially pushed the frontiers of economic ideas. In contrast to the philosophers and historians, they had little doubt about the benefits of pursuing material gains. During this era economics emerged from the shadows of ethics as economic literature increased in both volume and 'purity'. Political economy, as economics was then called, became a widely-debated subject as a critical portion of the new legislations being enacted was primarily economic in nature.

The birth of economics as a full-fledged discipline in the nineteenth century was a decisive moment. For the first time, human happiness and welfare were sought to be quantified in monetary terms. This quantification shifted the debate from the realm of morals to markets. Its most visible aspect was the change in the language of debates, where price replaced value.

As economists tried to bridge the two distinct concepts of value and price, a new concept emerged, that of marginal utility. This set the stage for the study of demand and supply of goods and services, laying the foundation for micro-economics.

The twentieth century not only marked the development of macro-economics but also saw it assume a prominent role. In the nineteenth century, material progress and economic cycles were both visible and pronounced. Economists analyzed the reasons for the coexistence of material prosperity and poverty, even as they advocated prescriptions for accelerating economic growth. For governments and corporations pursuing economic growth with single-minded devotion, their prescriptions were valuable. In this phase, economics moved from being a discipline that explained phenomena to a more predictive role. Economists began to play a dominant role in public policy formulation and shape an economic environment conducive to growth.

Chapter 2

Ethically Immersed: A Long Infancy 400 BCE to 1500 CE

He who thus considers things in their first growth and origin, whether a state or anything else, will obtain the clearest view of them.

— **Aristotle**, *Politica*[1]

Looking beyond Europe where modern economics was born, we examine here economic ideas from the Indian, Chinese, and Islamic civilizations. We identify one thought leader from each of these civilizations who considered issues that contain economic ideas. Their ideas are contrasted with the thinking of the Greek philosophers who inspired European thought, most specifically articulated through Aristotle's idea of the art of wealth-getting in contrast to the art of exchange. This contrast provides the evidence that economic ideas were restrained by ethical considerations. As we turn to Kautilya and Lord Chang – the Indian and Chinese contemporaries of Aristotle – we find more distinct economic ideas emerge through their debates on the administration of a kingdom. The focus on the unit of a kingdom permitted them to overcome the barriers of a self-centred and materialistic approach, which limited Aristotle's ideas, as he focused on the life of an individual (even while writing on the politics of city-states) when he examined the ideas closest to modern economics. Finally, in the ideas of Ibn Khaldun, the fourteenth-century Islamic historian who critiqued society and traced its evolution, we see the emergence of full-fledged economic concepts that come the closest to current economic thought. Even with the passage of time, economics did not emerge as a distinct discipline in these civilizations, as the third prerequisite – material pursuit – did not become the dominant goal of society.

Search for the Origin

The American economic historian and pioneer of business schools, Isaac A. Loos, insightfully observed, 'Economics seeks to discover and enunciate the rules, principles or laws, which underlie human activity in pursuit of a living.'[2] But it is important to consider when this search for rules, principles or laws began.

In the early stages of civilization, the challenge of reliably providing sustenance may not have been large, due to the conducive environment. As civilizations grew, a combination of the two factors – growing populations and increasing necessities for survival – would have dwarfed the available resources. With decreasing resources, intellectuals may have increasingly turned their attention to the challenge of meeting their material needs, on multiple levels, both individual and social. Today economics is studied from both these angles – the challenge of individual economic units under micro-economics, and in contrast, the working of an economy as a whole under macro-economics. Given this contemporary framework, it is interesting to see where the Greeks, the Chinese and the Indians, the three ancient civilizations for which written history is available, focused their attention, when it came to economic issues.

The Greek intellectual trinity – Socrates, Plato and Aristotle – placed significantly less emphasis on material life, instead preferring intellectual pursuits. Based on the records available to us today, Aristotle was the most prolific writer among the three. In addition, he followed the other two, which gave him the opportunity to critique and build on their contributions. Hence his writing offers a more complete view of the Greek thought of this era.

In India, the ancient manuscript of the *Arthasastra* written by Kautilya, a royal counselor, was discovered in the early twentieth century. Traced to the third century BCE, it provides us an insight into Indian thought of the time. The *Arthasastra* outlined a system of government. In *The Oxford History of India,* Vincent A. Smith opines that the system outlined in the *Arthasastra* is not what was practiced but only a model advocated by its author.[3] If we agree with this opinion, the *Arthasastra* becomes only a point of view and not Indian practice.

Preceding the *Arthasastra* by a few decades is the Chinese work *Shang-chŭn-shu,* now translated into English under the title *The Book of Lord Shang,* named after its author, who was also a royal counselor like Kautilya. A central theme in this book is the idea that all men are evil, seeking power, and therefore one should look out for oneself. This explicit endorsement for self-centred behavior resulted in many economic concepts being discussed, which in an ethically sensitive era that promoted altruism and social concern, was not commonly possible.

All the three authors identified above lived in the third century BCE. This provides us with an interesting contrast. Being a philosopher, Aristotle focused his writing on the individual's quest for a meaningful life. The two royal counsellors in contrast, answered the needs of a government planning its resources to build a strong kingdom. What did these scholars think about economic issues? A critical necessity as we look at their ideas is to discard our current economic lens which did not exist in their time. Many of their ideas captured here are the closest to the economic ideas of the time, though we might feel that they are more appropriately classified under trade and management practices or taxation and governance codes.

The Art of Acquisition

Aristotle dealt with what today we consider economic ideas when he examined human efforts to acquire material needs for life. In *Nicomachean Ethics* he searched for the end which all human beings target.[b] While a minority pursued the contemplative life, the majority, he noted, chased pleasure, honour and wealth. Narrowing down the choice to what a man should target, he dismissed the pursuit of pleasure as 'a life suitable to beasts'.[4] The pursuit of honour too he dismissed as superficial, as it depends on 'those who bestow honour rather than on him who receives it'.[5] Turning to wealth, Aristotle defined it as 'all the things whose value is measured by money'.[6] Analyzing the motive for its pursuit, he noted that it was only a means to an end and not the end itself, for it is 'merely useful and for the sake of something else'.[7]

Having dismissed the pursuit of wealth merely as useful when needed for other ends in *Nicomachean Ethics*, Aristotle gave it a little more attention in *Politics*, where he examined the art of acquisition, both in its theoretical nuances and its practical application. He split the art of acquisition into

---

b Aristotle at the end of his search finally concluded that 'Happiness, therefore, must be some form of contemplation'. However, he recognized that for a life of contemplation, a few other essentials were required: 'one will also need external prosperity; for our nature is not self-sufficient for the purpose of contemplation, but our body also must be healthy and must have food and other attention'.

two: the natural art of acquisition, which he called the art of wealth-getting; and the other, by inference unnatural, which he called the art of exchange. His classification is based on the relationship between an individual and their environment, both natural and social.

Aristotle divided economic life into two distinct segments. The first segment, he defined as the natural art of acquisition, including all forms of acquisition that do not involve exchange with another individual. This segment includes three categories: the first illustrated by the shepherd who obtains food from tame animals; the second category, containing hunters who depend for their livelihood on wild animals; and in the last were the cultivators who depend on plants for their food. Analyzing this segment, Aristotle concluded that bare livelihood was provided by nature herself. Just as milk is provided for young animals by their mother, Mother Nature too provides food that could be extracted by humans in the three forms identified above. This was the natural art of acquisition, which he termed the art of wealth-getting. Insightfully, he recognized that nature herself set a limit to the human appetite for its consumption.

In contrast to the natural art of wealth-getting, Aristotle identified the second segment as the man-made art of exchange. He illustrated it with the example of a shoe. A shoe could be worn or it could also be used in exchange for other goods. A shoe being worn is natural, since it was made for that purpose. However, a shoe used in exchange to get food or money is unnatural, as the primary purpose of the shoe is to be worn and not used in exchanges. Aristotle found another reason for classifying it as unnatural, observing that this 'art of exchange' was not used within a family, but resorted to only in larger societies.[8]

Aristotle once again classified the unnatural and therefore

justly censured art of exchange into three groups, namely commerce, usury and services for hire. Explaining the value of these activities, he identified risk as the source of gain in commerce. Further, he identified three types of commerce: overseas trade, inland trade and sale at the production point, remarking that the gain from these distinct activities was related to their inherent risk and noted their diminishing returns.[9] Usury, or breeding of money, he termed as the most unnatural mode of getting wealthy, as money was primarily intended for use in exchange and not for earning interest, 'because the offspring resembles the parent'[10] and therefore carries with it all unnatural elements, thereby deserving censure. Turning to services for hire, he identified the reasons why people engaged another individual: namely to eliminate the chance of failure, to perform menial tasks or repetitive tasks or tasks that deteriorated the body.

While the art of exchange existed during the barter period, Aristotle noted that the use of money increased its relative importance in society. He felt that money, which evolved from barter, gave birth to commerce. In the era of barter, commerce was at first a simple matter. But soon it became complicated, as people learnt from experience 'whence and by what exchange the greatest profit might be made.'[11] The art of exchange promoted by use of money had one major difference from the natural art of wealth-getting, i.e. it had no natural limit. This led Aristotle to remark that while the pursuit of riches had a limit, the hoarding of coins was without any limits.[12] Unlimited pursuit of wealth led to what Aristotle called 'this disposition in men that they are intent upon living only, and not upon living well.'[13]

This is the stage beyond which Aristotle refused to move in his exploration of economic goals. He recognized private property by acknowledging the art of acquisition. However, in choosing the pursuit of a contemplative life, he disregarded the materialistic outlook. And more importantly, in limiting the appetite for material resources, he also blunted the edge of the idea of a self-centred human. Thus, Aristotle did not give economics its distinct form and consigned it to a minor position in the domain of ethics.

Aristotle was not unique in his thinking. His guru, Plato also considered businessmen as the weakest in bodily strength and 'therefore of little use for any other purpose'.[14] This reflected a clear view of Greek society, where only slaves and foreigners engaged in economic activities.[15] For free citizens, commentators on Greek society noted, the first action on attaining economic independence was to invest in land and be insulated from the need to dirty their hands in any further economic activity.

However, another Greek who looked at a household managing its material needs gave our subject its current name. The Greek word *oikonomia* loosely translates to the science of household management or estate management. This word is the etymological root for economics.

Oikonomia – The Subject Named

In contrast to the Greek intellectual trinity, who searched for ways to live well, Xenophon, a student of Socrates, devoted his efforts in capturing the essence of 'living only' in his book, *Oikonomia* (usually referred to in English as *The Economist*). It covers a range of topics starting from the nature of economics and wealth and extending to the principles involved in wealth creation. The entire content is laid out in two sets of dialogues. In the first set, Socrates and Critobulus, an interested Greek citizen, discuss the nature of economics and refine a concise definition of wealth. In the second set of dialogues, between Socrates and Ischomachus, a successful and respected gentleman, the latter describes his techniques in creating wealth.

In contrast to Aristotle who gave a very precise but less useful definition of wealth as 'all the things whose value is measured by money',[16] Xenophon defined it as 'consist[ing] of things which benefit, while things which injure are not wealth'.[17] He also illustrated the subjective nature of wealth with the example of a flute, by showing that the flute is not wealth to an individual who does not know how to play it, as it does not benefit him. However, the same flute could benefit him if he chose to sell it. Thus Xenophon separated the benefit derived from the exchange of an object and the benefit derived from its use. He further differentiated between wealth and riches: wealth is absolute, while Xenophon defined richness as a relative concept. He demonstrated that Socrates, the less wealthy philosopher, was richer than Critobulus, the politician. The politician not only had to keep up a more luxurious lifestyle, but also had to meet public obligations due to his position, from his wealth. In contrast, Socrates with a significantly lower amount of wealth had to only defray a frugal lifestyle, leaving him a surplus – and was thereby richer. In the course of this dialogue, they establish that there is a science of wealth creation. Like a doctor who is well-versed in the science of medicine, a person well-versed in this science of wealth creation could be of assistance to another in need of his services.

The second set of dialogues between Socrates and Ischomachus dealt with the methods which lead to a surplus – the criterion essential for wealth creation. These methods included following the best practices in agriculture; educating wives to manage household affairs; and finally, selecting, training and developing integrity in the employees who administer the estate. The topics covered in this dialogue today would be classified under headings such as agricultural sciences, philosophy or management, with only a small portion coming under economics.

In contrast to the Greeks who accepted private property and studied how to meet their material needs at the individual and household level, the Indian and the Chinese counselors dealt instead with a government planning its budget. Maybe because they were looking at a government, much larger than an individual, they were able to accept the 'evil' (for it was recognized as an evil then) necessity of social sanction for a self-centred individual – the second prerequisite of economics. This larger canvas helped them grapple with more advanced economic issues. At around the same time, the Jewish Talmud, a repository of laws and wisdom, also acknowledged the need for self-centred behaviour in leading a comfortable life.

The Evil Spirits: Passion, Avarice and Greed

The Talmud is the repository of Jewish law and lore capturing ancient wisdom. Jewish legends trace the origin of the Talmud to Moses in Sinai. Captured in writing between the third and the fifth century BCE, the Babylonian Talmud contains among many other sections, 'The Fable of Evil'. Set in the context[c] of the Jews returning to Jerusalem after their first exile, in this fable, *Yetzer-Ha-rah,* the evil desire, is taken into custody and confined. The predicament after its capture is described in this fable. The concluding portion of the fable says:

---

c   King Nebuchadnezzar II conquered Jerusalem in 586 BCE. He then deported and exiled all the Jews to Babylon. The Persian ruler Cyrus the Great defeated the Babylonian rulers and permitted the Jews to return to Jerusalem.

For three days the "Evil Yetzer" was imprisoned;
Temptations vanished, greed and pride ceased.
Hurrah! The battle over, the sex-impulse is won –
Alas… a fresh egg is needed, there is none.
What shall we do? – they now intensely thought,
Shall we kill him? The world couldn't survive,
No one could build, nothing could be sold or bought
Neither shall one marry, no child, no drive.
At last it dawned – a truth profound
In schemes divine – a principal sound:
Vicious forces as passion, avarice, and greed
Are vehicles of progress the world doth need.
The tempter must live to tempt, so let no one dare
Deprive the Yetzer-Ha-Rah of his glare.[18]

The Talmud recognized the need for passion, avarice and greed as the vehicles of essential material progress. Even if the opportunity presented itself, it would not be beneficial to kill these evil spirits. This recognition of the need for Yetzer-Ha-Rah to have a thriving economy is not unique to Jewish culture. Similar sentiments were echoed in the *Sukraniti* or *Sukracharyya's System of Morals*[d] composed in fifth-century India. It stressed the benefits from greed, lust and intoxication, but with a caveat for moderation. In moderation, according to the *Sukraniti*, greed produces wealth, lust results in sons and intoxication stimulates the intelligence.[19]

After identifying the inspiration for wealth, the *Sukraniti* defined who is rich in terms of their need for wealth. Wealth

---

d The *Sukraniti*, *Arthasastra* and *Manusmriti* are among the three popular ancient Indian works that have dealt with commercial and economic ideas, concepts, policies and practices. The *Manusmriti,* being predominantly legal in nature, is not covered in this book.

equal to the amount needed to live for twelve years was considered sufficiently rich, enough for sixteen years was considered moderately rich and amply rich was defined as enough wealth to meet the requirements of thirty years or more.[20] This definition of a rich individual was not an academic exercise, as the duration of service to the king for the sufficiently and moderately rich was in proportion to their wealth. Individuals with ample wealth were mandated to serve the royal command for eight years without remuneration. Only the penniless were permitted to receive wages from the king for their service.[21] The rationale for compensating royal service providers based on their wealth was a logical one, considering the fact that the *Sukraniti* classified kingdoms based on their ability to collect tax without oppressing their subjects.[22] On that principle, paying the wealthy for their services would have amounted to oppression, as higher taxes would have to be collected from the rest of the population to pay the rich.

In contrast to the generic concepts and principles laid out in the *Sukraniti,* Kautilya's *Arthasastra*[e], from the third century BCE, focused exclusively on the policies and practices to be followed by a king in administering his kingdom.

The Science of Wealth

Kautilya[f], the author of the *Arthasastra,* was the guru and mentor of *Samrat* Chandragupta Maurya, the first emperor to rule over large parts of India in the third century BCE. As the legend

---

e   Loosely translated as 'the science of wealth'.

f   Kautilya was also known by two other names: Vishnugupta , his personal name, and Chanakya, the name derived from his home town, Chanaka. His name Kautilya denotes his lineage.

goes, Vishnugupta was insulted by the Nandas, the rulers of Magadha, when he visited their royal court. He vowed to avenge this insult by overthrowing them. In Chandragupta, he found a boy with promise. Taking him under his tutelage, Vishnugupta organized a revolt against the Nandas, with Chandragupta at its helm. After the Nandas were overthrown, Chandragupta assumed the throne and was guided by Vishnugupta, also known as Kautilya and Chanakya, as his minister.

The *Arthasastra* lists the duties of the king and ends with the conclusion that in the happiness of his subjects lies the king's happiness. Wealth and prosperity are the means to achieve this happiness, and the route to wealth and prosperity is via promoting robust economic activity within the kingdom. It goes on to highlight the absence of economic activity as the primary cause of declining present prosperity and lack of future prospects.[g] It recommends a multi-pronged approach to promoting economic activity. The importance of the army in keeping the kingdom strong is acknowledged, as well as the role of the treasury in strengthening the army.

Taxation and tax exemption are critical aspects of stimulating economic activity in the kingdom, according to the *Arthasastra*. The economy is segregated by it into four parts – agriculture, animal husbandry, manufacturing and commerce. Agriculture was promoted by providing tax exemption to newly-cultivated

---

g 'In the happiness of his subjects lies his happiness; in their welfare, his welfare; whatever pleases himself he shall not consider as good, but whatever pleases his subjects he shall consider as good. Hence the king shall ever be active and discharge his duties; the root of wealth is activity, and of evil its reverse. In the absence of activity acquisitions present and to come will perish; by activity he can achieve both his desired ends and abundance of wealth' Extract from Chapter IX, Book II.

land for a period of two years.[h] Exemption from water tax was granted for creating or restoring irrigation facilities: five years for construction of new tanks and embankments, four years for renovation and three years for clearing weeds. Animal husbandry was only second in importance to agriculture, as a result of the part played by animals in agricultural operations and war. In addition, they supplemented the dietary needs of citizens by supplying milk and milk products. Animal husbandry was promoted by preserving and growing livestock. Temple bulls, stud bulls and, for ten days after calving, cows, were exempt from payment of grazing charges.[i] Likewise, the slaughter of female and young ones and castration of male animals was prohibited.[23]

Manufacturing was classified into four groups in turn — state monopolies for weapons and liquor, state-controlled units for textiles, salt and jewellery, state-regulated crafts like goldsmithing, blacksmithing, weaving and dyeing and unregulated crafts like pottery and basket-making.[24] Although commerce was third in importance ahead of manufacturing, the general distrust towards traders was reflected in a well-regulated trade environment. Traders were clubbed along with beggars, buffoons and other idlers and called 'thieves in effect though not in name' and the *Arthasastra* recommended they should be 'restrained from oppression of the country.'[25]

---

h 'If uncultivated tracts are acquired (for cultivation) by mortgage, purchase or in any other way, remission of taxes shall be for two years' Chapter IX, Book III.

i 'Bulls, let out in the name of the village deity, cows which have not passed ten days inside the enclosure after calving, or bulls or bullocks kept for crossing cows shall not be punished.' Chapter X, Book III

Box 2.1
Trade Regulations and Labour Laws in the *Arthasastra*

Detailed trade regulations and labour laws were prescribed in the *Arthasastra*, even though the majority of trade was conducted by the state, leaving only a small portion to private traders. Trade was regulated by monitoring the demand for, and controlling the price of, goods.

The nature of demand decided the mode of distribution and sale between centrally-regulated distribution or locally-managed distribution. Centrally-regulated distribution was for goods widely in demand and they were produced under the royal command. In contrast, goods selectively demanded, including imported goods, were for sale only in some privately managed local markets. In both the modes, goods were to be sold at reasonable profits, as laid down by the precept, 'He shall avoid such large profits as will harm the people'.[26] Further, the interest of the consumer was protected by specific laws such as the one stipulating that the seller of ghee should give 1/32 more to compensate for decrease in density, due to measurements being done on liquid ghee instead of its normal solid state. Similarly, the seller of oil was to give 1/64 more to compensate for decrease in quantity due to overflow and adhesion to the measuring can.[27] In addition, private trade was regulated by collecting transaction taxes. Tax rates were based on the measure used. Tax for goods sold by volume was fixed at 1/16 of the price, by weight at 1/20 and by count at 1/11.[28]

Both imports and exports were actively promoted, encouraging foreign trade. The profit margin permitted on imported goods was 10 per cent, twice the profit permitted on domestic goods.[j] In addition, foreign merchants bringing

---

j   'The superintendent of commerce shall fix a profit of five per cent over and above the fixed price of local commodities, and ten per cent on foreign produce.' Extract from Chapter II, Book IV.

in goods were given immunity from being sued for debts. But their local partners could be sued, as this immunity did not extend to them. In cases where the local merchant directly imported the goods, they were exempted from taxation. Exports were promoted by conducting studies of profitable operations with foreign countries.

On the labour front, fair wages and conducive working conditions were promoted, as is reflected in the terms of engagement for weaving. Wages were fixed, based on the quality of thread spun and the quantity produced. Overtime for working on holidays was also provided for. In addition, a system of recognition for quality work was prescribed by providing awards of perfumes, garlands and other similar prizes. Considering the fact that women were employed in weaving, provisions were designed for eliminating any opportunity for sexual harassment. Women received their wages at dawn by exchanging their spinning. A conscious attempt was made to ensure that the light provided did not permit the cashier to look at the face of the woman while paying her wages.[k] Attempts by the cashier to look at the face of the woman or indulge in frivolous chit-chat were punished.

The *Arthasastra* can be evaluated as an economic treatise by seeing the extent to which it acknowledged and recognized the three prerequisites we have discussed in the previous chapter. The importance of private property was acknowledged by defining systems and processes for trade and exchange. It also

---

k   'Those women who can present themselves at the weaver's house shall at dawn be enabled to exchange their spinning for wages. Only so much light as is enough to examine the threads shall be kept. If the superintendent looks at the face of such women or talks about any other work, he shall be punished with the first amercement.' Extract from Chapter XXIII, Book II

recognized the self-centred nature of humans, by providing tax incentives to promote an activity. However, it did not permit this self-centred nature to be unrestrained. It sought to limit it by capping profits and specifying just wages. On the materialistic front too, by identifying the level of economic activity with people's happiness, the *Arthasastra* acknowledged the importance of material goods. It also sought to encourage material output by providing tax incentives. The only shortcoming in the *Arthasastra,* when compared with current economic texts, is that it did not give economics its distinct shape and form. By merely stating conclusions, the analysis behind these choices and the options examined and discarded were not captured. The result was that economics as a distinct discipline was not born in India in the third century BCE.

The Chinese view of this period is contained in *Shang-chŭn-shu,* now translated into English under the title *The Book of Lord Shang.* Preceding the *Arthasastra* by a few decades, this Chinese treatise has a lot in common with it. The parallels between Chanakya and Lord Shang are quite striking. They were both ministers, advising rulers in administering their kingdom. They both analyzed human nature and prioritized the end over the means, drawing criticism for this emphasis. Each individually drew an extensive blueprint to administer the kingdom using the two royal prerogatives: taxes and penalties. They both leveraged their understanding of human nature to execute their blueprints.

Shang-Chŭn-shu[1] –*A Chinese view*

Shang-Chŭn-shu, the Chinese book noted for its originality, is traced to the writings of an individual who lived in the third century BCE. Lord Shang was a counsellor in the state of Ch'in between the years 359 to 338 BCE. Born to a concubine of the Wei family, the counsellors of a marginal kingdom in the Western borders of China, he was given the name Yang and his family name was Kiung-sun. Failing to find an opportunity to use his talent in Wei his birthplace, Yang Kiung-sun responded to a call from Duke Hsiao for able men to join him in restoring the lost territory of his kingdom. Yang joined Hsiao's team and rose to prominence. He was instrumental in drafting the new laws for his country which contributed to the conversion of a marginal backward state into a dominant empire. Yang was awarded 15 cities in Shang as his fief when he brought his hometown Wei under the Ch'in rule and was given the title 'Lord Shang'.

The Book of Lord Shang outlines the end objectives to be achieved by a ruler and methods to realize them, grouped into five chapters. The ideas in the book have a few common points with Kautilya's in the use of taxation. In addition, it too looks to use rewards and punishments as a driving motive.

Lord Shang was clear about what a successful ruler should strive for: peace for the country and honour for its ruler. According to him, both these objectives depend on agriculture and war.[29] The strength of a country could be measured by thirteen indicators – granaries, able-bodied men and women, old and weak people, officials and officers, useful people, people

---

1 This book was translated for the first time from Chinese into French in 1928, and later into English by J.J.L. Duyvendak. This section is based on the English translation.

engaged in 'talking' (i.e.: unproductive work like merchants), horses, oxen, fodder and straw.[30] In all these indicators, more is not necessarily better. While a larger number of granaries, able-bodied people, useful people, horses, oxen, fodder and straw strengthen the kingdom, an increase in the number of old and weak people, officials, officers and people engaged in talking, makes the kingdom weaker.

The rationale for Lord Shang's line of thinking is found in his concept of wealth, which he explains is a result of large receipts and small expenditure. This is contrary to the current mode of thought that justifies a larger expenditure if it can generate a higher income. Shang believed that large receipts would be generated by all engaged in gainful occupation, while a small expenditure should be the result of frugal lifestyles.[31] Thus, wealth would be the source of peace for a country and honour for its ruler. While there can be only a few who will disagree with this stated objective of peace or its links to wealth, Lord Shang's analysis of human motives and, consequently, the means to achieve them, will find few supporters, as he opted to suppress human emotions and eliminate filial ties.

Lord Shang recognized three professions in the kingdom: farming, foreign trade and bureaucracy. He did not consider soldiers as being part of a separate profession, as he envisaged that during wartime farmers and bureaucrats would don the role of soldiers. He argued that the three professions give rise to 'six parasites', as he called them: old age care, living off others, beauty, love, ambition and virtuous conduct.[32] He saw these 'parasites' weakening the kingdom: farmers would not work hard if they were affluent, merchants would be distracted by beauty and love, and officials would pursue their personal ambitions and 'virtuous conduct' (that is, favour their near and dear ones). The result of farmers at leisure, distracted merchants and personally-driven officials would be a weak army, 'certain to suffer great defeat.'

Lord Shang sought to maintain a victorious army by abolishing ten evils, which he identified as rites, music, odes, history, virtue, moral culture, filial piety, brotherly duty, integrity and sophistry.[33] Recognizing that he was banishing the virtuous, he remarked, 'A country where the virtuous govern the wicked, will suffer from disorder, so that it will be dismembered; but a country where the wicked govern the virtuous, will be orderly, so that it will become strong.'[34]

In short, Lord Shang wanted a kingdom in which every individual was productive and earned not just their upkeep, but also at the same time set aside a portion of their income for future contingencies. Based on this idea, he advocated the guiding principle for administration:

> If the country is rich, but is administered as if it were poor, then it is said to be doubly rich, and the doubly rich are strong. If the country is poor, but is administered as if it were rich, it is said to be doubly poor, and the doubly poor are weak.[35]

Having defined a strong country, Lord Shang looked outside the kingdom for ways to strengthen it further. He advocated imports and immigration and discouraged exports, which seems counter-intuitive to current economic thinking that advocates export-led growth for development. He reasoned that promoting exports would lead to an increase of gold in the country at the cost of disappearing grain. In contrast, imports only reduced gold, while they increased grain. He argued that the increase of gold in the kingdom over time would drain both the granary and treasury as the prices would fall, reducing the incentive for producers to exert thereby gradually weakening the kingdom. But, if imports were promoted by keeping the prices high, over time both the granary and treasury would be full and the kingdom would be strong as measured by his thirteen parameters.[36]

After defining a strong kingdom and ways to strengthen it, Lord Shang turned his attention to the means by which he could attain the desired objective of a strong kingdom based on his understanding of human nature – primarily via taxation and rewards. Rewards included both the positive ones such as granting titles and the negative ones of punishments for non-adherence to the accepted code of behaviour.

Leveraging Human Nature

Lord Shang saw individuals primarily as self-centred.[m] Some individuals are motivated by profits and embrace unacceptable behavior, like robbers and thieves who deviate from their duty to their king and parents in pursuit of profit.[n] Others shun natural human desires in pursuit of fame, like scholars who increase their activity unmindful of the fact that 'their clothes do not warm their skins, their food does not fill their stomachs, they travail their thoughts, fatigue their four limbs and suffer in their five internal organs....'[37] These observations seem to have formed the basis for his scheme of rewards and punishments, which were meant to promote the desired conduct and restrain unacceptable behaviour respectively. The form of punishments and rewards too was based on human nature. He noted 'Shame and disgrace, labour and hardship are what the people dislike;

---

m 'It is people's nature, when measuring, to take the longest part, when weighing, to take the heaviest, when adjusting the scales, to seek profit.' p176

n If the people strive for gain, then they lose the rules of polite behaviour; if they strive for fame, they lose the eternal principles of human nature. p174

fame and glory, ease and joy are what the people pay attention to.' Rewards found a place in both peace and war time, being awarded based on agricultural production and on military merit as appropriate.[o] Lord Shang's major focus was to promote clarity on how to earn rewards. He considered ignoring merit in granting rewards akin to trying to fill a bottomless barrel,[p] as an individuals' incentive to do honest work is diluted if not destroyed, as it seems futile. Having identified the deficiency, he then laid out a clear plan for rewards. Lord Shang observed the use of standard scales for weights and measures. Drawing the analogy, he concluded that replacing standard scales with personal judgment would lead to indefiniteness and be ineffective. He extended this corollary by identifying effort as the standard scale for granting rewards and ranks.[38]

Moving to punishments, Lord Shang laid down the mandate that if light offences carry heavy punishments, heavy offences will not occur.[39] The inherent logic is that criminals start small and grow big and deterring them at the first stage is a sure way to prevent bigger crimes. Going further, he outlined a hierarchy for enforcing discipline, starting with the family at the base, bureaucracy at the next level and finally the prince at the apex. In strong states, he noted, discipline was enforced by the family

---

o   When the army is mobilized for an offensive, rank is given according to military merit, and reliance being placed upon the military, victory is certain. When the army is in reserve and agriculture is pursued, rank is given according to the production of grain, and reliance being placed upon farming, the country will be rich. If in military enterprises the enemy is conquered and if, when the army is in reserve, the country becomes rich, then it attains supremacy. p166

p   If a tube of no more than four inches has no bottom, it can certainly not be filled; to confer office, to give rank and to grant salaries, without regard to merit, is like having no bottom. p194 and in contrast, the need for a prince to enforce discipline resulted in weak states.[40] Rewards and punishments were not an end in themselves; their judicious use, he felt, would result in the poor getting richer and the rich becoming poorer, which was essential for a country to grow strong.[41]

While analyzing Shang's contribution to furthering the discipline of economics using the three prerequisites framework, we can see that the subject did not get its distinctive shape and form in his study. While Shang recognized humans as self-centred, a critical prerequisite, he did not fully approve of private property, another prerequisite. His attitude towards traders was reflected in his describing them as useless people who 'make a living by talking'. He sought to discourage traders as he believed that if people found an easy way of making money they would abandon agriculture and war, thus weakening the country. Hence, he opted for an active government that would regulate the life of its residents.

This championing of an active government seems an exception and an isolated call as it is in conflict with the more popular ancient Chinese view of a laissez-faire government. Lao-tse, in *The Book of Tao*, describes the art of government in these four lines that resonate with the right-wing intellectuals of today:

Therefore the Sage says:
I [government] do nothing and the people are reformed of themselves.
I [government] love quietude and the people are righteous of themselves.
I [government] deal in no business and the people grow rich by themselves.
I [government] have no desires and the people are simple and honest by themselves.[42]

In summary, we have an interesting situation: Aristotle represents the Greeks, who recognized private property, but not a self-centred human or materialistic outlook; Lord

Shang represents the Chinese, who recognized the self-centred nature of humans but did not fully acknowledge private property and attempted to curb trade and free exchange; and Kautilya represents the Indians, who recognized all the three prerequisites, but he did not explain the rationale for his analysis before presenting his conclusions. Elements essential to economics are found in the writings of all the three thinkers. But when and where did they merge?

By virtue of its geographical location in West Asia and the trade flows that linked the world, Islamic civilization was at the confluence of these three ancient civilizations. This is not to say that the ideas of all these three thinkers were available to all Islamic scholars. However, the closest approximation to current economic ideas and concepts emerged in Islamic society. It was not an abrupt arrival, but followed extensive deliberations on the commercial aspects of life. Among the prominent deliberations is the work by Al-Dimashqi, the twelfth-century businessman and scholar, who wrote *Kitab al-ishara ila mahasin al-tijara* translated as *Indication of the Merits of Commerce*. In this book, he analyzed the nature of wealth, the need for money, methods of evaluating commodities, investments in real estate, handicrafts and manufacture and the merits of business. But it was Ibn Khaldun, a fourteenth-century historian, who captured the essence of economics in his work *Kitab al-Ibar,* translated as *Book of Lessons.*

Ibn Khaldun – The Father of Economics?

Abd Ar Rahman bin Muhammed ibn Khaldun was born in Tunis, Granada on May 27, 1332. His family was a part of the ruling elite, serving the royal command. Over a career spanning multiple decades he served as a royal officer of the court, a tax collector, an ambassador and a judge. In 1375 CE, he retreated for seven years from public life to write his three volume work *Kitab al-Ibar*. Returning to public life, he spent the next 23 years as a professor, college principal and a judge. He died in 1406 while holding the office of a judge. One small part of his magnum opus is Chapter V of the first volume, *Muqaddimah* (translated as *Prolegomena*). This chapter deals with economics in a concentrated form, while in the rest of his work too, a sprinkling of economic thoughts can be found.

'On the (various) aspects of making a living, such as profits and crafts. The conditions that occur in this connection. A number of problems are connected (with this subject)', is the long title of the fifth chapter in *Muqaddimah* that more than adequately describes its content. Two of the three prerequisites of economics – private property and the self-centred nature of humans are identified[q] early in this chapter: 'Every man tries to get things; in this all men are alike. Thus, whatever is obtained by one is denied to the other, unless he gives something in exchange (for it)'.[43]

This chapter deals with a variety of economic concepts and principles set in a defined framework. In addition, the prevailing economic condition is adequately described, providing an insight into how Ibn Khaldun discovered these concepts and principles.

---

q   'Whatever is obtained by one is denied to the other' defines private property i.e. exclusive possession, and 'Every man tries to get things, in this all men are alike' defines the self-centred nature of humans. Chapter V, Section 1

Box 2.2
Muqaddimah by Ibn Khaldun

Usually shortened to *The History of the World*, Ibn Khaldun's *Book of Examples and Register of Subject and Predicate Dealing with the History of Arabs, Persians and Berbers*[r] was written in the 1370s. This chronicle of history was published in three volumes. The first volume deals with the nature of history and society, the second covers the history of Arabs and the third covers the history of Berbers. During the author's lifetime itself the first volume became an independent and renowned book, titled the *Muqaddimah*.

The *Muqaddimah* is organized in six chapters, of which only a small portion contains economic content. Containing around thirty thousand words, and placed in the penultimate chapter, this short portion nonetheless has a great deal of depth, as reflected in the thirty-two distinct headings under which this subject is covered.

Here, Ibn Khaldun covered a range of concepts and principles set in a well defined framework that would be rediscovered by the European economists between the eighteenth and twentieth century. The original manuscripts written during his lifetime are available today in Turkey. Franz Rosenthal translated *Maqaddimah* into English in 1958. Since then it has been a subject matter of intense study among the interested few, but is yet to gain mainstream recognition.

Ibn Khaldun took a detached view of society as he identified the need for economic activity, the options available to an

---

[r] The original work was titled *Kitab Al-Ishara Ila Mahasin Al-Tifara wa Matrifa Aljayyid Al-Atrad wa Radiha wa Ghushush Al-Mudallisinfiha*

individual to earn a livelihood, their relative merits and demerits and the influence of the economy on individual pursuits. In the process, he defined profit and its source, the evolution of livelihoods in human history, the traits required to succeed in each profession and the benefits that accrue from their pursuit. He also identified a few economic principles based on the observed relationship between events over time. These include the importance of rank in society, the reason why knowledge professionals like teachers, judges and religious scholars are underpaid, the desired price levels for a vibrant economy, and the relationship between demand and price.

Ibn Khaldun starts by asserting 'Profit is the value realized from labour'. Human labour is necessary to earn a livelihood, and profit is the surplus after meeting sustenance needs. He identified five facets of human labour – *collection* as seen in hunting and fishing, *partnering* with nature, as in agriculture and animal husbandry, *acquired skills* required in crafts like carpentry, weaving and medicine, *force* used in collecting tax and imposts and *knowledge of gainful exchange* required for undertaking commerce. These five facets of labour provide sustenance to the individual and where there is an excess, profit is the result. He made a critical distinction between natural ways of making a living based on an individual's own efforts as identified above, and the 'unmanly' livelihood of servants who live at the mercy of their masters.

The Importance of Rank

Ibn Khaldun logically built a case for linking the wealth in an economy to the human labour expended in it. Commenting on the then prevailing practice of men seeking riches by hunting for buried treasures, he reasoned that the property of earlier civilizations cannot be found in hidden treasure. He reasoned that it is human labour that causes wealth to increase or decrease and money is merely a representation of this wealth.[44]

After identifying human labour as the source of profit and property, Ibn Khaldun looked for the multiplier that accelerated an individuals' fortune. How could an individual accumulate a fortune that was in excess of their own efforts and property? The answer was through rank, i.e.: the position in the hierarchy that a person occupies in society. Rank, the multiplier he identified, does not dilute the principle of human labour being the sole source of profit and property. It is the factor that makes an individual voluntarily give up the benefits of their own efforts to the rank-holder. Explaining the need for rank, Ibn Khaldun recognized humans as social animals. They cannot survive except in groups, and to survive in groups they need to cooperate. This cooperation does not come to them voluntarily, he noted. Therefore God's plan for preservation of humanity included hierarchy. He justified hierarchy, by quoting the Koran which stated that some forced labour could be extracted by the higher ranks, but this was more than compensated by the mercy of the Lord.[45] In contrast, current justifications for hierarchy are based on managerial efficiency in increasing output.

Ibn Khaldun was fair enough to admit that hierarchy brought with it some evils. But he justified it as a matter of fact, by claiming much good often comes with a little evil. He further emphasized, 'The good does not disappear with the (admixture of evil), but attaches itself to the little evil that gathers around it'.[46]

Explaining the logic for individuals wanting to voluntarily part with the results of their labour and property to the holders of rank, Ibn Khaldun identified their motive as self interest. Their voluntary contribution was nothing but an investment made to avoid losses and, where possible, earn some gains.[47] This is not very different from the current phenomenon of making voluntary contributions for election campaigns by business-men. With remarkable insight, he noticed that the higher the rank, the greater the wealth accumulated by the individual. Higher rank translated to influence over a larger number of people. In addition to accessing a larger pool, people willingly shared a larger portion of their wealth with a person holding higher rank as they expected either a greater gain or hoped to avoid larger loss from their patronage. This benefit accrued not only to individuals in the ruling elite but also to merchants and craftsmen holding rank within their community.

Having outlined the need for and the benefit obtained from rank, Ibn Khaldun noted the qualities required for an individual to win rank and progress in the hierarchy. He noted that people who are subservient and use flattery gained rank. He reasoned that superiors bestow rank only to individuals under their control. Therefore, an individual who seeks and desires rank must 'be obsequious and use flattery'.[48] He then extended this logic to explain why teachers, judges and religious scholars are not as a rule very wealthy. Being in a noble profession, he noted that they are ill-equipped to be subservient and sycophantic and cannot 'prostitute themselves openly'.[49]

The Art of Trading

After dealing with the general aspects of making a living, Ibn Khaldun turned his attention to specific livelihoods. He found agriculture a simple and natural process, practiced by humble individuals who were dominated by the strong. In commerce, he identified the sole principle for earning profit and the two avenues to it. He quotes an old merchant to explain: 'I shall give it to you in two words: Buy cheap and sell dear. There is commerce for you'.[50]

The two avenues Ibn Khaldun suggested for success were by hoarding goods till the prices rose and transporting goods to a place where they were scarce. Laying down the guidelines for success to merchants transporting goods, he recommended dealing in medium-quality goods. Superior quality goods, he reasoned, have a restricted demand as only wealthy people, who are few in numbers, want them; therefore they may remain unsold. A third option he identified for enhancing profit was travelling to a distant land over dangerous terrain, as fewer goods would be transported and 'when the goods are few and rare, their prices go up'.[51] He illustrated this by highlighting trade with Sudan, a desert-encircled country. Merchants who dared to trade with Sudan, overcoming the danger of beasts and thirst faced in deserts, were wealthy and prosperous. In contrast, merchants who traded with nearby cities and countries earned 'a very small profit'.[52]

Turning his attention to hoarding, Ibn Khaldun defined the profitable strategy as that of waiting for prices to rise after buying at a low price. He however prohibited hoarding of food grains on the grounds that there is force involved. He quoted the Prophet who forbade taking property without giving anything in return. Even though food grains are exchanged in trade, there is an element of compulsion as the grains are a necessity, essential for life. Hence, he approved the hoarding of luxury goods as people buying them were not under any compulsion, and could live without these goods. He illustrated it with an interesting anecdote narrated to him by his teacher. Judge Abul-Hasan al-Malili was offered the option of selecting the tax from which he would be paid his salary. After due deliberation, the judge choose to be paid from custom duty on wine, to the amusement of observers. Answering their questions he remarked.

> All tax money is forbidden. Therefore, I choose the tax that is not haunted by the souls of those who had to pay it. Rarely would anybody spend his money on wine unless he were gay and happy with the experience of (drinking wine), and did not regret it. His soul, therefore, does not cling to the money he has had to spend.[53]

Both in the case of transporting goods, and hoarding them, a higher price translates to a higher profit for the merchant. Given this, Ibn Khaldun answered the question of what price level would be conducive to the livelihoods and profits of people in society. He first enumerated the adverse effects of low price levels in an economy by highlighting that merchants will go out of business when low prices prevail. If low prices continue for long, even for food grains, farmers will make insignificant or no profits at all and the implication is that craftspeople dependent on farm outputs like millers and bakers, will also be under economic stress. The cascading impact of this will reduce the taxes collected by the ruler, and consequently the life of the soldiers too would be adversely affected. In short, low prices destroy livelihood by drying up employment opportunities. Now turning his attention to high prices, Ibn Khaldun noted that occasional high prices will result in a one-time profit for the merchant. But what is conducive for livelihood are, 'medium prices and rapid fluctuations of the market that provide people with their livelihood and profit.'[54] Further reflections on this topic resulted in Ibn Khaldun finding an exception to this rule. He advocated low prices for essentials like food grains on the ground that the majority of the people would benefit from it and this was more important that pure commercial considerations.[55]

The economic rationale of self interest and material acquisition that is visible throughout Ibn Khaldun's writing in this chapter is replaced by social concern when it comes to necessities – especially food. This is seen in his advice to merchants on hoarding necessities and again on the need for low price levels for food grains, even at the cost of hampering commerce. He saw that low prices for necessities resulted in population growth in cities and towns, which in turn increased the number of crafts. These he split into necessary crafts, like agriculture, architecture, carpentry, tailoring and weaving, and noble crafts, like midwifery, medicine, singing, book writing and book production. While the logic for classifying midwifery and medicine as noble crafts is quite apparent, due to their close links with the origin and sustenance of human life, the logic he uses for classifying music, book writing and book production is very distinct. These crafts become noble crafts as their practitioners need contact with the rulers in privacy and at their intimate parties. He identified singing as the last craft to develop in a civilization as it is a luxury and serves no other purpose than leisure and gaiety. Hence, it is also the first to disappear when a civilization is in decline. Finally, Ibn Khaldun also identified the reason for destruction of a dynasty, saying that in their days of their ascension, rulers bestow rank on competent individuals and look upon them as equals. The dynastic decline starts with the rulers' intolerance of dissent, which results in capable individuals being replaced by sycophants who willingly support the ruler in all undertakings, no matter how ill-advised, 'until the dynasty is destroyed.'[56]

Ibn Khaldun described and analyzed an economy from its inception to its destruction. As a historian he took a dispassionate view which enabled him to trace the economic aspects of a society without any personal bias. In the process, he identified private property as a critical feature in society. He saw the wide prevalence of self-interested human behaviour and only advocated restraint in pursuit of profit where essential goods were involved, as human welfare would be hampered. He also recognized that vibrant economic activity was desirable, though not when accompanied by high prices.

The Bottom Line

Ibn Khaldun, Kautilya, Lord Shang and Aristotle had a few thoughts in common. They all analyzed the different types of livelihoods prevalent in their society. However, they did not consider all livelihoods to be on an equal footing. Except for Ibn Khaldun, the other three looked down upon trade and commerce as unnatural and harmful to society. They preferred livelihoods that leveraged nature and used physical effort, as in agriculture and animal husbandry. In contrast, Ibn Khaldun was neutral to trade, disapproving only of profiteering with essential commodities in a way that put the masses to hardship.

Each of the four saw economic activity with a different lens. Aristotle saw it as subservient to a bigger purpose – to 'living well'. Kautilya and Lord Shang viewed it as a means to building a stronger state. Only Ibn Khaldun among the four gave it an independent view, but it was a small part of his larger work on human history. For economics to evolve as a distinct discipline, it would need a different environment, where it was recognized for its own merits.

Economics came of age as a distinct and independent discipline only after the sixteenth century. Europe, the abode of Christian civilization, was the place. The seeds were sown when the idea of an individual as a self-centred being started to gain social sanction. The result was the birth of economics as a distinct discipline, no longer a 'slave' to larger purposes. This emancipation would soon see it command greater attention and dominate the world of social sciences, as human life became increasingly dominated by economic pursuits.

Endnotes

1   Aristotle, *The Basic Works of Aristotle*, The Modern Library, 2001, p1127

2   Loos, I. A., Historical Approaches to Economics, *The American Economic Review*, Vol.8, No.3, (Sept., 1918), p550

3   Smith, V. A., *The Oxford History of India*, Oxford University Press, Fourth Edition, 1958, p96

4   Aristotle, *The Basic Works of Aristotle*, The Modern Library, 2001, p938

5   Ibid p938

6   Ibid p984

7   Ibid p939

8   Ibid p1138

9   Ibid p1141

10 Ibid p1141

11 Ibid p1138

12 Ibid p1139

13 Ibid p1139

14 Plato, *Republic*, p371

15 Lind, L. R., Man in Ancient Athens, *The Classical Journal*, Vol.35, No.1., (Oct., 1939), p31

16 Aristotle, *The Basic Works of Aristotle*, The Modern Library, 2001, p984

17 Xenophon, *The Economist*, Translator H. G. Dakyns, August 20, 2008, [E Book #1173], Guttenberg

18 Ohrenstein, R. A., Economic Self-Interest and Social Progress in Talmudic Literature: A Further Study of Ancient Economic Thought and its Modern Significance, *American Journal of Economics and Sociology*, Vol.29, No.1, (Jan., 1970), pp 62-63

19 Sarkar, B. K., *The Sukraniti*, Oriental Books Reprint Corporation, Second Edition, 1975, p17

20 Ibid pp42-44

21 Ibid pp106-08

22 Ibid pp365-67

23 Rangarajan, L. N., *Kautilya Arthashastra*, Penguin Classics, 1992, p97
24 Ibid p84
25 Shamasastry, R., *Kautilya's Arthasastra*, Mysore Printing and Publishing House, Sixth edition, 1960, p231
26 Ibid p105
27 Ibid p116
28 Ibid p105
29 Duyvendak, J.J.L., *The Book of Lord Shang*, Wordsworth Classic of World Literature, 1998, p157
30 Ibid p166
31 Ibid p217
32 Ibid p223
33 Ibid p163
34 Ibid p163
35 Ibid p162
36 Ibid p165
37 Ibid p174
38 Ibid p199
39 Ibid p168
40 Ibid p170
41 Ibid p168
42 Yutang, L., *The Wisdom of China and India*, The Modern Library, 1942, p613
43 Ibn Khaldun, *Muqaddimah*, translated by Frank Rosenthal, Chapter V, Section 1
44 Ibid Chapter V, Section 4
45 Ibid Chapter V, Section 6
46 Ibid Chapter V, Section 6
47 Ibid Chapter V, Section 6
48 Ibid Chapter V, Section 6
49 Ibid Chapter V, Section 7
50 Ibid Chapter V, Section 9
51 Ibid Chapter V, Section 10
52 Ibid Chapter V, Section 10
53 Ibid Chapter V, Section 11
54 Ibid Chapter V, Section 12
55 Ibid Chapter V, Section 12
56 Ibid Chapter V, Section 6

Chapter 3

Socially Shackled: A Brief Childhood 1300 to 1776 CE

For the first discovery of every science is the discovery of itself.
— **Joseph A. Schumpeter,** *History of Economic Analysis*[1]

Europe is arguably the birthplace of economics as a distinct discipline. The plague epidemic of 1348-50 in Europe – and its economic impact – coincides with the beginning of accelerated economic growth. Prior to this epidemic, the social and moral climate in Europe was not very different from that in India and China, the two largest economies in the world at the time. Trade practices had very strong ethical restraints on the pursuit of profit. The royal sanction of monopolies, which started in England in the wool trade, in return for advance tax payments to fund the Hundred Years War, is significant for its departure from the strong ethical nature of the policies followed hitherto. As monopolies increased in number, the right to grant them in England shifted from the monarchy to Parliament. Since Parliament consisted of a large number of individuals, a new class of pamphleteers emerged, with the specific agenda of mobilizing support for granting monopolies. These pamphleteers collated the prevailing economic thoughts across the European continent and built on them to advocate their individual cases, thereby providing material for the development of economics as a distinct discipline. Two centuries later, Adam Smith consolidated these thoughts in his magnum opus, *The Wealth of Nations*, setting the stage for a new discipline.

Why Europe?

Around the tenth century, Europe was a backwater of the global economy. India and China, the two dominant economies, each contributed about 28.9 per cent and 22.7 per cent respectively to the estimated global GDP.[2] In contrast, Europe accounted only for 10.9 per cent. This income distribution was broadly in line with the population estimates of their respective geographies.[a] In a relatively short span of 500 years, Europe almost doubled its GDP contribution to 20.5 per cent. This growth was not driven by population growth, which was much slower, with Europe accounting for only 16.2 per cent of the global population at the end of that period.[3] Neither colonial expansion nor the Industrial Revolution can explain this change, as they started only after 1500 CE. These two factors merely accelerated the initial momentum that was brought into play, placing Europe on the top of the world. This gives rise to the significant question: *what was the initial force that shifted this inertia to propel Europe ahead?*

European society was synonymous with Christianity during this period. As J.M. Roberts in *The Penguin History of the World* noted, only a few Jews, visitors and slaves were outside the domain of the Church.[4] Starting in 1000 CE, the population began to grow rapidly. from around forty million to around seventy three million by 1300.[5] The majority of this increase was in France, England, Germany and Scandinavia. This growth seems to have been primarily driven by increased food production, a result of larger areas of land brought under cultivation, concomitant with improved agricultural techniques. The population increase was stalled by the

---

a   The population in the three geographies of India, China and Europe was 28, 22.1 and 11.9 per cent respectively of the global whole at the time.

outbreak of epidemic diseases. The 'Black Death' of 1348-50, brought about by the outbreak of plague was a demographic disaster. The total loss was estimated at around a quarter of the population of Europe, with specific areas losing between half to one-third of their population.[6] The magnitude of this loss seems to be the highest in recorded human history. In comparison, the loss of life during Word War II as a ratio of the population of the countries engaged in the war was between 3 and 4 per cent.[7] This loss of around ten times the magnitude of what was seen in World War II resulted in multiple reactions.

As is to be expected, witnessing this humungous human tragedy prompted many people to look inward and seek refuge in religion and turn to the Church. A belief emerged among many that the plague was a sign of God's wrath against sinners. Konrad Von Megenburg writing in 1350 interpreted the meaning of the Black Death as a consequence wished by the society upon itself by its sinful behaviour.[8] In 1308, Dante Alighieri had written the epic three-part *Divine Comedy*. The first part, Inferno, vividly depicted the nine stages of hell. Purgatory, the second part, represented the cleansing required before reaching the final part – Paradise. Such graphic depictions of hell further frightened the survivors. Some people also saw it as a sign of the Return of Christ to rule the earth.[9] As redemption, many private chapels and charities were set up. Catholics, for whom it was stipulated to participate in communion once a year, now sought to participate in it more frequently.[10] Various forms of penance were also adopted as repentance for sins committed to appease god. Public flagellation as repentance was more visible in continental Europe. The Brothers of the Cross, for example, formed teams in Germany who flogged themselves publicly twice a day for thirty-three and a half days, one day representing a year in the life of Jesus Christ. However, not everyone turned inwards. Those who looked outwards on the material front saw a silver lining in these dense dark clouds.

Silver Lining in the Dark Clouds

Paradoxically, the plague epidemic that had such a huge human cost resulted in some material benefits. Survivors from all sections of society stood relatively better off afterwards. Among the landed class, large-scale death resulted in accelerated inheritances. In contrast to wars which also cause human death in large numbers, in a pandemic, physical assets are not destroyed. With wealth remaining the same, the remaining survivors got larger shares. Increased mortality also contributed to a sharp drop in rents and in some cases rent was even eliminated for houses, shops and fisheries.[11] Among the other classes too, one immediate impact of this human disaster was an acute labour shortage, which resulted in a shift in the rural workforce from serfdom to paid labour. Many landlords gave in to the peasants' demands for higher wages, resulting in improved standards of living.[b] An effect of these changes resulting in paid labour was the gradual shift, even in the rural economy, away from the barter system to money-based exchanges.[12]

Labour, which till then was abundant, suddenly became a scarce commodity. In many areas, crops rotted in the fields and farm animals wandered loose with no one to care for them.[13] The search began for methods to optimize labour. In England, sheep rearing gradually displaced cultivation, as it required

---

b There was an attempt to suppress wage levels by enacting the Statute of Labourers, 1351 in England.

lesser manpower.[c] This led to wool production being much in excess of domestic demand. Exports of wool began to grow, leading to the establishment of the first regulated company, the Merchants of the Staple in 1353.[14]

There was a deeper psychological impact too. The prolonged epidemics that wiped out a sizeable fraction of the population led to a few even doubting the existence of a providential God.[15] These individuals observed that plague epidemics were not halted by prayers and the mercy of God. It was in fact better sanitation and improved hygiene that stemmed this disease. This promoted a belief in reason. Logical decisions started to displace faith and authority, which had hitherto ruled the day, in a small way. In commercial life, it emerged in the concept of prudent economic reason.

The growth of a money-based economy in place of barter–trade, the rise in exports as distinct from local trade and the concept of prudent economic reason guiding decision–making, all played a major role in promoting economics as a distinct discipline in Europe. However, it was not elevated in a single move. The first step was taken by the 'physicians of the soul' who were at the centre of these three forces. As the popular saying goes, well begun is about half-done.

Private Property Justified

Most of Europe was under the decisive influence of the Church in the first half of the second millennium. The influence of the Church strengthened with the growing popularity of two practices – communion and confession. In the thirteenth century, the theory of transubstantiation, a mystical process through which the bread and wine used in the communion

---

c   See Chapter 1, 'The Urban Tilt' for more details on this transition

process becomes the body and blood of Christ, was propounded, leading to frequent communions.[d] Along with it, the practice of individual confessions, a powerful instrument to control the religiously-minded, was also practiced.[16] The requirement to confess led to the need to define sins and the occasions when sinning occurred in the routine life of an individual.

The nature of commercial transactions made them a potential cause and location of sin, as defined by the rules of that era. Trade was the major area of focus. During this period, perishable goods, such as food, dominated trade. In addition, transportation was expensive and limited, and so too were the number of transactions. These factors confined trade to a local, intra-community exchange. Given this, a trader could profit only at the cost of his consumer – his brethren. This then raised a few critical ethical and moral questions. Was profit then a result of avarice and greed? Would earning profits result in sin? If so, how could one live without any commercial transactions? The priests who administered the communion and heard the confessions needed answers to these delicate questions.

Around this period, the twelfth century, Arabic, Hebrew and Greek manuscripts of Aristotle and other Greek scholars reached Europe for the first time. Aristotle's use of logic to further arguments caught the imagination and appealed to the reason of the European intelligentsia, most of whom were from the religious fraternity. A new sect of theological scholars, who attempted to use logic to explain the doctrine and mysteries of the Church, emerged. They were called the Scholastics. Albertus Magnus (1193-1280) led this attempt to

---

d   Communion is the practice in which bread and wine, representing a part of Jesus Christ, is given to a Christian thereby forging the bond between Jesus Christ and the Christian, and thereby connecting all the Christians.

supplement faith-led obedience to the Bible.[17] In this process, Magnus and his disciples interpreted the Bible in the context of the prevailing situations. These interpretations provided the merchant guidance on prudent commercial conduct, as trade was seen to endanger the salvation of souls by exposure to the temptations of usury, cheating and unlawful gain.[18] The reasoning that led to these recommendations provided the first stepping-stone in shaping economics as a distinct discipline.

St. Thomas Aquinas, a student of Magnus, is the most reputed of the Scholastics. In his book *Aquinas Ethicus: or Moral Teachings of St.Thomas, vol.2 (Summa Theologica – Secunda Secundae Pt.2)* dated 1274 CE, he answered a series of questions of which only a handful pertained to commercial transactions. He acknowledged the existence of private property, the first prerequisite of economics, in answering the question, 'Is it lawful for anyone to possess anything as his own?'[19] Thomas Aquinas identified property as essential for human life and listed three reasons to support it. First, humans take care of their private assets better than what is owned in common. Second, human affairs are managed in an orderly fashion and confusion is avoided when property is individually owned. Finally, owning in common can lead to disputes, which private property eliminates. However immediately in the next paragraph, he qualified his approval for private property, with a covenant: 'a man ought not to hold exterior goods as his own, but as common possession, so as readily to share them with others in need.' These ideas seem to have set the foundation for his views on the exchange of goods and trade.

Fair Trade Identified

Thomas Aquinas answered a series of questions on what constitutes fraudulent dealing in buying and selling. In the process he laid out the principles for prudent commercial conduct that would not endanger the soul. He started his analysis by bifurcating commercial exchanges in society. In the first category he included exchanges that are necessary for life or occur naturally in the course of daily existence, and in the other category he placed the rest, which are commercial transactions motivated by gain.

Thomas Aquinas held that trade is mutually beneficial. This mutual benefit requires that the principle of equality be honoured. He emphasized that money was invented only to measure the benefit derived by an individual from a product. Considering this, he laid down the rule, 'And therefore to sell a thing dearer or to buy it cheaper than its worth, is a proceeding in itself unjust and unlawful.'[20] As a rule is validated eminently by its exceptions, for this rule too, he listed the exceptions in dealing with incidental transactions that are not commercially motivated. He realized that in some situations, the seller may suffer more from parting with the goods than the ordinary worth of the good. In these cases, the seller was permitted to receive a higher price, as equality was to be measured in specific instances and not in general situations.

Reflecting on the duties of the seller, Thomas Aquinas turned his attention to flaws in the goods sold. First dealing with an apparent flaw like a horse with one eye, he expected the seller to offer a reduced price considering its handicap. On the other hand, he did not expect him to specifically declare the flaw as it was apparent and visible. Turning to flaws that were not so obvious, he used Cicero's two widely-quoted examples[e] to illustrate prudent conduct. In the first instance of the merchant in Rhodes, St. Thomas held that the merchant had no obligation to share knowledge that would have reduced his price with the buyers, as the expected fall in the price of goods would occur only in the future. If the merchant shared this information or provided a rebate in price, he would be acting in virtue, without any obligation of duty. In the second instance, his advice to the honest seller is not to advertise the defect in his house, but to share it with a potential buyer in private, when he 'draws near to purchase it.' He then explained the logic for his advice by stating that one fault by itself did not reduce the usefulness of the article sold and it was for the buyers to compare the good and bad together in making their decision.

Finally, Thomas Aquinas answered a purely economic question: 'Is it lawful to sell an article at more than its cost price?' In reply, he segregated natural trade arising from necessity which he approved of, and isolated it from trade for gain, which he had reservations about. In this bifurcation, he included exchanges made by a domestic household and a statesman trading for his country under natural trade. He approved of trade that resulted in meeting the needs of a family, providing relief to the distressed and supplying the necessities for one's country. Moving to trade for gain, he

---

e   Cicero quoted these two instances in his book *On Duties,* written to advise his son on moral challenges in commercial situations. In the first, a merchant from Alexandria transporting food grains to Rhodes, a city hit by famine, is faced with the question of his duty to Rhodes' residents. As the first merchant reaching Rhodes, should he tell the residents that other merchants were on their way with more merchandise? In the second instance, an honest man offering his house, which he believes is infected with termites, for sale faces the question, should he share his apprehension with his potential buyer?

further divided it into two. When it yielded only a moderate gain in the nature of fair wages for the trader, he saw it as neutral, neither a vice nor a virtue. In contrast, he disapproved of trade that resulted in gains disproportionate to the efforts of the trader.

Fairness, like Beauty, is in the Eye of the Beholder

In the thirteenth century, ideas about commercial aspects of life in Europe were not very different from thoughts elsewhere in the world. European thinking as reflected in the writings of the Scholastics dealt with many more economic concepts than 'just' or a fair price. They also provided guidelines on usury, just wages, debasement of currency, just taxation, monopoly and the likes. A stock taking at this stage would show that Europe, like much of the rest of the world, looked down upon self-centred individuals who were indifferent to the needs of their brethren.

A new line of thinking emerged as fresh guidelines were needed for evolving commercial practices. Dedicated works on commercial practices, distinct from ethical treatises soon came to be written. *De Contractibus Mercatorum*[f] written by Johannes Nider, the Dominican friar, was posthumously published in 1468.[21] In the preface to this treatise, Nider identified himself as a physician of the soul, working to separate the just from the unjust in the operations of the merchant.[22] In this treatise, Nider defined a just price using a very different concept from that used by Thomas Aquinas. His concept of a just price was,

> A thing is worth as much as it can be sold for, that is, according
> to how purchasers can be got to buy, when at liberty and by

---

f   Translated as *On the Contract of Merchants*

free choice, and assuming that the purchasers are not fools, pinched or deceived.[23]

While the seller deciding on a just price could be suspected of furthering his own interests, Nider reasoned that using the buyer to define a just price was an ethically safe choice, as no one could accuse the buyer of ignoring his own interests. This new concept of a just price, based on the buyer's view and not seen as a just wage, probably captured the emerging sentiments of his time. While this was a significant move towards the social sanction for self-centred individualism, the Scholastics did not shape economics into a distinct subject. In this, they too, like non-European thinkers, were limited by their framework. They saw economic transactions in the context of a larger purpose – the salvation of the soul. The Bible acknowledges this limitation in multiple places, as in Luke 16:13, where it clearly articulates 'No servant can be the slave of two masters: he will hate one and love the other; he will be loyal to one and despise the other. You cannot serve both God and money'.[24] This limitation was finally overcome by replacing the clerics with merchants, who served a sole master: money. But how did the merchants overcome the strong social and religious sanctions, fortified by individual perceptions of ethics?

Royal Sanction for Self-Centred Behaviour

A strong moral duty to support brethren, reinforced by an organized religious institution which monitored it over the centuries could not have been overcome by conventional forces. Heightened passion, fuelled by an intense contest that stretched over multiple decades provided, as it were, the escape velocity for economics to emerge as a distinct discipline. The setting was England. Three principal parties

– the royalty, the merchants and the Parliament – entangled in financing the Hundred Years' War[g] with France, resulting in a detached view that actually led to socially sanctioned monopoly. This royal sanction of a monopoly on the wool export trade was the seed that germinated into economics as a distinct discipline.

Material life in the fourteenth century revolved around, food, clothing and shelter. The luxuries of gems, perfume and spices were relevant only to a miniscule elite. Trade during this period was local, as food was perishable and transportation expensive, so the small towns that emerged during this period were supported by their surrounding rural communities. Trade gradually expanded from providing local supplies to longer distances. The bulk of it was in non-perishable items, such as clothes, especially the raw material for cloth. Given the cold climate in Europe, wool was a significant part of the long-distance trade. Burgundy, the Spanish peninsula, and England were the three major sources of supply.[25]

In the English economy, sheep occupied a distinctive position. They transformed sand into fertile soil with their manure. In addition to providing input to agriculture, they were a source of food too. These utilities supplemented their primary role – providing wool for clothes. Sheep rearing was a major occupation carried on at varying scales. Small flocks were owned by tenant farmers, while manors and monasteries housed large flocks. In contrast to the manure and mutton that was locally consumed, wool was a 'cash crop' that needed a market outlet. Foreign merchants were the main conduit of sale for the large manors and monasteries. The small flocks owned by the tenant farmers were too small for the foreign merchants

---

g   The Hundred Years' War was fought between 1337 and 1453 CE.

to consider, as they wanted scale. A 'woolman', a specialist who consolidated stocks from the tenant farmers, emerged to bridge this gap. It was a very profitable business that provided significant value-addition. Their importance can be gauged by the fact that an act passed to prevent the woolman from procuring wool resulted in the entire community of Halifax, an area dominated by tenant farmers, facing an economic downturn. To halt the decline, this act was quickly repealed in 1555 CE.[26]

Italians, who collected the papal taxes from the monasteries, viewed the wool trade as a logical extension to collecting taxes, as the monasteries were often short of cash, but rich in wool.[27] Given its commercial importance, wool was also a critical source of revenue to the royal exchequer. In times of war its attractiveness only increased, as it could be sold overseas and money realized to fund wars.[28] The lure of the wool tax was in its liquidity. It was collected from the wool merchants, whose wealth permitted the royal exchequer to draw advances. It was in this context that King Edward I had called for an assembly of merchants in 1275, as collecting taxes with their assent made it easier. In the face of competition from Burgundy and Spain, raising the selling price of their wool was not a viable option for the merchants. Despite this, the wool merchants provided little resistance to the royal tax claims, as they passed the cost of the tax onto the sheep farmers by reduced their purchase price. Parliament, the other advisory body comprising mainly knights and burghers, represented the interest of the farmers, and expressed its concern, but also put up with these temporary hikes in taxes.

The Hundred Years' War that began in 1336 increased the royal demands. With the outbreak of the war, King Edward III again convened the Assembly of Merchants and Parliament for consultations. The three parties were entwined in a power struggle that lasted almost two decades during which a few critical practices emerged.[h] All the three parties achieved their goals. The royal exchequer got its taxes. The farmers got a minimum price fixed for their wool. The merchants, who forfeited their flexibility by having to pay a minimum price to the farmers, got the monopoly of the wool trade that gave them their pricing power.[29]

This right to monopoly over the wool trade evolved through three distinct phases – preferential staples, compulsory staples and monopoly. In the first phase, in 1294 Edward I, who had collected tax on wool in kind by taking a portion of the produce itself, ordered that all the wool exported from England along with his own share to be sold in a fixed place to realize better prices. This process was called the *preferential staple*, as there was no compulsion or enforcement of this instruction. In 1313 for the first time, the compulsory wool staple was introduced. All wool merchants were required to sell only at the town of St. Omer. The third phase began with the advent of the Hundred Years' War, which resulted in the merchants advancing money to the monarch. In return, they received royal sanction allowing them to exclude others from exporting wool, creating a monopoly in favour of the royal lenders. Over time, these individual monopoly grants were institutionalized into the Company of the Staples of Calais. Over centuries, this precedent paved the way for the granting of monopolies to companies.

---

h   Refer to *The Wool Trade in English Medieval History,* by Eileen Power, The Ford Lectures, 1941 for a detailed narrative of this struggle

Box 3.1
Monopoly: A Capital Offense?

Social and religious sanctions against monopoly have deep roots. Quoting the instance of a merchant who purchased all the iron in the market to become the sole seller, Aristotle in *Politics*, remarked that he made a hefty 200 per cent profit, having discovered monopoly. However, he noted that Dionysius, the Stoic philosopher and mathematician, told the merchant to take his money and leave Syracuse, as 'that man had discovered a way of making money which was injurious to his own interests'.[30] The Romans too followed this Greek thought. In 301 CE an edict of the Roman Emperor, Diocletian, prescribed the death penalty for any attempt to cause artificial scarcity of commodities by eliminating competition, especially in food articles. Though four years later, this stringent punishment was withdrawn, monopolies remained illegal in their empire.[31]

With the advent of Christianity, canon law recognized monopoly profits as *turpe lucrum,* or ill-gotten gains, subject to restitution failing which the monopolist would suffer eternal damnation. While gains from usury were to be returned to the suffering borrower, gains from monopolies came at the expense of the general public, and hence were to be given away as alms to the poor, charity to hospitals and other such public benefits. The sanction against monopoly was based on three beliefs. First, goods being sold for more than their worth was unjust, second, it went against charity and brotherly love and finally it destroyed public welfare by creating an artificial scarcity.

Around the time when a wool monopoly was being granted to a set of merchants in England, it was harshly punished in the rest of Europe. In France, Philips VI in 1339 passed an ordinance that banned *harelles* or seditious associations for the purpose of improving bargaining power.[32] In 1345, a Florentine woolcarder was arrested and executed for trying to organize a labour union, in the nature of a monopoly.[33] The opposition to monopolies continued right through the fifteenth and sixteenth century. The rationale for it was more explicitly expressed in the French Ordinance of 1519, where the rates charged by innkeepers were fixed. The ordinance stated that, driven by avarice and cupidity, the innkeepers had endangered the salvation of their souls by overcharging their customers. Hence, the government decided to be kind and save their souls by reducing the price to a reasonable level.[34]

Finally, in England too, the unilateral right of the monarch to grant monopolies was restrained by the Statute of Monopolies in 1623. But by then, the basic foundation for economics as a distinct discipline had already been laid, with the advent of the second prerequisite, social acceptance for self-centred individuals.

Patents: A Monopoly with a Difference

Around the fifteenth century, a monopoly of a different kind was emerging in the Italian city-states. Contrary to the conventional kingdoms that depend on a larger area and population for prosperity, the city-states realized that producing knowledge-intensive goods can enrich them. The knowledge in these goods was distinct from the raw materials and the labour need to produce them. They also realized that this knowledge was embedded in the master craftsman. The city-state rulers, both the princes and the republics, competed to attract master craftsmen to their city by providing tax relief, prizes and incentives.[35] One distinct incentive offered by the city-states was 'privilege,' which gave the inventor the exclusive right to commercially exploit the invention for a defined period. This incentive was formalized when Venice enacted the statute of 1474 guaranteeing this right to every inventor for a period of ten years.[i] Gradually this system spread across to the rest of Europe, with each country customizing it for their needs.

Initially in England patents[j] were granted by the monarch to attract foreign artisans to bring advanced technologies. The objective seems to have been import substitution. By inviting foreign artisans who would ply their trade in England, the need to import these goods could be eliminated. The earliest of these go back to 1331 when John Keyes of Flanders was given the exclusive right to introduce advanced weaving techniques in England. Likewise in 1449, John of Utyman brought in new methods of making stained glass.[36] This system seems to have functioned efficiently till the end of the sixteenth century when the royal privilege of granting patents was abused by the

---

i   The operating provision of the statute was 'Be it enacted that, by the authority of this Council, every person who shall build anything new and ingenious device in this City, not previously made in this Commonwealth, shall give notice of it to the office of our General Welfare Board when it has been reduced to perfection so that it can be used and operated. It being forbidden to every other person in any of our territories and towns to make any further device confirming with and similar to said one, without the consent and license of the author, for the term of next ten years. And if anybody builds it in violation thereof, the aforesaid author and inventor shall be entitled to have him summoned before the Magistrate of this City, by which Magistrate the said infringer shall be constrained to pay him hundred ducats; and the device shall be destroyed at once.' From *On the Origin of Patent Law* an essay by Robert P. Merges, pp 4-5.

j   These privileges were called patents in England as they were issued in the form of an 'open letter', which the recipient could show others.

monarchs in return for monetary contributions. Patents were granted for common products like producing playing cards and running ale-houses, resulting in a revolt against this royal right. In 1610, in the midst of intense debate in Parliament, James I publicly announced the withdrawal of all monopoly rights previously granted. These debates ended in the termination of the royal right to grant monopolies and the enactment of the Statute of Monopolies in 1623 by the Parliament.

The Statute of Monopolies recognized 'sole buying, selling, making, working, or using anything' as a monopoly. New monopolies under this statute could be given for a maximum period of fourteen years, to the first and 'true' inventors and manufacturers. This monopoly, by virtue of creating new products or new methods of manufacture, resulted neither in an increase of the domestic prices nor in hurting the domestic trade. All grants of monopoly given prior to this act were to be terminated within forty days of its enactment. There were two exemptions to this revocation. The first exempted the judicial system, which had a monopoly on delivering justice, and the charters granted to the towns for their local self administration. The second exemption covered all companies or societies of merchants created for the maintenance, enlargement or regulation of trade or merchandise.

The substance of the statute approved monopolies that were beneficial for the domestic economy. This in turn created a new brand of professionals who wrote essays and argued cases to enable their merchant corporations win monopolies that would 'benefit' the English economy. The availability of printing technology and the need to win a majority in the parliament ensured that these essays were produced in larger numbers and many of them survived.

Out Of The Shadows, For A Place Under The Sun

The intense debate on monopolies in England and the imminent enactment of a statute to regulate them got interested parties lined up to advance their briefs. In 1856, the Political Economy Club in London put together *A Select Collection of Early English Tracts on Commerce* by reprinting the original essays written in the seventeenth century as an anthology. The importance they accorded to these essays can be seen from the stated objective of this exercise, which was 'to provide against the imminent risk of their being lost, and render them accessible to future inquirers.'[37] Three of the eight[k] essays in this collection pertain to the English East India Company that had obtained its royal charter of monopoly to trade with the East in 1600. Thomas Mun, a leading London merchant and Director of the East India Company wrote two of the three treatises that advocated the benefits of trade with the East.

In the preface to this collection the editor, J.R. McCulloch, noted that at the beginning of the seventeenth century, bullion was seen as the only real wealth of a country. The national policy derived from this popular wisdom was to ban the export of precious metals. But in trade with the East, bullion was the most favourable article of export, and public opinion was against this export by the East India Company. In 1621, Thomas Mun wrote the essay titled, *A Discourse of Trade, from England vnto The East-Indies; answering to diuerse Obiections*

---

k   Of the eight essays two were written by directors of the East India Company, one by a director of Levant Company, who was also a shareholder of the East India Company, and one more essay was attributed to William Petty who also advocated foreign trade.

which are vsually made against the same, to defend this policy.[1] Swimming with the tide of the popular sentiments, Mun first highlighted the amount of bullion earned by the East India Company. He quantified the bullion exported by the East India Company to purchase goods in the East and compared it with the bullion it imported from the rest of Europe. The purchase of goods in the East Indies cost England a fraction of the price it would have paid if the same goods had been purchased in Europe. In short, the East India Company exported a small amount of bullion and leveraged it to import a much larger amount. With this he advanced the idea of the Balance of Trade as a critical criterion in settling national economic debates. In his view, what was to be seen was not the export of bullion in isolation, but the balance generated by a completed trade cycle.

A balance of trade as the measure of wealth of a country achieved such prominence that it pushed into background the more obvious measures i.e. the state of agriculture, commerce and manufacture, that reflect its prosperity. More than two centuries after it was first expounded, the editor of this anthology remarked

> No sophistry was ever more completely successful. Its confines was not just limited to England, but extended to most other countries. The rule that in dealing with strangers, "we must ever sell more to them yearly than we consume of theirs in value" was looked upon as infallible. Its merits were proclaimed

---

1 Thomas Mun answered the four objections raised against the English trade with the East Indies. The first objection was to the East India Company exporting bullion, the second dealt with East India trade reducing the availability of ships in England, the third argued that the East India trade impoverished the English economy and finally the last objection related to disinformation on East India trade.

alike by philosophers and merchants, while statesmen exerted themselves to give it a practical effect.[38]

Even today, the pride with which a trade surplus is globally greeted by the popular press is a tribute to Thomas Mun and his persuasive logic. Given the potency, its influence in the seventeenth century, especially on growth in the volume of trade with the East, increased the anxiety of the general public about the health of English economy. The visibility of large bullion outflows from England to the East seemed to fuel these concerns.

The 'Petty' Impact

It was in this setting that William Petty wrote *Political Arithmetick*[m] to examine these concerns using a novel method. His work was posthumously published by his son in 1690. Petty addressed public concerns about the welfare of the English economy. He saw this concern manifested in fears of declining rents, scarcity of gold and silver, heavy taxes, the burden imposed by their colonies and the lack of trade and employment for the people of England despite their small population To compound this, the English public apprehended that Holland, Zealand and France would progress ahead, leaving the English behind. To examine these concerns William Petty used a novel method of quantification. He described his method:

----

m   The long title of the essay he wrote was *Political Arithmetick or A Discourse concerning The Extent and Value of Lands, People, Buildings, Husbandry, Manufacture, Commerce, Fishery, Artizans, Seaman, Soldiers, Publick Revenues, Interest, Taxes, Superlucration, Registeries, Banks, Valuation of Men, Increasing of Seamen, of Militias, Harbours, Situations, Shipping, Power at Sea, &c. As the same relates to every country in general, but more particularly to the Territories of His Majesty of Great Britain, and his Neighbours, of Holland, Zealand and France.*

for instead of using only comparative and superlative Words, and intellectual Arguments, I have taken the course (as a Specimen of the Political Arithmetick I have long aimed at) to express myself in Terms of *Number, Weight or Measure*; to use only Arguments of Sense and to consider only such Causes, as have visible foundation in Nature; leaving those that depend upon the mutable Minds, Opinions, Appetites, and Passions of particular Men, to the Considerations of others...[39]

Holland of the seventeenth century was the European economic leader. Analyzing the richness of Holland, Petty dismissed the popular claims that attributed its success to pursuit of the right trade and policies. He refers to many writers on this subject who made the Hollanders out to be 'angels' and all the other country men to be 'fools, brutes and sots' in matters of trade and policies.[40] He instead identified the reasons for their wealth with some critical and incisive analysis backed by numbers. He quantified the advantage derived by Holland from their geographical location and topographical features, which he enumerated one by one and quantified as having a worth of more than £1.15 million. To put this number in perspective, he quantified the entire trade of Europe with the whole world at £45 million and concluded by remarking that people who can undersell others with their intrinsic advantage of £1 million, can 'easily have the trade of the world without such Angelical Wits and Judgments, as attributed to the Hollanders.'[41]

Table 3.1

Benefits derived by Holland by virtue of their geographical location as quantified by William Petty[42]

	Benefit from	**Basis for quantification**	**Worth (pounds sterling)**
1	Urbanization	Increased specialization and division of labour	£100,000
2	Cheap Energy	Use of windmills resulting in human labour saved	£150,000
3	Trade	Favourable location at river mouth facilitating manufacture and trade	£200,000
4	Navigation	Cheap navigation due to extensive network of rivers and canals	£300,000
5	Defense	Naturally favourable defense fortifications due to dikes, marshes and sea coast	£200,000
6	Harbour	Better quality of harbour resulting in savings on shipping	£200,000
		Total benefit from Location & Topography	£1,150,000
7	Fishing	Profit derived from trading herring with rest of the world	£3,000,000
		Total benefit	£4,150,000

Petty demolished the prevailing myth that only labour and land contribute to riches, by quantifying the relative positions of France, Holland and Zealand. He noted that France had thirteen times the population of Holland and Zealand, and in terms of good land, it was eighty times bigger. However these attributes translated only to three times as many riches to the French.[43]

The use of quantitative measures like numbers and weights in the place of qualitative values utilized by scholastics was only one of the contributions made by Petty. His second contribution was much more significant. Petty looked at Holland's history and noted that a hundred years earlier, despite its tangible advantages, it was a cold country inhabited by poor and oppressed people. Given this, he turned his attention to the factors that could have changed their status and identified 'Liberty of Conscience' as a key factor. He noted that Holland broke with Spain to avoid the imposition of clergy. By liberty of conscience he identified the right of people to dissent from the Church. He then noted, 'Dissenters of this kind, are for most part, thinking, sober, and patient men, and such as believe that Labour and Industry is their Duty towards God. (How erroneous soever their Opinions be)'.[44] He then went on to observe that in most countries trade is carried on by the 'Heterodox', who hold a different belief from the majority, and concluded by stating that three quarters of the trade in Europe was carried on by people who separated from the church like the inhabitants of England, Scotland, Ireland, United Provinces, Denmark, Sweden, Norway and the German Protestant Princedoms.[45]

By reasoning thus, Petty was the first European to identify the use of public policy and trade in transforming a country like Holland, inhabited by poor and oppressed people, into the dominant position of an economic leader. Specifically, he identified 'Liberty of Conscience', low taxes, banking facilities and legal infrastructure as the major important factors that promoted trade.

With these two contributions, William Petty formally transplanted economics which was under the shadow of the banyan-like realm of ethics into its own place under the sun, as a distinct discipline. This provided a favourable environment for economics to flourish, in the years to come.

Laissez faire: *The Idea*

'Good ideas are, usually, not new ideas, but old ideas resurrected at the right time'[46] remarked Charles Handy, the Irish business philosopher. This principle is evident when we examine the idea of free markets and the power of the 'invisible hand' that came to prominence when Adam Smith wrote *The Wealth of Nations* in 1776. Today, its publication is popularly seen as the first super-structure of economics as a distinct discipline. As in buildings, where the depth of the foundation that remains hidden underground reflects its strength, for this idea too, the submerged foundation is deep. Similar ideas had emerged in more than one place and across long time periods.

Adam Smith had several predecessors of whom we know very little. Preceding Smith, Althusius, a German town administrator and political theorist, highlighted the ill effects of monopoly and advocated free markets, Quesnay, a French intellectual, laid out its philosophical foundation, while Turgot, a French minister, was the first to implement it, though not with success; and in Sweden, Andres Chydenius, the parliamentarian, was its loyal advocate. Each of them started from a different base to reach the same conclusion. But Adam Smith, the professor, presented this idea on a broader canvas and set it in England, the dominant and fastest-growing economy of the time.

Highlighting this, Arnold Toynbee remarked, 'He was the first great writer on the subject; with him political economy passed from the exchange and market-place to the professor's study'.[47] But what did Adam Smith and his predecessors say about free markets? How did they justify it?

The terms laissez faire and free markets, used in the eighteenth century were very different from the call for free markets and hands-off policy of the government that they represent in the twenty-first century. Words have a contextual meaning arising from the circumstances in which they are used. Over time, it is possible for a word to be understood differently from what it originally meant. In eighteenth-century Europe, the right to hold land was restricted, choice of profession regulated, working for wages limited, lending money for interest censored and large chartered corporations usurped monopoly in their lines of trade. It is against this backdrop that the revolutionary idea of laissez faire or free markets was promoted to stimulate and accelerate economic growth.

Johann Althusius, a German town administrator and a prominent political theorist[n] who lived between 1557 and 1638, described himself as a staunch defender of free trade, individual bargaining and freedom to contract.[48] He went on to define a monopoly as a restraint on trade to the benefit of select traders and to the detriment of the public. He felt that there were three drawbacks to monopolies. The first was that necessities of life cannot depend on the whims or discretions of a few, as shortage due to restriction on trade is against charity. Second, free commercial intercourse is a public right given to

---

n   Althusius was among the first few advocates of federalism as an idea for administering the state and sharing of sovereign rights between the centre and the provinces.

every individual to barter, buy, sell, acquire and alienate. Finally, commerce is meant to facilitate exchange necessary for survival and to deny anyone this right is to take away life itself. He identified nineteen forms of monopoly to show its widespread presence, classified under the three heads, commercial, industrial and political. These monopolistic practices included illicit agreements, secret pacts, conspiracies, abuse of professional guilds, exorbitant fees, free labour extracted from apprentices by the master craftsman and use of political power to restrict competition. This reasoning led Althusius himself to advocate free trade.

The French Connection

In France, the call for action to promote free trade came from a deeply depressing situation of abject poverty. In 1707, Marshal Vauban printed *Dixme Royale* anonymously for private circulation. In this work, he noted that about 10 per cent of French families begged for a living, 50 per cent were too poor to give any alms, 30 per cent had debts and were embroiled in law suits with only the balance 10 per cent of families a little better off.[49] He counted only half a per cent of the households as wealthy families, made up of rich merchants, officials and the beneficiaries of royal patronage.

France, a reasonably prosperous nation in the seventeenth century, had come to this disastrous state through a combination of expensive wars, public indulgences, imprudent fiscal policies and bad administration. In a short span of five decades ending in 1715, a public debt of more than 3.3 billion French francs was contracted and due to a combination of war, declining birth rates and the expulsion of Protestants, the population declined by 20 per cent. Two-thirds of the tax collected went to pay for its collection.[50] Despite this, the royal court and the nobility maintained their glittering lifestyle. The nobles and clergy were exempt from tax as they owed only their personal service to the king, not money.[51] The entire burden of tax was borne by the commoners. Collection of taxes was contracted out to tax-farmers who paid a fixed sum in advance to the Royal treasury and subsequently collected it from their constituents. The tax-farmers had stringent powers to seize goods to recover tax dues, making the peasants' lives miserable. Adding to their misery, the peasants did not have the freedom to move grains from one province to another even within France.[52] In 1737, *corvee,* a new obligation was imposed upon the peasant to provide free labour to repair roads across the whole of France.[53]

It was in this setting that Francois Quesnay, a surgeon by qualification and profession, started writing economic articles in *Encyclopedie.*[o] These articles reflected his analysis of an economy which consisted of three segments – agriculture, producing food and raw materials; manufacturing, supplying clothes and shelter; and landowners, only receiving rent without contributing anything productive. He further depicted the relationship between the three segments using hypothetical figures. He presented two contrasting situations of restricted inter-segment flows prevailing in France at that time and unrestrained flows showing that the latter would increase overall wealth. These articles also reflected his belief and the ideas[p] prevailing at that time that agriculture was the sole

---

o   A general encyclopedia published in France between 1751 and 1772 to promote consolidation of knowledge

p   Richard Cantillon, an Irish-born French economist, who preceded Quesnay, had quantified the intrinsic cost of labour as the land required to support an individual. In estimating the value of slaves in a plantation, he arrived at the judgment that the value of the lowest, unskilled slave's labour was twice the value of the land required to support the slave.

value creator in an economy. In his words, 'The state is a tree, agriculture its roots, population its trunk, arts and commerce its leaves'.[54] Just as without healthy roots a tree cannot survive for long, he observed that the other two segments depend on agriculture for their prosperity, and so thriving agriculture is essential for a prosperous state. He also emphasized that the state of unrestricted flow, which he felt was natural, is the most conductive for economic growth. Any barriers to this flow would harm the entire economy. His followers took this clue and called themselves *physiocrate,* a French word meaning the rule of nature.[55]

Quesnay proposed two major changes to arrive at the unrestricted flow scenario that would promote economic growth. He advocated a single point tax on the landowners, moving the burden of tax away from the peasants. This was based on his belief that taxing manufacture would reduce output, as manufacturers did not create any surplus. Following a similar rationale, he felt that taxing agriculture, the most productive sector, would reduce subsequent investment in it thereby reducing its output. His second change was to permit the free flow of goods among the nations. This was on the belief that the free flow of goods would lead to better prices, resulting in increased production of goods, which was the basis for prosperity. This view was in variance with the policy advocated by English merchants who preferred a favourable balance of trade, resulting in the accumulation of bullion.

Laissez Faire: The Debut

Anne-Robert Jacques Turgot, a physiocrate, had the chance to implement the ideas proposed by Quesnay much sooner than expected, when he became the Controller General of France. This position combined the role of the Chancellor of the

Exchequer, Home Secretary, and Minister of both Transport and Agriculture.[56] On September 13, 1774, he implemented the policy of laissez-faire by issuing the 'Six Edicts'. The preamble to this policy explained the rationale for its implementation. The aim was to promote free and full competition both within and among the countries. It stemmed from the belief that surplus in any one section should be gainfully exchanged in places where it was needed. The preamble invested this idea with divine sanction by noting that 'exchange of superfluities for necessities … is conformable to the order established by Divine Providence'.[57]

The 'Six Edicts' included the right for free trade in grains, abolition of the system of guilds that restricted new members from joining the profession and the abolition of *corvee*, the system of extracting free labour from peasants to maintain roads. Using the principle of free trade, Turgot explained his logic for banning *corvee*. He noted that a man forced to work without wages will work slowly and produce inferior output. In addition, since only time was required from the labourers, they daily spent three hours in commute, which was totally unproductive.[58]

All the good intentions of Turgot were in vain when the vested interests that he took on to implement his laissez-faire policies succeeded in getting him dismissed within three years.[59] With Turgot's dismissal his 'Six Edicts' too were withdrawn, leaving the implementation of the laissez-faire system to be deferred for the time being. By a sheer coincidence, Adam Smith in the same year published the *Wealth of Nations* to keep this idea alive for a more successful implementation.

Around the same time, Andres Chydenius, the Swedish parliamentarian, was advocating for free trade in Sweden. Preceding the *Wealth of Nations* by a decade, in 1765 he wrote a pamphlet titled *The National Gain*. In this short pamphlet, he crisply identified the core principle of self-centred humans who sought their own gains. He also noted that self-seeking humans were natural and the basis for all communities in the world. In their absence he saw all social norms fail, while their presence promoted economic pursuits in society. He summarized from this the key economic principle that, 'The work that has the greatest value is always best paid and what is best paid is the most sought after'.[60]

The Swede differed from the French physiocrates who recognized a nation's wealth in its increasing agricultural production. He opted for the measure of a favourable balance of trade, in line with the English merchants. Based on this measure he quantified Sweden's gain for the year 1764 at 6 million dalers.[61] Using a series of anecdotes from Swedish history, Chydenius went on to build a case for greater division of labour, freedom for workers to choose their trade, abolition of incentives for exports and promotion of new trades, abolition of the institution of apprenticeship; in short the removal of all impediments that come in the way of the free pursuit of vocation and commerce. Identifying the wealth of a nation with the diligence of its workers, he recognized 'liberty, quick returns and individual gain' as its source. He further argued for competition which would encourage large production, after noting that 'limited production makes idle hands and expensive goods'. A statute in place at that time in Sweden banned farmers from selling their produce locally. It also prohibited peddlers from visiting rural areas. Seeing this statute violated, he expressed his happiness and commented that a quarter of the country was saved from misery by this breach. Turning to the value of free competition for the consumer, with sharp insight he noted that they would benefit from lower prices and the only way for the producer to earn a higher profit was to 'be content with less profit on each commodity, but must instead turn it over much more frequently'.[62] Thus free competition would result in lower prices for consumers and larger markets for the producers, benefiting the whole economy.

The Wealth in The Wealth of Nations

Adam Smith, though by far its most popular proponent, was not the first to champion free trade even in England. This credit probably goes to Edward Misselden, who wrote a treatise in 1622 titled, *Free Trade or the Means to Make Free Trade Flourish,* when the debate on the Statue of Monopolies of 1623 was at its peak.[63] Considering the fact that almost everything we know today to be the benefits of the free markets and fair competition, were clearly articulated before Adam Smith published his *Wealth of Nations,* what made his book so popular? What did he add that the others had missed?

Two centuries after Smith's book was published, economic historians concurred on its greatness, but held widely differing opinions on their reasoning. In 1960, Overton Taylor of Harvard University, writing in his book *A History of Economic Thought,* praised it as 'one of the world's, or all history's, truly great books, and a rich mine of wisdom on a very wide range of subjects – economics, psychological, and sociological, and historical, moral and political'.[64] In contrast, Joseph Schumpeter in his classic, *History of Economic Analysis,* attributed its success to ungrudging labour spread over twenty-five years, of which ten years were exclusively concentrated on it. Highlighting the critical reason for its wide appeal, Schumpeter remarked on its simplicity in addressing such a novel and complex subject and the ingenious use of trivialities and homely observations to keep the average reader interested. At the same time, serious readers were engaged with deep insights and analysis. Commenting on this fine balance, he remarked, 'While the professional of his time found enough to command his intellectual respect, the "educated reader" was able to assure himself that, yes, this was so, he too had always thought so'.[65]

As in the story of the elephant and the six blind men, Taylor and Schumpeter seem to have touched different parts. Schumpeter's book has a short section titled 'The Reader's Guide to the *Wealth of Nations*', in which the book is described in brief. He noted that nobody either before or after Smith gave such a prominent place to the division of labour in human society, which was its unique feature. On most other aspects, Smith had either provided a logical extension of his predecessors' ideas or had restated them by providing analogies and elaboration.

Within three decades, the book had run through nine English editions, and was translated into Danish, Dutch, Italian and Spanish, with multiple editions in French and German. Soon thereafter, it was also published in Russian in 1806.[66] Schumpeter comments that this spectacular success was minor compared to the really significant success achieved in the next fifty years when Adam Smith became the 'teacher not of the beginner or the public but of the professionals, especially the professors'.[67] It is only then, Schumpeter remarks, that Adam Smith 'was invested with the status of 'founder' – which none of his contemporaries would have thought of bestowing on him'.[68]

In contrast to Schumpeter who evaluated *The Wealth of Nations* as a standalone book for its incremental contribution to economic theory, Taylor viewed it as a continuation of Adam Smith's earlier book, *The Theory of Moral Sentiments,* in which the author analyzed human motives. More importantly, the Harvard professor saw parallels between Isaac Newton's discovery of gravity and the grand universal symphony and Adam Smith's idea of self-interest and the functioning of economic system. In fact this extract from *The Theory of Moral Sentiments* reinforces the basis for such a belief:

> The administration of the great system of universe, however, the care of the universal happiness of all rational and sensible beings, is the business of God and not of man. To man is allotted a much humbler department, but one much more suitable to the weakness of his powers, and to the narrowness of his comprehension; the care of his own happiness, of that of his family, his friends, his country.[69]

After the publication of *The Wealth of Nations,* economics truly became a distinct discipline. It began to examine the major questions that faced human society in meeting material needs. Accepting private property and a self-centred individual as an essential virtue, the immediate focus now shifted to identifying the logical method to divide the wealth generated and analyzing value to explain the inherent conflicts visible in paradoxes such as the high price commanded by the superfluous diamond in contrast to water, the elixir of life, remaining without a price. A parallel track that continued away from the mainstream discourse examined the basic premise of Adam Smith: do individuals focusing on their own self-interest promote 'the universal happiness of all rational and sensible beings'?

Endnotes

1   Schumpeter, J. A., *History of Economic Analysis*, George Allen & Unwin Ltd., 1955, p107

2   Maddison, A., *The World Economy,* OECD, Development Centre Studies, Indian Edition, 2007, p641

3   Ibid, p638

4   Roberts, J. M., *The Penguin History of the World,* Third Edition, 1997, p473

5   Ibid, p495

6   Ibid, p500

7   Haddock, D. D., & L. Kiesling, The Black Death and Private Property, *The Journal of Legal Studies,* Vol.31, No.2, Part 2: The Evolution of Property Rights, p546 footnotes

8   Getz, F. M., Black Death and Silver Lining: Meaning, Continuity, and Revolutionary Change in Histories of Medieval Plague, *Journal of the History of Biology,* Vol.24, No.2, (Summer, 1991), quoted in p274

9   Ibid, p267

10 Watson, P., *Ideas, A History from Fire to Freud,* Weidenfeld & Nicolson, 2005, p390

11 Mate, M., Agrarian Economy after the Black Death: The Manors of Canterbury Cathedral Priory, 1348-91, *The Economic History Review,* New Series, Vol.37, No.3, (Aug., 1984), p341

12 Roberts, J. M., *The Penguin History of the World,* Third Edition, 1997, p501

13 Getz, F. M., Black Death and Silver Lining: Meaning, Continuity, and Revolutionary Change in Histories of Medieval Plague, *Journal of the History of Biology,* Vol.24, No.2, (Summer, 1991), p269

14 Carr, C. T., *Select Charters of Trading Companies, CE 1530-1707,* Selden Society, 1913, p xxi, footnote 5

15 Watson, P., *Ideas, A History from Fire to Freud,* Weidenfeld & Nicolson, 2005, p390

16 Roberts, J. M., *The Penguin History of the World,* Third Edition, 1997, p477

17 Wren, D. A., Medieval or Modern? A Scholastic's View of Business Ethics, circa 1430, *Journal of Business Ethics,* Vol.28, No.2, (Nov., 2000), p111

18 De Roover, R., Scholastic Economics: Survival and Lasting Influence from the Sixteenth Century to Adam Smith, *The Quarterly Journal of Economics,* Vol.69, No.2 (May, 1955), p179

19 Rickaby, J., *Acquinas Ethicus: Or The Moral Teachings of St. Thomas, A translation of the principal portions of the Second part of the 'Summa Theologica',* Burns and Oats, 1892, Question LXVI, Article II

20 Ibid, Question LXXVII, Article I

21 Wren, D. A., Medieval or Modern? A Scholastic's View of Business Ethics, circa 1430, *Journal of Business Ethics,* Vol.28, No.2, (Nov., 2000), p110

22 Ibid, p111

23 Ibid, p112

24 *Good News Bible, With Deuterocanonical Books / Apocrypha,* Today's English Version, 1979, p102

25 Power, E., *The Wool Trade in English Medieval History,* The Ford Lectures, 1941, p11

26 Ibid, p29

27 Ibid, p32

28 Ibid, p39

29 Ibid, p46

30 Aristotle, *The Basic Works of Aristotle,* The Modern Library, 2001, p1142

31 De Roover, R., Monopoly Theory Prior to Adam Smith: A Revision, *The Quarterly Journal of Economics,* Vol.65, No.4 (Nov., 1951), p493

32 Ibid, p503

33 Ibid, p504

34 Ibid, p501

35 Belfanti, C. M., *Between Mercantilism and Market, Privileges for Invention in Early Modern Europe,* paper presented at the 4th EPIP Conference, European Policy and Intellectual Property: History and Economics, Paris, October 2-4, 2004, p5

36 http://ipo.gov.uk/types/patents/p-about/p-whatis/p-history.htm

37 *A Select Collection of Early English Tracts on Commerce,* Political Economy Club, 1856, p iii

38 Ibid, p vi

39 Petty, W., *The Economic Writings of Sir William Petty, vol.1,* The Online Library of Liberty, p207

40 Ibid, p213

41 Ibid, p215

42 Ibid, pp213-215

43 Ibid, p213

44 Ibid, p218

45 Ibid, p219

46 Handy, C., *the hungry spirit,* Arrow, 2002, p61

47 Toynbee, A., *Lectures on the Industrial Revolution in England,* Blackmask Online, 2001, p25

48 De Roover, R., Monopoly Theory Prior to Adam Smith: A Revision, *The Quarterly Journal of Economics,* Vol.65, No.4 (Nov., 1951), p513

49 Higgs, H., *The Physiocrats, Six Lectures on the French* Economistes *of the 18ᵗʰ Century,* Batoche Books, 2001, p12

50 Ibid, p8

51 Ibid, p9

52 Ibid, p10

53 Ibid, p9

54 Ibid, p16

55 Pressman, S., *Fifty Great Economists,* Rutledge, 1999, First India Reprint, 2004, p13

56 Hill, M., Property Rights and Public Administration, *Geophilos,* Spring 2001, No.01 (1), p100

57 Rothbard, M. N., Concepts of the Role of Intellectuals in Social Change Towards Laissez Faire, *The Journal of Libertarian Studies,* Vol. IX, No.2 (Fall 1990), p 56

58 Claessen, M. & I. Nijenhuis., *Turgot: The Dutch Connection,* A Contribution to the Lantheuil Conference, 2003, p17, footnotes

59 Wendel, J. M., Turgot and American Revolution, *Modern Age,* Summer, 1979, p282

60 Chydenius, A., *The National Gain,* www.chydenius.net/historia/teckset/e_kansallinen_johdanto.asp., p5

61 Ibid, p3

62 Ibid, p26

63 Mehary, T. Y., *A Short History of Economic Thought,* University of Asmara and Groningen, 2002, p68

64 Taylor, O. H., *A History of Economic Thought,* McGraw-Hill Book Company, 1960, p28

65 Schumpeter, J A., *History of Economic Analysis,* George Allen & Unwin Ltd, 1955, p185

66 Ibid, p193

67 Ibid, p194

68 Ibid, p194

69 Smith, A., *The Theory of Moral Sentiments,* Glasgow Edition of the Works and Correspondence Vol.1, The Online Library of Liberty Collection, p246

Chapter 4

Market Based: A Promising Youth 1776 to 1929 CE

Man can see more with the light of intellect and reason than with his physical organ of sight.

– Otto von Guericke, German scientist, inventor and politician

The human quest for perfection has often taken expression in the form of describing an ideal society. These utopian writings had a strong ethical streak as they eliminated, or at least downplayed, the role of private property and a self-centred or materialistic outlook. In the writings of Adam Smith we see a strong ethical streak in his first book, *The Theory of Moral Sentiments* and a radical departure from it in his second book, *The Wealth of Nations,* which focuses on the self-centred actions of individuals. In this chapter, the link between the two books is analyzed to identify why the second book assumed prominence. As the focus shifted away from ethics to wealth, economics developed rapidly as a distinct subject with the factors of production identified and a rationale articulated for their fair price. However, the reality of the marketplace conflicted with such abstract conclusions; a conflict most prominent in the price commanded by diamonds and water in relation to their ability to satisfy basic human needs. Labeled as the water-diamond value paradox this conundrum challenged the minds of economists in the second half of the nineteenth century. These inquiries led to the concept of marginal utility. A by-product of this development was the formulation of economic 'Laws' that placed the subject of economics on a completely distinct plane among the social sciences, giving it its dominant status.

The Quest for Perfection

The human mind's quest for perfection has found expression in numerous ways. Perhaps the highest level of this pursuit is in visualizing an ideal society. Over the last three millennia, vivid descriptions of utopias – ideal societies – have been captured not once but many times over. Among the first of these descriptions is found in Plato's *Republic*. Plato perceived an individual's inability to be self-sufficient as the main reason for the formation of society. He thought that once in society, an individual would be better off specializing in one occupation and depending on others to meet his remaining needs. He thus visualized all transactions between individuals as motivated by mutual gain. Exchanges needed to be facilitated by retailers in the marketplace who, in his view, performed a menial job. He went on to describe the retailing class in a well-run community as, 'those who are least fit physically, and unsuitable for other work. For their job ties them to the marketplace, where they buy goods from those who want to sell and sell goods to those who want to buy'.[1]

In his ideal society, Plato sought to abolish private property for the guardians, those who occupy positions of power. In fact, he prescribed no private possessions beyond the barest essentials for the ruling class. They were to live in public housing with food provided by other citizens in a common mess. In addition, they were to be forbidden to touch or handle gold and silver, wear them as ornaments, or drink from utensils made of them. If a guardian were to acquire private property, he was to be automatically expelled from the ranks of rulers and become a farmer and a man of business. Plato saw the societies in which ruling class owned private property as 'heading for destruction that will overwhelm themselves and the whole community.'[2] Turning his attention to the non-rulers, that is, those who could hold private property, Plato held that both wealth and poverty was detrimental to society. He said, 'One produces luxury and idleness and a desire for novelty, the other meanness and bad workmanship and the desire for revolution as well'.[3]

Plato in his *Republic* went against the three basic prerequisites of economics – private property, a self-centred outlook and materialism. Since then, there have been many more[a] such utopian dreams, sprinkled across three millennia. The consistent thread that runs across these themes is their negation of the three essential prerequisites of economics. The scores of attempts to actually create a utopian society over the centuries attest to the singular fact that all of them have, regretfully, failed. Thus, utopia, which can be translated as both the ideal place and the elusive place, has lived up to its second meaning.

In contrast to Plato who negated private property, Adam Smith accepted both private property and a self-centred human instinct. The basic reason for this difference could lie in the way they saw the link between community and an individual's welfare. It looks as if Plato perceived an individual's welfare as being derived from community welfare. In contrast, Smith saw social welfare as a summation of individual welfares.

---

a   Some of the prominent ones are: *On the Commonwealth* by Cicero, *The City of Gods* by St. Augustine, *Utopia* by Thomas More, *The New Atlantis* by Francis Bacon, *Oceana* by James Harrington, *Erewhon* by Samuel Butler, *A Modern Utopia* by H. G. Wells, *Kibbutz: Venture in Utopia* by Melford Spiro.

Inspired by the ideas of Adam Smith,[b] in 1890 Theodor Hertzka, an Austrian economist, designed a society in which perfect liberty and economic justice would flourish, trying to combine the conflicting ideas of Plato and Smith. He set forth his ideas in his book *Freeland: A Social Anticipation,* first published in 1889. Hertzka described perfect liberty as the unqualified right of every individual to control his or her own actions, in line with the concept of laissez-faire[c] and, economic justice as the right of all workers to the full and uncurtailed enjoyment of the fruits of their labour. The International Free Society outlined by Hertzka was based on six fundamental principles:

1. No exclusive right of property in land, either to the individual or to the collective community,
2. Self-governing associations for all productive activities, with profit-sharing amongst the members in proportion to each member's labour contribution,
3. The right to join and leave any association at the individual's discretion,
4. Capital for production given from community revenue, which is to be returned by the producers,
5. All individuals incapable of labour to have a right to receive adequate allowance for living from the community revenue, which he called 'competent maintenance,'
6. Community revenue to be raised by a tax levied on the total production.

---

b   In the Preface to his book *Freeland*, Hertzka described Adam Smith 'Then arose the giant of our science, one of the greatest minds of which humanity can boast – Adam Smith.'

c   A system where economic activities are not regulated by public authorities.

A critical aspect of this utopian endeavour was the combination of rewarding individual exertion, which upheld private property, and at the same time catering to the needs of individuals incapable of labour. Unfortunately, Theodor Hertzka's utopian dream too followed its predecessors' path of failing to be sustainable and did not survive.[d] Around the same time, realization dawned on many that combining economic freedom with benevolence was not yet feasible. With this, the ideas in Adam Smith's first book, *The Theory of Moral Sentiments* came to be regarded as an ornamental luxury, like the role he held out for benevolence in society. Instead, his second book, *The Wealth of Nations* became a necessity, nay an essential in the years, decades and centuries that followed.

From Good to Goods

Adam Smith's first book primarily examined what is good for mankind. In his subsequent book, *The Wealth of Nations*, he made a smooth transition from good to goods. As subsequent events show, this shift from moral theory to practical political economics once and for all cut the umbilical cord linking economics with ethics. However this outcome appears contrary to Smith's intention, as he built a strong link between good and goods in his first book, which unfortunately was not reiterated in his second book. What was the link between good and goods that Smith envisaged?

The Theory of Moral Sentiments explored what motivates humans to a life of virtue, identifying three principal factors: prudence, justice and benevolence, and self-command. Smith

---

d   The concept failed due to differences among the participants on administering the Freeland.

defined prudence as superior reason and understanding combined with self-command. This superior reasoning and understanding, he theorized, would result in individuals appreciating the consequences of all their actions and evaluating what to do using a cost-benefit framework. To act on this understanding, self-command was important, as abstaining from immediate pleasure or enduring temporary pain could lead to a greater pleasure or avoiding a greater pain, later.[4] Turning to justice and benevolence, Smith saw it as the glue that held a society together. Justice at its core was a negative virtue, as it only prevented an individual from hurting his neighbor. He saw justice as protection operating at three distinct levels. Protecting life and person was at the core, property and possession in the middle, and personal rights and enforcement of promises at the periphery.[5] In contrast to justice, which is essential for a society to exist and hence enforced using punishment, benevolence was an embellishment that improved the society and therefore is only encouraged by rewarding the benevolent individual with a 'pleasing conscience'.

Structurally, it looks as if Adam Smith saw self-command as the foundation, prudence as the building blocks and justice as the pillars that functionally hold the society together. In benevolence he only saw an ornamental embellishment to this structure. Rewards too followed this architectural design. Health, fortune, rank and reputation, in short, security for the individual, were the rewards of prudence.[6] In Smith's schema, prudence combined with industry resulted in wealth and external honours.[7] On the other hand, truth, justice and humanity, (all reflecting benevolence) rewarded their practitioners with confidence, esteem and the love of their fellow citizens.

Smith placed the joy of being loved higher than riches. Ranking the relative importance of these two distinct types of reward, Smith wrote, 'Humanity does not desire to be great, but to be beloved. It is not in being rich that truth and justice would rejoice, but in being trusted and believed, recompenses which those virtues must almost always acquire'.[8] In addition, he felt that an individual would not pursue higher rewards without having secured the lower ones. In the most illuminating part of the book, Smith expressed his opinion that for an individual to feel for others, he or she must first be comfortable himself or herself. Elaborating on this, he wrote,

> If our own misery pinches us severely, we have no leisure to attend to that of our neighbour; and all savages are too much occupied with their own wants and necessities, to give much attention to those of another person.[9]

Probably stemming from this view, Adam Smith sought to increase the goods in a society, an essential prerequisite for the development of benevolence, which in turn would usher in the good. In the absence of goods, did Adam Smith foresee an absence of the good? Could this be the reason for the focus on wealth and wealth creation in his second book?

Role Play for Success

In an insightful article,[e] Jeffery Herbener, Senior Fellow of the Ludgwig von Mises Institute in Austria, developed an interesting hypothesis to show consistency between Adam Smith's two books and thereby, the link between goods and good. He explored how free markets develop benevolence.

---

e   'An Integration of *The Wealth of Nations, The Theory of Moral Sentiments,* in the *Journal of Libertarian Studies,* Vol. VIII, No.2 (Summer 1987), pp275 -288.

Herbener saw Smith's capitalistic system as a 'non-violent, voluntary exchange, limited-government, largely spontaneous, ordered society where individuals interact within a system of natural law'.[10] This capitalist system rested on two important natural laws: the right to private property and the existence of a mechanism for free exchange. The right to free exchange institutionalized in the markets was characterized by the absence of any threat or use of violence. Given this feature, the only means available to an individual to influence others in the free market would be by adopting their value system. Division of labour and the resultant specialization make it mandatory for every individual to cooperate with others in a market-based society. As each individual seeks to prosper, they need to allocate their own resources in line with the value system of all the others in society. This results in a system of mutual influence which strengthens society. He identified the source of this strength in sympathy, a basic human emotion.

Herbener pointed out that Adam Smith also recognized in each individual not only their propensity for self-love but also their ability to feel sympathetic. In *The Theory of Moral Sentiments,* Smith defined sympathy as the ability to step into the shoes of another and feel their emotions. In addition, he also recognized that there is an increased ability to feel sympathetic, when the feelings are reciprocal. This mutual sympathy was identified as the bond on which a society is built.

Turning to *The Wealth of Nations,* Herbener went on to identify the central role of sympathy as vital for free market exchanges. He reasoned,

> Each participant in each exchange must gain the voluntary cooperation of the other party. By role switching, each individual comes to understand the viewpoint of the other

party and thus how to induce them to trade. If initially, the buyer bids a price lesser than the price the seller offers, they bargain until a coincidence is reached. The result of this moderation is a working market system of interaction—analogous with Smith's moderation of sentiments producing a society. Capitalism provides a fertile ground for the development of the internal impartial spectator.[11]

The 'internal impartial spectator' was the voice in an individual's mind pointing out his counterpart's interest. Likewise, the *external* impartial spectator represented the voice of other participants in evaluating an individual's activity. These voices converse with each other in the dialect of bids and offers, creating a new language of market prices. Adam Smith hypothesized that material success would only come to individuals who developed their internal impartial spectator. By inference, it looks as if Smith deduced success in the marketplace was assured only to the individuals with a sympathetic heart. Consequently, this meant that success in the marketplace would naturally lead to the pursuit of justice and benevolence. Adam Smith therefore concluded, 'individuals at ease with themselves would now turn to the needs and necessities of others', in their desire to be loved and respected.[f]

While Smith's logic looks plausible, the basic question is whether his assumptions about human nature's propensity for both self-love and sympathy are grounded in reality. Did the language of market prices, as Adam Smith visualized, speak for benevolence and justice after the basic needs were met? Or did this also remain a utopian dream?

---

f   We see the reality of this observation today when the rich and wealthy direct portions of their wealth to the benefit of others in society, in the last phases of their careers

A Framework for Wealth Creation

While a small section of idealistic social thinkers continued their work on creating a utopia sans private property, in the belief that humans are virtuous by nature and benevolence is a necessity in society, the belief amongst the majority was that the absolute equality resulting from diluting private property and censoring self-centred individuals would only culminate in universal poverty. Consequently, this majority accepted private property and self-centred individuals as necessary evils, if not essential virtues, in building a prosperous society. With wealth creation, or goods, as the primary focus, Economics could emerge as a distinct discipline. The attention of the growing tribe of economists then turned to analyzing how to reward the various participants in economic activity fairly, in order to fully engage them in the process of accelerated wealth creation.

At the turn of the nineteenth century, wealth creation was the subject of intense study among economists. The French School of economists, also known as the Physiocrates, argued that it was **land** that supported the other factors of production, including labour, and therefore it was the primary factor of production. Hence, amongst them it was viewed as the basic source of wealth creation. They were countered by the articulate Marxists, for whom **labour** was the basic factor, as they claimed that land without labour is barren. In the process of arguing their claims, these two groups identified two major factors of production and therefore, of wealth creation.

The Classical School of economists, consisting of Ricardo and Malthus in addition to its founder Adam Smith, considered that, in addition to land and labour, **capital** (i.e. machinery, tools and equipment), as a major factor of production. This was not accepted by other schools of thought: 'Capital is dead labour, that, vampire-like, only lives by sucking living labour, and lives the more, the more it sucks'.[12] retorted Karl Marx in *Das Capital*, re-emphasizing labour's place as the primary factor.

Moving a step ahead, the Austrian School of economists, including Carl Menger and Ludwig Von Mises among others, considered **entrepreneurship**[g] the most critical input. To them, land, labour and capital, though essential ingredients, were not adequate by themselves to create wealth. They need to be blended and further processed, by the spirit of entrepreneurship.

With the four factors of production – land, labour, capital and entrepreneurship – identified, theories about their value evolved as well, providing a basis by which their intrinsic share in the wealth created could be computed. Economics continued to define itself as a distinct discipline as the bases for rent, wages, interest and profit were debated and articulated.

David Ricardo was the first to outline a precise theory of rent rates in 1817. A successful merchant and parliamentarian, he analyzed the impact of the Corn Law in England, which levied a sliding-scale duty on corn imports to keep their prices high, thereby protecting local landlords. Ricardo noted that the rent received by the landlords increased in tandem with the price of food grains. Analyzing this, he moved away from the

---

g   Carl Menger in his *Principles of Economics* defines entrepreneurship to include the following four activities, '(a) obtaining *information* about the economic situation; (b) economic *calculation* – all the various computations that must be made if the production process is to be efficient (provided that it is economic in other respects); (c) the *act of will* by which goods of higher order (or goods in general – under conditions of developed commerce, where any economic good can be exchanged for any other) are assigned to a particular production process; and finally (d) *supervision* of the execution of the production plan so that it may be carried through as economically as possible.'

then-prevailing concept of rent as the compensation received by the landlord. Ricardo classified the income received by a landlord as partly rent and partly interest: the higher income received for a piece of land due to things like better irrigation and buildings was actually a reflection of the interest earned on capital invested by the landlord to provide these things. By segregating the income like this, he showed that the rent paid for 'the original and indestructible power of the soil' for similar plots was identical. As high corn prices brought inferior land into cultivation, the rent rates on superior land automatically went up. This led him to conclude 'that [rent is the] portion of the produce of earth, which is paid to the landlord for the use of the original and indestructible powers of the soil'.[13]

In a similar vein of inquiry, the origins of, and the reasons for variation in wages were identified by Adam Smith in his *Wealth of Nations*.[14] He noted that in the early stages of society, when land was not scarce and the use of tools yet to evolve, the time expended on a job was a measure of its value. He illustrated this measure in a primarily hunting-based economy by tracing the exchange value of a beaver and a deer to the time taken to hunt each of them. Gradually, the value of the time expended on a job was adjusted to also take into account the severity of the job – the greater the hardship or dexterity and skill required (which translates to longer time taken in training), the higher the value. While these factors were precise in theory, in practice other considerations came into play. In a society in which land is privately owned, Smith noted, the superior bargaining position was with landlords who could survive 'a year or two, when many workmen could not subsist a week', without mutual dependence. He then logically envisaged that the landowner would appropriate most of the value of the good, leaving only the bare minimum possible as wages for the labourers.

Adam Smith defined this bare minimum as including not just enough for the subsistence of the individual labourer, but also what is necessary for him to maintain a family – to ensure a continuous flow of labour in the future. Endorsing the computation made by Richard Cantillon, the French economist, he quantified the amount required for the lowest types of labour as twice the amount required for his or her maintenance. The rationale for this computation was based on equating the maintenance cost of four children to that of one adult. Four children per family were required to maintain a continuous flow of labour, given the child mortality rate of that time, as only two were likely to survive and live to be adults.[15]

Of Interest and Profit

Although the ethics of receiving interest were dubious for a long time, the basis for computing it was settled a lot earlier than those for either rent or wages. It was embedded in the word used for interest in the two ancient languages, Sumerian and Egyptian – *mash* or *mas,* both of which meant calf. When property was borrowed, as in the case of cattle, the borrower had to return not just the original cattle borrowed but also the calves that were born in the interim; likewise, capital consisting of tools, equipment and machinery similarly fetched for their owner an additional portion of what could have been earned by their owners, had they used their capital themselves.

In contrast, even though profit was recognized quite early, entrepreneurship as a factor of production took a longer time to be defined. This was due to the multi-faceted role played by the entrepreneur who received profit. In most cases, the entrepreneur also provides capital and labour, with the result that his income derives from three streams: the interest on capital invested, wages for labour provided and profit. Segregating these was a challenge to academicians or theorists, but it was finally effectively conquered by Frank Knight in 1921, when he wrote the book *Risk, Uncertainty and Profit*. In this book, Knight surveyed the thoughts of his predecessors on profit in economic writings and concluded with his own inference that profit was the reward for risk-taking or uncertainty. Profit, he argued, was a result of uncertainty and the reward for successfully managing the risk. The greater the uncertainty, the higher would be the potential for profit. He went on to remark,

> The presence of true profit, therefore, depends on an absolute uncertainty in the estimation of the value judgment or on the absence of the requisite organization for combining a sufficient number of instances to secure certainty through consolidation.[16]

(Knight not only isolated profit in the stream of income that goes to an entrepreneur, he also saw it in the return obtained by an investor in the form of interest. With great insight he noted that 'pure interest is almost as rare a phenomenon as pure profit'. The extra interest earned by an investor in a venture, over the amount that would be returned by investing in 'gilt-edged' securities, where the risk factor is negligible, is 'pure profit' in the sense in which economic theory uses this term).[17]

With profit, the four factors of production and their intrinsic value were identified. However, the real world differs significantly from the conceptual world and the actual remuneration received by the factors of production often deviates significantly from their intrinsic values. During periods of scarce supply or excessive demand, their share is inflated and likewise, it is suppressed when the market situation is reversed. In addition, rent control acts and legislation for land holding, minimum wage policies influencing rent and wages, monetary policies to stimulate the economy or control inflation, and a host of other actions influence the prevailing interest rates. Given this, what is the role of the intrinsic contribution made by the four factors of production? Do they provide a centre of gravity around which their actual shares revolve or are there other generic factors that influence this?

The Paradox of Value

'Labour was the original, is now and ever will be the only purchase money in dealing with nature'[18] claimed the economist Thomas Hodgskin in a much-publicized debate with William Thompson at the Mechanics Institute, London in 1827. The debate was organized with the intent to bring knowledge closer to the general public, and brought up, among other ideas, the concepts of natural price and social price. Natural price was defined as the usefulness of a product to humanity – what is today called the intrinsic value. In contrast, social price was extrinsic value – the value placed by humans for exchanging the product among themselves. The contrast between the two is best seen by the relative prices prevailing for water and diamonds. The diamond-water paradox, also called the paradox of value, was a conundrum that engaged the minds of economists from the days of Adam Smith[h] and before.

The challenge before the economists was to explain the deviation between the natural price and social price of water and diamonds. Water, the elixir of life is absolutely free, whereas diamonds which have only a cosmetic use, command premium pricing. Scarcity, the most obvious explanation, is a

---

h   Adam Smith had explained the higher value commanded by diamonds in contrast to water by noting that value in exchange was determined by labour. He said, 'The real price of everything, what everything really costs to the man who wants to acquire it, is the toil and trouble of acquiring it.'

necessary but not essential criterion. In a desert, for example, water is both naturally and socially valuable, but this logic of scarcity as the basis for social price is not universally extendable. While it explains the premium price of diamonds, the same logic does not extend to, for example, antique books, which may be also scarce, but do not command a high social price. (While it is true that some antique books can have a high social value, not all do, and usually their social value is not directly linked to their scarcity). This paradox in value continued to haunt the minds of economists until it was satisfactorily explained just before the beginning of the twentieth century.

The foundation for this solution was laid more than two centuries earlier in an insightful and short essay written by Nicholas Barbon, a medical doctor and a fire insurance pioneer, who is now recognized as one of the early advocates for free trade. Barbon's *A Discourse of Trade,* published in 1690, contains a chapter titled 'Of Value and Price of Wares' which begins with the sentence: 'The Value of all Wares arise from their Use; Things of no Use have no Value, as the *English* Phrase is, *They are Good for Nothing*'. He went on to identify use as what was necessary to supply the wants and necessities of a person: the wants of the body and of the mind. Food, clothing and shelter were identified as the three wants of the body, but he qualified this by saying that only food was an absolute want, as clothing and shelter became a necessity only much later in human evolution. In short, he quantified the wants of the body as finite. In contrast, the wants of the mind were infinite. Barbon identified desire as the source of the wants of the mind, saying 'It [desire] is the appetite of the Soul; and is as natural to the Soul, as Hunger to Body'.[19] The mind wants everything that promotes ease, pleasure and pomp of life and its wants explode as its senses get refined and provide it with more delight, he observed. He went on to claim that the mind craves things which are difficult to get, such as pearls, diamonds and precious stones, and hence 'Things Rare are proper Ensigns of Honour, because it is Honourable to Acquire Things Difficult'.[20]

Nicholas Barbon illuminated the paradox of value by highlighting the distinction between the wants of the body and of the mind; in short between necessities and luxuries. Hence, it was clear that the natural price of a good adjusted for scarcity would provide the social price, in the case of necessities. However, the logic underlying the social price for comforts and luxuries could not be identified as precisely, and its workings were left unanswered for other economists to explore.

The Initial Answers to the Value Paradox

Major developments in the field of political economy followed the publication of *The Wealth of Nations*. Two decades later in 1798, Thomas Malthus published *An Essay on the Principles of Population*. In this short and insightful essay, Malthus noted that population grows geometrically, while the food required for the subsistence of a population grows only arithmetically. He felt that the implication of this insight was the future growth of misery and vice, with misery being absolutely unavoidable, whereas vice was merely highly probable.[21] With this observation, Malthus moved away from postulating principles for future interpretation based on an analysis of the past, to conclusively forecasting a life of misery for humanity. This prediction earned for the discipline of economics its distinctive label, coined by Thomas Carlyle, as a dismal science, which has since then stuck to it firmly.[22]

In 1817, within the next two decades, David Ricardo, published his treatise *On the Principles of Political Economy and Taxation*. In this, he analyzed the principles regulating the distribution of rent, profit and wages, which he considered the primary subject matter of political economy. It was in this book that Ricardo defined rent with a precision that stands the test of time even today. In contrast to these two relatively short but impactful essays, John Stuart Mills wrote a lengthy treatise in 1848 titled, *Principles of Political Economy with some of their Applications to Social Philosophy*. In the preface, he briefly summarized his objective for writing this book. He noted that Smith's *Wealth of Nations* comprehensively covered the discipline of political economy, but many of the concepts had become obsolete. He wanted his treatise to present an updated version of the subject, which in addition was to 'be more than a mere exposition of the abstract doctrines of political economy',[23] therein expressing a desire that his work would be a guide for practical applications as well.

Turning his attention to the water-diamond paradox, Mills reiterated the logic used by Adam Smith in identifying exchange value with labour, or the sacrifice made by an individual in terms of time and effort needed to produce the object. He went on to explain the premium value that diamonds command by redefining the term 'value in use'. According to Mills, Adam Smith had erred in assigning a broader meaning to the words; he felt that in political economy the words had a limited meaning, compared to their meaning in philosophy or morals. In the economic sense, he felt that the 'value in use' of a good indicated 'its capacity to satisfy a desire, or serve a purpose. Diamonds have this capacity in a high degree, and unless they had it, would not bear any price'.[24] Thus, he thought he solved the paradox by blurring the distinction between value in use and value in exchange. With this conclusive reasoning, as he saw it, he ended by saying, 'Happily, there is nothing in the laws of value which remains for the present or any future writer to clear up'.[25]

Mills thought that further deliberation was only needed to define the real-world applications of the concepts and asked for the patience of his readers as these were formulated. In line with this, after a detailed commentary on how prices are determined in the real world, Mills noted three distinct points. The first is that demand and supply define value in the real world. Secondly, the minimum value of a good is set by its cost of production. Finally, if the supply of a good can be increased over time, then demand and supply define value only for the interval during when supply cannot be increased.[26] However, history subsequently revealed that the value paradox remained unsolved.

Calculus of Pain and Pleasure

The water-diamond paradox was successfully taken up again by another English economist, William Stanley Jevons, who questioned the existing economic doctrine and Mills's conclusion that the last word on value had already been written. He began a completely new line of enquiry by viewing economics as a calculus of pleasure and pain. Since it dealt with quantities, he saw it as a mathematical subject, an aspect which had been ignored by the doyens of the discipline: Adam Smith, Malthus, Ricardo and Mills.

As a matter of fact, not only did Jevons change the line of enquiry in the discipline, he also gave it its current name in his book *The Theory of Political Economy*, published in 1879. Explaining the logic for this name change, in the preface to the second edition he reasoned:

Among minor alterations, I may mention the substitution for the name Political Economy of the single convenient term *Economics.* I cannot help thinking that it would be well to discard, as quickly as possible, the old troublesome double-worded name of our Science. Several authors have tried to introduce totally new names, such as Plutology, Chrematistics, Catallactics, etc. But why do we need anything better than Economics? This term besides being more familiar and closely related to the old term, is perfectly analogous in form to *Mathematics, Ethics* and *Aesthetics,* and the names of various other branches of knowledge, and it has moreover the authority of usage from the time of Aristotle.[27]

Returning to the water-diamond paradox, Jevons explained it in sync with his new line of enquiry by defining a few basic underlying concepts. He defined a commodity as 'any object, substance, action or service, which can afford pleasure or ward off pain'.[28] After defining a commodity, he defined utility as the abstract quality that converts an object into a commodity. With this foundation, Jevons now equated value in use to the utility offered by the total mass of that commodity, which he called total utility. For instance, water is amongst the most valuable commodities for sustaining human life, as life cannot exist in the absence of water. Hence, water as a commodity in totality has one of the highest possible values in use, second only to the air that we breathe.

In contrast, Jevons equated value in exchange with the 'intensity of desire or esteem for a thing'.[29] He noted that the intensity of desire or esteem for a thing varies with the quantity consumed at any given point of time. He then quoted from Richard Jennings,[i] a pioneer in linking economics to physiology,

---

i   In 1855, Richard Jennings wrote *Natural Elements of Political Economy,* establishing the linkages between Economics and Physiology.

about the impact of incremental consumption on satisfaction, or in Jevons' language, utility:

> To turn from the relative effect of commodities, in producing sensations, to those that are absolute, or dependent only on the quantity of each commodity, it is but too well known to every condition of men, that the degree of each sensation which is produced, is by no means commensurate with the quantity of commodity applied to the senses.… These effects require to be closely observed, because they are the foundation of the changes of the money price, which objects command in times of scarcity and abundance; we shall therefore here direct our attention to them for the purpose of ascertaining the nature of the law according to which the sensations that attend on consumption vary in degree with changes in the quantity of the commodity consumed.[30]

By extracting these insightful observations from Jennings on incremental consumption of a commodity, Jevons differentiated between the total utility of a commodity and the marginal utility, which he called 'the final degree of utility.' He noted that value has three aspects often confused with each other – value in use, intensity of desire or esteem and purchasing power. He equated value in use with total utility, esteem or value in exchange with marginal utility, and purchasing power as the ratio of exchange between any two commodities exchanged. Jevons then explained the role of labour, which Adam Smith had held to be the primary basis for exchange value: 'Value depends solely on the final degree of utility. How can we vary this degree of utility? – By having more or less of the commodity to consume. And how shall we get more or less of it? – By spending more or less labour in obtaining a supply'.[31]

In short, Jevons resolved the water-diamond paradox by pointing out that all of the water available to humanity was much more valuable than all of the diamonds available. This, then, is what is commonly understood to be value in use, i.e. the value of that commodity at large. But value in exchange depends on the incremental benefit provided by an additional unit of that commodity to an individual buyer and seller. Thus a new source of water will bring little exchange value for its owner, due to water not being a scarce commodity in general, whereas a diamond in contrast, being in short supply, will command a large value in exchange for its dealers. It is here that diamonds command a premium over water for individual traders. While Jevons identified this rationale, the relationship between exchange value and price was better illustrated by Carl Menger, the Austrian economist, who arrived at the same conclusion as Jevons at around the same time, independently.

The Continental Supplement

Like Jevons, Carl Menger too was dissatisfied with the line of enquiry adopted by his predecessors into the discipline of economics. He found that practical businessmen had no use for the science of economics. He inferred that this indifference could not be due to lack of interest or ability on their part, but could be accounted for by, 'the sterility of all past endeavours to find its empirical foundations'.[32] He then set about filling in this lacuna by following the empirical methods used in natural sciences to examine this discipline. Based on his empirical observations, Menger extracted and set out in his *Principles of Economics* the theories on goods, economy and economic goods, value, exchange, price, use value and exchange value, commodity and money.

Menger began by noting the universality of the cause and effect principle. Any things that satisfy human wants were termed as useful things. If human beings recognized the causal connection and directed the use of the thing to the satisfaction of their needs, the things could be termed goods, according to him. In the process, he identified four essential criteria for a thing to become a good: there should be a human need, the thing in question should be able to satisfy the human need, this causal effect between the need and the thing's properties should be known, and finally, such things should be able to be commanded. While identifying these features, Menger had the insight that goods can be both tangible and intangible. In addition, the human need in question may be real or illusionary. Likewise, the causal effect may be real or erroneously attributed. But in all these cases, if these four conditions are met, the things become goods.

Menger noted that as human societies evolve, there comes a time when the need for goods exceeds their supply. This change can arise when either the demand for goods goes up due to population increases or the availability of goods decreases. In either case, when the availability of goods is lower than the demand for goods, humans begin to 'economize', i.e. as all humans cannot satisfy all their needs, they prioritize which ones to pursue, leading to some needs remaining unfulfilled. With the advent of economizing, goods are transformed into economic goods. The distinction between goods like air, and economic goods like food, is the relationship between the quantity of goods needed and their availability. In an interesting observation, Menger noted that for a good to become an economic good, human labour is not essential – contrary to the opinion held at that time by many experts. Then he went on to conclude that the natural consequence of advanced civilization is the conversion of non-economic goods into economic goods, as human needs expand.

In some aspects, the advancement of civilization also reverses certain economic goods into non-economic goods. Menger illustrated this reversal by noting that government intervenes to increase the supply for certain goods held to be of social importance, like public education or the provision of drinking water, by transforming them back to non-economic goods.

Turning his attention to the water-diamond paradox, Menger arrives at the same conclusion as Jevons did, by noting that all the diamonds available to mankind can be kept in a single container, while all the drinking water on the earth cannot be confined to a single conceivable reservoir. Thus, while a diamond is an economic good, water, despite its ability to satisfy essential human needs, remains outside the realm of economic goods. He then theorised further than Jevons by describing the factors that determine the price of an economic good and its relationship with use-value.

Of Trading Cattle

Menger described the hypothetical situation of two individuals living in isolation. Both the individuals need cows to meet their dietary needs and horses to supplement their work and transportation. One cow meets basic food requirements, the second cow provides for an adequate diet, and the third cow for food variety; similarly they need one horse for transportation and a second horse for their riding pleasure; additional cows and horses serve as contingency demands. Menger then assigned a numerical value for the use-value of each animal at 50, 40, 30, 20 and 10 from the first to fifth animal respectively. With this background, he envisaged a situation where one individual, A, has six horses and one cow, while other individual, B has six cows and one horse:

Number of Animals	Person A		Person B	
	Use Value of Horses	Use Value of Cows	Use Value of Horses	Use Value of Cows
1	50	50	50	50
2	40			40
3	30			30
4	20			20
5	10			10
6	0			0

Source: Menger, Carl. *Principles of Economics,* p183

Menger then proceeds to show that it is beneficial for A and B to exchange horses for cows as the overall use-value of the animals will increase by exchanging. The first exchange of a horse for a cow increases the use-value for both individuals, from a total use-value of 200 each, before the exchange of the first animal, to 240 each after the exchange. Each person has given up a surplus animal with zero use-value, and in return obtained an animal yielding 40 units of use-value:

Description	Gain in Use-Value resulting from Exchange						Gain from Exchange	Use value of A & B
	Person A			Person B				
	Horses	Cows	Total	Horses	Cows	Total		
Pre-exchange								
Number of animals	6	1	7	1	6	7		
Use-value units	150	50	200	50	150	200		400
First Exchange of animals	-1	1	0	1	-1	0	0	
Change in Use-value units	0	40	40	40	0	40	80	480

With the exchange of the second animal, each of them loses 10 units of use-value from their initial total, but makes up for it by gaining 30 units of use-value. After the second exchange their use-value is at 260 each.

Description	Gain in Use-Value resulting from Exchange						Gain from Exchange	Use value of A & B
	Person A			Person B				
	Horses	Cows	Total	Horses	Cows	Total		
Second exchange								
Number of animals	1	1	0	-1	1	0		
Use-value units	-10	30	20	30	-10	20	40	520

If they undertake a third exchange their total use-value remains at 260 each, as they give up an animal worth 20 units of use-value and get another animal also worth 20 units of use-value. Hence, there is no incentive for them to do the third exchange.

In this illustration, Menger demonstrates that the use-value of goods declined with an increase in the total quantity exchanged.

	Gain in Use-Value resulting from Exchange							
Description	Person A			Person B			Gain from Exchange	Use value of A & B
	Horses	Cows	Total	Horses	Cows	Total		
Third exchange								
Number of animals	-1	1	0	1	-1	0		
Use-value units	-20	20	0	20	-20	0	0	520

If the parties continue to exchange further, after the fourth exchange there would be a loss of 40 use-value units.

	Gain in Use-Value resulting from Exchange							
Description	Person A			Person B			Gain from Exchange	Use value of A & B
	Horses	Cows	Total	Horses	Cows	Total		
Fourth exchange								
Number of animals	-1	1	1	1	-1	0		
Use-value units	-30	10	-20	10	-30	-20	-40	480

As depicted in the tables above, after the first exchange the gain from exchange is 80 use-value units. After the second exchange the gain drops to 40 use-value units, but it is still a gain. However after the third exchange increase in use-value is nil, and thereafter, it goes into negative figures. From this, and other similar but more complex illustrations, Menger arrived at a few critical inferences:

- For an individual, goods have two distinct benefits: the direct benefit or use-value and the indirect benefit or exchange-value,
- All goods with use-value cannot be converted into goods of exchange value, (for example, the notes of a writer, the crutches for a disabled person, family photographs and other personal effects have very high use-values, but practically negligible exchange-values in most circumstances),
- All goods with exchange-values need not have a use-value for their owner, (for example, foreign language books to a book seller who doesn't read that language, surgical instruments to a manufacturer or trader and the like are not valued by them for their use-value but for their exchange-value),
- Where goods have both use-value and exchange-value to their owner, the use-value is the minimum value to the owner and the exchange-value is the maximum value; if the exchange-value is lower than the use-value, the owner will use the good and not exchange it,
- Use-value is not constant and changes with the life stages of an individual, (for example, children outgrow toys, adolescents no longer need study materials, adults past their work-life dispose of their work equipment, etc). Use-value also changes with external defects in goods like clothes, horses, dogs, modes of transport, etc, while their exchange-value remains relatively unaltered,
- Exchange-value can fall, while the use-value remains constant, (for example, in the case of goods with external defects that do not alter use value; Menger gave the instance of innkeepers and grocers using food materials with external defects, or shoemakers, tailors and hatters

who use goods with external defects, but with their use-value intact).

After identifying all these different facets in considerable depth, Menger highlights the universal factor: use-value declines with an increase in the quantity available to an individual, while exchange-value remains intact. He also saw the apt contrast between the exchange-value and use-value of goods. A commodity held for sale is exclusively prized for its exchange-value while goods held for consumption derive their utility exclusively from their use-value.

The works of the trio of Jevons and Menger along with Leon Walras,[j] changed the focus of economics from its supply-side and macro orientation, to the concept of utility and demand, with the spotlight shifting to the study of individual consumer behaviour and its impact on the demand for specific products/services. This major shift was a trigger for Alfred Marshall, the English professor of economics, to develop 'laws' of economics, along with their attendant limitation: *ceteris paribus* or 'all other things being equal'. He, too, provided a solution for the value-paradox, using a different logic.

Money: The Generic Measure

Alfred Marshall also reached the same conclusion about the value paradox as the other three, solving it using the concept of marginal utility. But he took the route of studying consumer surpluses to get there, and in the process, elucidated an important point about the role of money. Marshall's

---

j   Leon Walras independently and concurrently arrived at the concept of marginal utility. However his approach to marginal utility came from a macro analysis of the economy, hence his contribution to the development of economics is not dealt with here.

example noted that salt, an essential food item, was priced lower than tea, an optional addition to a diet. He then went about illustrating a hypothetical case of tea purchase to show the link between use-value and exchange-value through the medium of consumer surplus.

Marshall's resolution of the value paradox is based on the key concept of measuring human motives using the yardstick of money. By using the measure of money, he converted all goods and services into their exchange-value equivalents, as expressed in monetary terms. Money, which till then was primarily seen as a medium of exchange and store of value, acquired its third and most critical function as a *measure* of value, setting the stage for fiat money.

Box 4.1

Fiat Money: The Birth of Legal Tender

'Money is what money does' is a very popular definition. Even though it does not throw any further light on money, why did this definition gain such wide acceptance? A probable reason for this could be the wide range of products that have served as money over the course of human history, including, among others, items of daily use like salt, tobacco, coconuts, rice, beads, fish hooks, feathers, cowries and other shells, fur, wampum, arrows, whale teeth, cattle, fish, rum, sugar and leather.[33] The only common factor among all these items is that they all performed the functions of money. A more functional definition of money lists its three functions as, 'a medium of exchange, a measure of value and a store of value'.

Speculating on the origin of money, Carl Menger attributed it as 'a natural product of human economy.'[34] He identified its origin to economizing individuals in social situations who realized that they could further their economic interest by the exchange of goods. Money was the lubricant that facilitated this exchange. He then went on to identify the reasons why, in the early pastoral societies, cattle were the most common form of money. First, cattle had universal acceptability and so could be an effective medium of exchange. As they transported themselves, they could be used even in exchanges between individuals from distant places. A cow, for instance, was of considerable durability and maintained itself in an era where pastures were not in short supply, thus proving to be a relatively stable store of value. The only shortcoming of cattle as money was in their function as a measure of value. They could not be sub-divided into smaller units. Further, the variance in qualities between two sets of cattle could be large as they were not homogenous.

Metallic Money

The early use of metals and coins seems to have been a device to overcome this shortcoming of cattle in performing the third function of money, as a measure of value. Menger identified the Greek lawmaker Solon as the first to convert fines to be paid in cattle into coin money, when he equated a sheep to one drachma and a cow to five drachmae in 430 BCE.[35] Another factor that could have contributed to the shift to metallic money is the advent of agriculture and the complement of handicrafts required to sustain it, which led to the recession of pastoral economies. This would have diluted the acceptability of cattle as a medium of exchange. With reduced pastoral land for the cattle to feed, their effectiveness as a store of value too would have declined, paving the way for metals and coins to act as money in agricultural economies.

The quantity of money required in an economy is directly proportional to the volume of its exchange transactions. Over the centuries, as the proportion of exchange transactions increased in human society, metals considered as money expanded from silver and copper to include gold. In addition, a pecking order of value too evolved among the three metals, based on their relative scarcity. Gold assumed the pinnacle, followed by silver, even as copper exited this domain.

The transition from a sustenance economy to an exchange economy required frequent transfers of large amounts of money, with its attendant costs. Initially, these metals were deposited with goldsmiths, who could assay its purity. As the deposits increased, the need for a reliable warehouse became acute, leading to the formation of the gold standard.

Under the gold standard, the government of the land received gold in their central bank and gave a token to acknowledge this receipt. The ingenuity and trust inherent in humans resulted in the acceptance of these tokens, called bank notes, in place of large amounts of metal or coins. The government and the bank also undertook to return the gold whenever these bank notes were presented to the bank. England was the first country to adopt the gold standard, when it enacted the Gold Standards Act in 1816.[k] However, the act providing for the convertibility of bank notes into gold came into effect only five years later.

Fiat Money

The English government went one step further when it made the Bank of England's bank notes legal tender, by enacting the

---

k Conceptually the idea for a gold standard came up in 1763, when an act was passed in England that forbade banks to create more money than the amount of bullion they had.

Bank Notes Act in 1833. Prior to this, economic exchanges in England could be settled in any commodity mutually agreed to between the contracting parties. After 1833, it was obligatory on the part of the seller to accept payment tendered in bank notes. Refusal to accept bank notes in discharge of an obligation in an economic exchange was a crime punishable under the laws of the land. This move gave bank notes the sole role of money in the economy and central banks the monopoly over issue of bank notes. More importantly, it set the stage for the advent of fiat money at a later date.

Once England, the dominant economy worldwide at the time, entered the gold standard, it was merely a matter of time before other countries in the world too followed it. The impetus for this was also provided by the growing global trade, a result of industrialization with its large-scale production. This required an international measure and store of value, which the gold standard provided. By the end of the nineteenth century most of the countries in the world were under the gold standard, either directly or indirectly. However, what worked during peaceful times did not survive the First World War.

The outbreak of the First World War put a decisive end to the gold standard in a two-step process. In the first stage it made holding bank notes a patriotic duty. As economic instincts got better of patriotic obligations, it forced the introduction of fiat money that replaced the gold standard, first in England and later across the world. With the declaration of war, uncertainty increased. People opted to hold their wealth in the form of gold, in preference to its paper token. As holders of bank notes opted to convert their holdings into gold, the Bank of England increased the bank rate, i.e. the base interest rate in the economy from 3 to 4 per cent. This was intended to provide an incentive to the holders of bank notes, which earned interest, in contrast to barren gold. A day later on July 31, 1914, as the initial trickle of people converting bank notes into gold snowballed into an avalanche, the bank rate was doubled to 8 per cent to arrest the momentum. In addition, the Stock Exchange was also shut.[36] Even the idea that that it was unpatriotic to demand conversion of bank notes into gold at a time when the country was at war and needed to use all its resources to defeat its enemy, could not stem the tide.

During the war, the role of the British government increased as their responsibilities expanded from managing war activities to providing essential services to the entire British population. Measured as a share of national income, government expenditure increased from 8 per cent in the pre-war period to about 50 per cent during the war.[37] Much of this increased expenditure was funded by the Bank of England, which did not have the backing of gold reserves. It started issuing new bank notes called Bradburys, as they bore the signature of Sir John Swanick Bradbury, the Chief Cashier of the Bank of England. These notes did not promise to pay their value in gold as the earlier notes had. Looking at the intrinsic value of these bank notes a clear decline is visible. The pre-war gold standard pound sterling traded at US \$4.86 (the US dollar was backed by gold). During the war, the British government supported the pound sterling at around this rate. As the war ended, the British government withdrew its support, and by February 1920, one pound sterling was trading at US\$3.20, reflecting the dilution in its gold backing.[38]

The First World War ended the Gold Standard. The bank note, with its position reinforced as legal tender, assumed the role of fiat money. Fiat money in the form of paper money got its value not from its ability to be converted into gold or any other valuable commodity, but from a government mandate that it must be accepted as the sole mode of payment in the domestic economy, giving it the status of legal tender.

Marshall begins his book, *Principles of Economics,* by noting that historically religion and economics are the two dominant influences in human life. He observed that while the influence of religion is intense and limited to short spells, the influence of economics is more persistent. He defined economics as 'a study of men as they live and move and think in the ordinary business of life. But it concerns itself with those motives which affect, most powerfully and most steadily, man's conduct in the business part of life'.[39] In the study of motives in conduct of business, Marshall found money to be an ideal measure, a methodology which enabled economics to progress ahead of all other social sciences. Using money, economists could measure the force of a motive: the amount of money humans gave up, i.e.: the price they paid to secure a pleasure, or the money they demanded to undergo a fatigue, was a precise measure amicable to further analysis.

To resolve the value paradox, Marshall described a hypothetical situation, based on observations in the marketplace of individuals buying larger quantities when the price of a product fell. For this illustration, he defined a situation where a consumer would buy one pound of tea annually if it was priced at 20 shillings per pound and two pounds if they were priced at 14 shillings. From this he inferred that at 20 shillings a pound of tea, the minimum benefit derived by the consumer would be 20 shillings. If the benefit was lower, there would be no purchase. Given this, when the price of the tea came down to 14 shillings, the benefit derived by the consumer would be the equivalent of 34 shillings, the total of the first pound giving a 20 shillings benefit, and the second pound giving a 14 shillings benefit. However for this 34 shillings benefit, the cost incurred by the consumer would only be 28 shillings, i.e. he would only pay the price equivalent to the benefit derived for the last unit consumed for both the units purchased.

In the above illustration, the use-value to the buyer of the last unit purchased declined with every incremental purchase. However the total benefit derived by the buyer was a summation of all the individual purchases. In contrast, the exchange-value – the price paid by the buyer for the entire quantity purchased – was based on the benefit derived from the last incremental quantity bought. This explains why the exchange-value deviated from the use-value in the case of not only water and diamonds but also in all instances where use-value and exchange-value diverge, as for salt and tea and other such examples containing contrasts between socially desirable and ornamental services.[1]

Marshall, in contrast to his contemporaries, took an incremental step that placed economics on a distinct pedestal. He converted his insights from the study of this subject into economic 'laws'. He summarized the results of his study in the value paradox into a general observation which goes under the title of 'The Law of Marginal Utility'. He wrote,

> The larger the amount of a thing that a person has the less, other things being equal (i.e. the purchasing power of money, and the amount of money at his command being equal), will be the price which he will pay for a little more of it: or in other words his marginal demand price for it will diminish.[40]

---

[1] Incidentally this also explains why certain essential professions like nursing and teaching are paid a pittance compared to more superfluous professions like tax advising and investment banking, which rake in millions. While the total salary paid to all the nursing and teaching staff in an economy is a lot higher than the total salary paid to all the tax advisors and investment bankers, reflecting their value in use, what each nurse or teacher individually gets is much lower than each tax advisor or investment banker, reflecting their marginal utility.

All Other Things Being Equal

The importance Alfred Marshall attached to what he called the economic laws is reflected by an entire chapter devoted to them in his book, *Principles of Economics*. This book attained status and fame comparable to books like Adam Smith's *Wealth of Nations.*

While formulating these economic laws, Marshall realized that they were not precise and universal, like the law of gravity and other such inferences from the natural sciences. He described them as 'nothing more than a general proposition or statement of tendencies, more or less certain, more or less definite'[41] comparing them to the science used to predict water levels during high tides. While the influence of the sun and moon on the tides is well known, the impact of heavy rains and strong ocean winds cannot be accurately predicted, so the prediction of tides contains an element of probability. The reason that he still went ahead and formulated these laws was the need to frequently refer to them in any discussion on the subject. After a quick cost-benefit analysis, he concluded that frequent use in discussions justified the use of general statements in place of formal technical statements.[42]

To reduce the uncertainties of these 'laws' and make them more definite, Marshall sought to diminish these uncertainties with his most visible contribution to the discipline of economics: the term *ceteris paribus* or 'other things remaining the same'. One illustration of its use is in the interesting example of the market for fishes when the demand for fish has gone up due to a panic about disease infecting the farm stock that would otherwise be wanted, such as poultry and cattle. In this case, with *ceteris paribus* he disregarded the vagaries of the weather, such as a stormy day or good fishing weather, on the supply of fishes. His logic for this was that weather extremes are of short duration and will cancel each other out and therefore will not be important. Likewise, long-term events like an increase in number of sea-faring men increasing the supply of fishes can also be excluded from this study, as they cannot make a difference to the immediate affects of this scare. After eliminating the two extreme time periods in this case, Marshall wanted to study the impact of the unexpectedly good fishing wages resulting from the higher demand for fishes due to the scare: they drew in sailors who otherwise would have sailed on long non-fishing voyages, and increased the number of fishing vessels as older/other non-fishing vessels were being pressed into service. After these observations he concludes, 'Here we see an illustration of the almost universal law that – the term Normal being taken to refer to a short period of time – *an increase in the amount demanded [of fishes] raises the normal supply price[of fishing wages]*'.[43]

Following a similar approach, Marshall evolved a cluster of economic Laws: the Law of Diminishing Utility, Law of Demand, Law of Increasing Returns, Law of Diminishing Returns, Law of Constant Returns, Law of Substitution and Law of Supply, among others. These generalizations had a revolutionary impact on the discipline. They influenced the study of economics at that time and converted it into a celebrated discipline to be taught in educational institutions. Their influence is visible even today in most elementary economic textbooks that teach the Laws of Demand and Supply. But somewhere down the line, the important limitations identified by Marshall have faded into the background, leaving the laws standing by themselves in the limelight and being compared to those of natural science.

At the beginning of his thesis, Marshall named religion and economics as the two most significant factors that impact human life. As the twentieth century unfolded, the religious impact which Marshall recognized as being intense and of short duration, reduced in its intensity and frequency for a variety of reasons, even as economic factors, which he perceived as persistent, increased their intensity while retaining their persistent influence on human life. A consequence of this development was an increased insulation of human sensitivity from their ethical and social obligations.

Just as the law of gravity, when it pulls a falling child to death towards the ground, does not evoke any moral outrage as it is part of nature, so too did the 'Laws of Economics' insulate the human conscience when a 'free' market nudged and pushed the weak and the innocent to an inhuman existence. Unintended by Marshall, the canonization of the Laws of Economics, with their pretense of equating economics to a natural science, made the break between economics and ethics complete, as judgment about natural science is outside the realm of morality. Nowhere is this more clearly reflected than in the words of Marshall's contemporary, Carl Menger, who in his *Principles of Economics* examining the ethical questions around rent and interest collection noted, 'But it seems to me that the question of the legal or moral character of these facts is beyond the sphere of our science'.[44]

Jevons, Menger, and Marshall, with their new approach to the discipline of economics, altered its very nature by studying utility to the consumer and individual market. The result was a shift in focus to individual consumers and business firms, the domain of micro-economics. It took a sharp and continued demand contraction that began in the United States of America in the year 1929 and sent ripples round the world for economists to shift their focus from individual consumers and business firms to the overall economy.

Endnotes

1 Plato, *The Republic,* Penguin Classics, Second edition, 1987, p120

2 Ibid, p185

3 Ibid, p188

4 Smith, A., *The Theory of Moral Sentiments,* The Online Library of Liberty Collection, PLL V4, January 6, 2009, p207

5 Ibid, p127

6 Ibid, p226

7 Ibid, p188

8 Ibid,p189

9 Ibid, p220

10 Herbener, J., An Integration of *The Wealth of Nations, The Theory of Moral Sentiments,* in the *Journal of Libertarian Studies*, Vol. VIII, No.2 (Summer 1987), p276

11 Ibid, p279

12 Mark, K., *Das Capital Volume 1 The Process of Production of Capital,* First English edition of 1887, Progress Publishers, Moscow, Online version: Marx/ Engles Internet archive, www.Marxists.org, p154

13 Ricardo, D., *The Principles of Political Economy and Taxation,* Third Edition, 1821, p39

14 Smith, A., *The Wealth of Nations,* Bantam Classic, March 2003, p67

15 Ibid, p96

16 Knight, F., *Risk, Uncertainty and Profit,* Hughton Mifflin Company, 1921, Online Library of Liberty, p146

17 Ibid, p155-6

18 Hodgskin, T., *Popular Political Economy. Four Lectures delivered at the London Mechanics Institution,* London, Charles and William Tate, 1827, p112

19 Barbon, N., *A Discourse of Trade,* The Online Library of Liberty Collection, p12

20 Ibid, p13

21 Malthus, T., *An Essay on the Principle of Population,* Printed for J. Johnson, in St.Paul's Church-Yard, 1798, p5

22 Carlyle, T., *Occassional Disclosure on the Negro Question,* published in Frazer's Magazine for Town and Country, London, Vol. XL, 1849, p532

23 Mills J.S. *Principles of Political Economy with some of their Applications to Social Philosophy,* (Ashley ed.) 1848, p23

24 Ibid, p314

25 Ibid, p314

26 Ibid, p327

27 Jevons, W. S., *Theory of Political Economy*, 1871, p10

28 Ibid, p46

29 Ibid, p71

30 Ibid, p56

31 Ibid, p120

32 Menger, C., *Principles of Economics*, Ludwig Von Mises Institute, 2007, p46

33 Tandon, P., *Banking Century*, Penguin Books, 1989, p5

34 Menger, C., *Principles of Economics*, Ludwig Von Mises Institute, 2007 reprint, p262

35 Ibid, p264

36 Mayhew, N., *Sterling, The History of a Currency*, Penguin Books, 1919, p200

37 Ibid, p202

38 Ibid, p207

39 Ibid, p14

40 Ibid, p62

41 Ibid, p25

42 Ibid, p25

43 Ibid, p216

44 Menger, C., *Principles of Economics*, Ludwig Von Mises Institute, 2007 reprint, p173

Chapter 5

Ideologically Designed: A Rich Adulthood 1929 to 2009 CE

Ultimate decisions, the valuations and the choosing of the ends, are beyond the scope of any science. Science never tells a man how he should act; it merely shows how a man must act if he wants to attain definite ends.

– Ludwig von Mises, in *Human Action, A Treatise on Economics*

The nineteenth century witnessed the birth and evolution of two opposing schools of thought in macro-economics, reflected in Say's Law of the Supply-side school and the opposing Demand-side school. A century later, this debate resurfaced triggered by the Supply-side school's inability to explain the American Great Depression of the 1930s. The British economist, John Maynard Keynes, offered an explanation asserting Demand-side ideas, even as the Supply-side school headed by the Austrian economist, Hayek gamely fought on. The Keynesian victory was short lived, as the 1970s oil crisis and stagflation presented them with an unanswered question, reviving the fortunes of the Supply-side school for the next three decades. The debate has since raged on and resurfaced in our times. The financial crisis of 2008 once again brought up the debate, threatening the seemingly unassailable position of the Supply-side school at the end of the second millennium.

A Case for 'Free' Business

After the publication of *The Wealth of Nations* in 1776, signaling the birth of economics as a distinct discipline, the 1820s produced the first depression when economists could analyze their theories 'live'. The long war between the English and the French that ended with the defeat of Napoleon Bonaparte triggered this slowdown. During the war, English industry had expanded rapidly to meet growing war needs. Even their enemy the French army, who were fighting the Russians in 1807 on the remote Eastern borders, were wearing British greatcoats. The English not only clothed the French, but even the Russian, Prussian and Swedish armies.[1] In addition to the textile industry, their iron trade too prospered on the war-fed demand. Along with the war, the good times of robust business too ended. The resultant glut provided the first platform for economists to debate their theories of demand and supply in a real setting. The solutions they proposed were not just academic speculations. With parliamentary democracy as the national decision-making process in Britain, the potential for these deliberations to influence policy decisions was real.

'*Traite D'Economie Politique*' published by Jean Baptiste Say in 1803 was considered one of the most influential books after Adam Smith's *Wealth of Nations*. David Ricardo, the English economist, remarked that this work 'has succeeded in placing the science in a more logical, and more instructive order; and has enriched it by several discussions, original, accurate and profound'.[2] Say sought to outline in this treatise a way to realize all rational human desires using human will and intelligence.[3]

Say began his treatise which dealt with wealth creation, distribution and consumption, with a unique take on wealth production, laying the foundation for his distinct approach. Viewing wealth production through a new lens, he acknowledged that humans can neither create nor destroy matter, but what they can and do create is utility. He then defined production as 'the creation, not of matter, but of utility. It is not to be estimated by the length, the bulk, or the weight of the product, but by the utility it presents'.[4] Taking this line of reasoning based on utility further, Say identified services as wealth. This was in contrast to the prevalent mode of thought at that time when only products were considered as wealth. Viewing services through the product framework, he called them 'Immaterial Products or Values Consumed at the Moment of Production'. Say identified the principle that is linked to his name even today by inferring the link between production and consumption in services: Say's Law,[a] which states that 'supply creates its own demand'.

Say's Law and the rationale for its formulation were a matter of interest to the debaters of the first depression. The French economist noted that the primary interest of the merchants was in seeing consumption grow and prices increase, saying 'The grand object of their desire is a consumption brisk enough to quicken sales and keep up prices'.[5] While concurring with the logic and importance underlining the desire of the merchants, he disagreed with their request for protection and their advocacy for balanced trade in their country and advanced his reasons in the new line of enquiry contained in his book.

Say knew that the prevailing explanation for lack of demand in the economy was that money[b] was in short supply.

---

a F.M. Taylor in his book, *The Principles of Economics,* for the first time accorded this principle, the status of a law, by noting, 'I shall therefore put this proposition we have discussed in the form of a principle. This principle, I have taken the liberty to designate Say's Law; because, though recognized by many earlier writers, it was particularly well brought out in the presentation of Say.'

b Money during this time was primarily metals: gold and silver. The prevailing view was that net imports by a country drained the country of its money supply, thereby reducing demand for domestic production.

He went on to discard this reason, stating, 'For after all, money is but the agent of the transfer of value'[6] and cannot by itself cause a glut: a state when the supply is greater than the demand. Identifying scarcity of money as the reason for lack of demand was, he added, mistaking 'the means for the cause'. After dismissing the prevailing explanation, he advanced his new counter-intuitive conclusion, 'that it is production which opens a demand for products'.[7] He observed that when people complained of dull sales, it was not because of a scarcity of money but because of reduced economic activity, reflected in the scarcity of products being produced. Lack of money in an economy could not be the reason for dull sales, he reasoned, as merchants were resourceful and would find substitutes for the money. Once a substitute is found for money, he noted that its supply would increase as, 'all produce naturally gravitate to that place where it is most demanded'.[8]

To support his conclusion that production creates its own demand, Say pointed out empirical evidence, such as a good harvest translating to good demand for other industries, while a bad harvest resulted in poor demand.[c] Similarly, he noted that the success of one branch of commerce opened up the market for the products of many other branches. A general glut, which is the result of inadequate demand for all commodities, was not feasible, he concluded, though he admitted that there could be gluts in some select commodities, due to overproduction or the reduced production of other commodities. He saw in profit a powerful stimulus to correct such a situation and

---

c   We see the same logic advanced in India today, where the monsoon and the resultant food production influence the demand for consumer goods in rural markets, which is further amplified by the stock markets.

identified the sole reason for a continued glut in some products as 'a violent means, or an extraordinary cause, a political or natural convulsion, or the avarice or ignorance of authority, to perpetuate this scarcity on one hand, and consequent glut on the other'.[9]

The belief that supply creates its own demand led Say to infer a number of relationships, all of which had profound implications on his recommendations to abstain from promoting consumption. For one, he believed that more producers and products translated to more demand for the product; secondly, that the success of one trade promoted success in all other trades; and finally, that unrestrained foreign trade is beneficial, following the logic that what is good for an individual, i.e. free trade within a country, would be good for the country too. He concluded by stating that encouraging consumption was counter-productive to stimulating demand and therefore it is production that must be encouraged to grow demand, and not consumption.

Say's rationale and recommendations formed the basis for a proposal advocated by the nineteenth-century English economists, Ricardo and Mills, to counter the lack of demand in the market, thereby bringing this idea into the English economic debate. These recommendations today fall under the rubric of supply-side economics. Advocated by the votaries of free trade, supply-side economists propose measures to encourage production, not consumption. They also advocate free trade, both local and foreign, and believe that a profit stimulus will redress the situation by generating demand through the mechanism of price corrections. Government intervention, they believe, is required only to eliminate 'the violent means or the extraordinary cause'. In short, they advocate a policy of *laissez faire* or 'let it be'.

In contrast to the supply-side economists' proposals, another French historian and economist, Jean Charles Leonard Simonde de Sismonde proposed an alternative approach, in which he looked beyond production. This proposal was forcefully taken forward by Thomas Malthus, the English economist of the 'population bomb' theory fame, in his lesser-known work, *The Principles of Political Economy*. Interestingly, both of them were drawn by the distressed conditions prevailing in England at the birth of the nineteenth century; Simonde by the impact of the Industrial Revolution where prosperity and poverty jointly flourished, and Malthus by the depression triggered by the end of the French-English war.

Wealth Sans Welfare

Jean Charles Leonard Simonde de Sismonde, the French historian and economist, was bewildered by the paradox he saw in England. Poverty thriving amidst plenty stunned him. The England he knew at the beginning of the nineteenth century was in the full flow of the Industrial Revolution. Steam and hydro-power combined with mechanization had multiplied production beyond the wildest imagination of that time. Yet, Simonde was puzzled. In the preface to his economic treatise, *Political Economy and the Philosophy of Government*, he noted with concern the developments taking place in England, where production grew even as enjoyment declined and the basic idea was forgotten that '[the] increase of wealth is not the end in political economy, but its instrument in procuring the happiness of all'.[10]

Considering the contradictory states of widespread poverty and increasing wealth created in the economy, Simonde redefined national wealth as 'the participation of all in the advantages of life',[11] in place of the then prevailing concept of total wealth creation. Talking about the poor, he identified their needs as food, clothing, and shelter, along with the belief that their future will not be worse off than their present if they continued to put in the same level of labour.[12] Turning to the rich, in addition to their food, clothing and shelter (which he acknowledged would be 'better for some than for others') Simonde identified a new need. It was their need for leisure or, as he put it '[the] subsistence of the rich must be independent of their labour'.[13] Leisure could only be assured by their command over wealth. The two benefits from leisure that Simonde visualized were in the development of intellectual faculties and in providing relief against 'all kinds of wretchedness'[14] in society.

Simonde saw the rich class as essential to a nation's progress. He saw them as the source of knowledge creation, civilization and altruism. In the absence of the rich who enjoyed leisure, he reasoned, a nation could descend into ignorance, barbarism and selfishness.[15] He viewed the development of intellectual faculty as advancing the frontiers of knowledge, and charity undertaken by the rich as necessary to negate the streak of selfishness and barbarism in society. In addition, he believed that the wealth of a nation was better serviced by a large number of moderately rich people, rather than a few super-rich individuals. He reasoned that the moral and social impact of the charitable activities and intellectual pursuits of a larger number of reasonably rich individuals serving as a role model for others would be far greater than of a few super-rich individuals.

Turning to the Industrial Revolution in England, Simonde saw it entwined with the spirit of free competition among businesses. Free competition fueled by self-interest, he noted, led businesses to 'produce the greatest possible quantity of work at the cheapest rate.' As every business tried to reduce costs and produce more, the competitive spirit became more intense, as one could succeed only at the cost of the other opponents. In short, Simonde noted that a competitive environment bred ill-will, leading him to conjecture, 'perhaps, you will be called on to say to your rival, your death is our life'.[16] In their endeavours to produce at the cheapest rate, Simonde noticed a change in the approach of businesses towards using labour. Their goal now was to make more things with the same quantity of labour, or alternatively, to make many things with a smaller quantity of labour. This naturally resulted in the use of machinery, which replaced labour. Based on this analysis, Simonde concluded that in an environment of free competition, collective progress will tend to depreciate the value of labour, thereby causing hardship to those who depended solely on labour for their livelihood.[17] This profound conclusion by Simonde has stood the test of time, as even today we see businesses in their quest for market-share and profits lay off employees to reduce costs.

Simonde also identified management practices that, down the line, gave birth to the 'outsourcing' industry, thereby causing hardship to labour in the domestic economies of the businesses. He identified initiatives to replace highly-priced labour with low-cost substitutes. In England, this was clearly visible in the local English labour being replaced with cheap Irish immigrants, resulting in an overall drop in welfare. Simonde elaborated that, 'She [England] has found it more economical to feed the Irish with potatoes, and clothe them in rags; and now every packet brings legions of Irish, who, working for less than the English, drive them from every employment'[18]

In this new mode of production under free competition, Simonde observed that supply by itself does not create a demand. When the labourers are able to earn lower and lower incomes, even as more goods are produced, the total demand declines. For production to become wealth, he realized that there must be willing consumers with income to buy. This was a fact which Say and his followers had ignored, but Simonde forcefully highlighted, He asserted that:

> By neglecting a quality so essential to be determined, Say and Ricardo have arrived at the conclusion that consumption is an unlimited power, or at least having no limits but those of production, whilst it is in fact limited by income.[19]

The job of detailing the arguments against Say's law was left to Malthus who articulated them with vigour and clarity, when he analyzed the reason for slack economic activity in England after the French-English war in 1815 and identified three fundamental errors in Say's Law.

The Three Fundamental Errors

The concluding chapter of Thomas Robert Malthus's book, the *Principles of Political Economy*, was an analysis of the prevailing economic conditions in England, where the labour found it tough to get employed. Popular reasoning attributed this inability to create employment opportunities to lack of capital in the country. The war, it was noted, had drained the country of its capital, resulting in this undesirable situation. Beginning an independent analysis, Malthus could not find an explanation for the stagnation in Say's Law, which believed that production is the only source of wealth.[20] Malthus provided an alternative explanation that answered this conundrum.

In an earlier chapter,[d] Malthus had identified the 'fundamental errors' of the line of thinking that was

---

d   Section III, *Of Accumulation, Or The Savings From Revenue To Add To Capital, Considered As A Stimulus To The Increase of Wealth* propagated by Say, Ricardo and James Mills who all held that production was the key to increasing wealth. Listing out the three fundamental errors, he placed at the top of the list the tendency to treat articles of consumption and the wants of customers as mathematical figures to set off against another set of numbers that represent production or supply. Malthus noted that increased production can coexist with constant or declining wants, due to parsimony which leads to surplus production and supply, creating a mismatch. Malthus went on further to identify an observation made by Ricardo in support of his own conclusion. Ricardo had remarked that 'If men cease to consume, they would cease to produce,' before adding, 'This admission does not impugn the general principle'.[21]

Ricardo made this contradictory observation to his own theory, when he pointed out the sole exception he saw where a general glut could exist for short duration: when wages increased and profits declined. He foresaw this situation when low food prices prevailed, along with large capital accumulation. To attract labour, higher wages would be offered at the cost of lower profits. Malthus pointed out that this rationale could be extended to a larger set of exceptions, negating the basic principle itself. He gave the example of a situation where an increase in the supply of necessities could be consumed only by an increase in population, which would take a long period of time to realize, thereby letting the general glut continue during this intervening period.

Turning his attention away from necessities to luxuries, Malthus identified the second fundamental error, which was ignoring a principle in human nature of 'indolence or love of ease'. Illustrating this principle with a hypothetical case of farmers and manufacturers suddenly being able to increase their production with the same labour, Malthus pointed out:

> The cultivator, now being enabled to obtain the necessaries and conveniences to which he has been accustomed with less toil and trouble, and his taste for ribands, lace and velvet, not being fully formed, might be very likely to indulge himself in indolence, and employs less labour on land; while the manufacturer, finding his velvets rather heavy for sale, would be led to discontinue their manufacture, and to fall almost necessarily into the same indolent system as the farmer.[22]

Malthus then opined that the taste for luxuries and conveniences and a demand for it are of slow growth. He noted that it was an important error to take for granted that mankind will chase luxuries and conveniences and not prefer 'indolence to the rewards of industry.'

In a different context, Say himself had identified luxuries and conveniences as a separate category of wants. He added a prefix to this kind of consumption and called it 'unproductive consumption' to differentiate it from productive consumption or investment. For him, unproductive consumption was 'a mere exchange of a portion of existing wealth on the one side, with human gratification on the other, and nothing more'.[23] Even within unproductive consumption, Say identified positive wants and negative wants. Among positive wants, he included all that which is required for the existence, health and general contentment of mankind. In contrast, negative wants were generated by 'refined sensuality, pride and caprice.' He recommended that a judicious nation should spend only on positive wants and ignore the negative wants if it wants a better economy and illustrated it with interesting maxim: 'the more linen and the less lace, the more plain and wholesome dishes, and fewer dainties; the more warm clothing, and the less embroidery, the better'.[24] In short, the lacuna Malthus identified of 'indolence to rewards of industry' was in a different context endorsed by Say himself, who advocated shunning luxury consumption and preferring necessities, on moral grounds.

The third fundamental error identified by Malthus was, in his words 'the most important of the three'. This was the belief that savings ensure demand. Ricardo had noted that additional resources available to a rich person would be either spent on consumption or invested in productive activity. If they were spent on consumption, it created a demand for luxuries and conveniences. Even if they were invested in productive activity, Ricardo noted that that they created a demand for necessities for the new set of labourers who were employed by the money invested. After a detailed description of how the situation could play out if this continued, Malthus identified the crux of the problem. In the initial stages, if the savings of the rich were consumed by the poor, it would only temporarily halt the growth of wealth. But if the conversion of income into capital by the savings of the rich extended beyond a point, resulting in a large scale investment in machinery, it would displace labour, leading to unemployment. From this rationale Malthus derived the consequence of such unemployment: initially a reduction in wealth, followed subsequently by a reduced population.

Based on this detailed critique, Malthus dismissed the conclusion drawn in Say's Law that supply creates its own demand, and proposed in its place an idea to resolve the depressed conditions prevailing in England. He noted that during wars, which did not interrupt commerce, 'loans to government convert capital into revenue, and increase demand at the same time that they at first diminish the means of supply'.[25] The consequence of a simultaneous decrease in supply and an increase in demand is higher prices, translating to higher profits for the manufacturers.

A climate of high profits both increases the capacity for, and the reward of accumulation. This, then, one could say, is 'Malthus' Law', which claims that 'loans to government create demand for businesses and profit for investors.' This was especially true of a time when fiduciary or paper money and deficit financing by government were yet to make their debut. The additional money available to the government in the form of loans or taxes, Malthus recommended, was best spent on employing the poor in building public infrastructure and roads. Likewise, the rich too could beautify their property and thereby create employment. He insightfully observed that during the war, the government had converted labourers into soldiers and sailors, and in peacetime, they could balance the gap between production and consumption by engaging the discharged soldiers and sailors as productive labourers.[26]

Malthus's recommendations about how to combat the depressed economic situation did not find favour with policy makers, despite his logical analysis, His ideas remained dormant for more than a century, before they were revived by John Maynard Keynes. In the intervening period, both Simonde and Malthus were branded heretics[27] and ignored by the orthodox economists who dominated the scene in the nineteenth century.

Malthus Resurrected

John Maynard Keynes is considered one of the three giants in the history of economics, the other two being Adam Smith and Karl Marx.[28] The impact of his influence was conceded even by his staunchest critics, as his ideas formed the basis for global economic policies for more than a quarter of the twentieth century. Keynes was crowned the guru when he published his magnum opus, *The General Theory of Employment, Interest and Money* in 1936. Published at the right time, it revived and built on the ideas proposed by Simonde and Malthus to solve a burning problem that engulfed the world: The Great Depression. This depression conclusively showed the flaws in the Classical economic theory that supply creates its own demand. The general glut created by evaporation of demand that prevailed during this decade was the final verdict against it.

The Great Depression began in 1929. Triggered by the New York stock market crash, the global economy collapsed. Not surprisingly, this collapse was most visible in the country where it began – the USA. The contrast between the years 1929 and 1933 was the starkest. In this short period of four years, the nominal value of the GDP of the US fell from $103.8 billion to $56.4 billion, a fall of 46 per cent. The decline in prices softened the fall in real terms to 27 per cent. The human face of this collapse is clearly seen in the unemployment figures which galloped from 3.2 per cent to 24.9 per cent.[29] With one in four unemployed in the United States of America, for the first time in democracies, economic issues were at the core of the political debates. This brought the professional economists from lecturing in the classroom to advocating in public domain.

In his magnum opus, Keynes first demolished the orthodox/Classical economic theory advocated by Ricardo and his followers, which was crisply represented in Say's Law. On its ruins, he built the new edifice for 'heretics' by acknowledging Malthus as the originator of his new theory. Keynes described this change in his flowery writing style, captured in the paragraph below,

> Malthus, indeed, had vehemently opposed Ricardo's doctrine that it was impossible for effective demand to be deficient; but vainly. For, since Malthus was unable to explain clearly (apart

from an appeal to the facts of common observation) how and why effective demand could be deficient or excessive, he failed to furnish an alternative construction; and Ricardo conquered England as completely as the Holy Inquisition conquered Spain. Not only was his theory accepted by the city, the statesman, and by the academic world. But controversy ceased; the other point of view completely disappeared; it ceased to be discussed. The great puzzle of effective demand with which Malthus wrestled vanished from economic literature.[30]

Keynes explained the disappearance of the Malthusian idea of deficient demand, and the prominence attained by the orthodox economists representing Say's Law, as the play of vested interests. He reasoned that the capitalist class advocated for these ideas as they gave them a free-trade environment. The governing authorities on the other hand were attracted to it as it insulated them from the responsibility of redressing the injustice and cruelty of society. This insulation was justified as the supply-side economists saw it as an inevitable by-product of progress, justified by the net total outcome.[31]

Away from the socially-patronized academic world of the orthodox economists, Keynes did identify the lineage of the Malthusian idea of deficient demand as living in 'the underworlds of Karl Marx, Silvio Gesell or Major Douglas'. After identifying the submerged thread, Keynes revived the Malthusian idea, by both forwarding new ideas and dispelling the erroneous platform on which Classical economics was built. (*For details see Box 5.1*). In the process, he brought back the idea of deficient demand from the underworld to the center-stage.

Keynes borrowed the Malthusian idea of new investment in public works and roads by the government to generate new employment as a cure to the rampant and widespread unemployment plaguing the world. Conscious of the serious objections that orthodox economists believing in the free-markets could raise to his unconventional recommendations, Keynes sarcastically suggested that the Treasury buy old bottles and stuff them with banknotes to be buried at random depths along with rubbish in disused coal mines. Then the government could invite tenders from private enterprise to dig up and reclaim the banknotes thereby generating employment and money flow in the economy. Fully aware that the objections to his proposals were political in nature, he shared his real idea, 'It would indeed be much more sensible to build houses and the like; but if there are political and practical difficulties in the way of this, the above [stuffing old bottles with banknotes] would be better than nothing'.[32]

Given the compelling need and the ease of execution by governments in power, Keynes's suggestion for public expenditure to fund new employment opportunities found wide acceptance. The absence of any other viable alternative also speeded up its implementation. With this, the macro-economic challenge shifted from fueling growth to ensuring full employment in the economy. The power of Keynes' idea is most visible in the policy changes it triggered. The British White Paper on Employment Policy in 1944, the 1946 Employment Act in the USA and the full employment commitment enshrined in the United Nations charter[e] are glimpses of his global influence. When Keynes died in 1946, a decade after

---

e   Article 55 of The United Nations Charter 'With a view to the creation of conditions of stability and well-being which are necessary for peaceful and friendly relations among nations based on respect for the principle of equal rights and self-determination of peoples, the United Nations shall promote:
 a. higher standard of living, **full employment**, and conditions of economic and social progress and development' [emphasis mine]

the publication of his magnum opus, Keynesian economics was well on its way to attaining the status of a dominant religion, and Keynes was the new God of economics.

Box 5.1
Keynesian Economics in a Nutshell

The core of Keynesian economics is enshrined in *The General Theory of Employment, Money and Interest.* The introduction to this book contains three parts where Keynes first outlined his general theory, stated the postulates of Classical economics and finally concluded by spelling out the principle of effective demand, based on which he built his new theory. Right through this book, Keynes contrasted the Classical theory of employment, money and interest with his new conclusions.

The Classical theory of employment is based on the laws of demand and supply for labour. The demand for labour arises from its marginal productivity, while the supply of labour is regulated by the 'disutility' caused by that employment. Keynes defined disutility to labour, in such a way as to include 'every kind of reason which might lead a man, or a body of men, to withhold their labour rather than accept a wage which had to them a utility below a certain minimum'.[33] The point at which the demand and supply for labour intersected determined the level of employment in an economy. According to this theory, there could only be fictional unemployment, which arose due to the time taken for an individual to move between two jobs, and voluntary unemployment or labour unwilling to work at the prevailing wages.

Keynes found that the unemployment prevailing during the period of the Great Depression was not explained by the Classical theory of employment. People willing to work at any wage level found employment hard to come by. In addition to fictional and voluntary unemployment, the Great Depression threw up involuntary unemployment in significant numbers. Classical theory could not explain involuntary unemployment in an economy. According to it, involuntary unemployment just could not exist, as a larger workforce hunting for jobs would drive down the wage levels; and at lower wage levels, the demand for labour would rise and the enterprises would employ them gainfully. This lacuna prompted Keynes to abandon the Classical economics in which he was educated and find a new framework to explain the prevailing conditions. Based on his revised analysis, he formulated The General Theory of Employment.

The General Theory of Employment in short considered the entrepreneur to be at the core for generating employment. The level of employment in an economy would be determined by the point at which aggregate demand price intersected with aggregate supply price. Aggregate supply price is the cost incurred by the entrepreneur for engaging various factors of production for a given level of output. Aggregate demand price is the total realization that an entrepreneur **expects** to collect by selling all the output. As an entrepreneur seeks to maximize his profits, he determines the level of employment in the economy based on his expectation of aggregate demand price. By calibrating the level of operations to his current expectations, the entrepreneur decides the employment level in the economy.

Keynes studied this analysis and concluded that the level of employment in an economy was both a cause for, and the result of, demand expectation in the economy, which he called the effective demand. Based on this conclusion, he recommended that governments promote employment by making investments in public works as the first step to increase effective demand in an economy. He reasoned that an increase in demand would set off a virtuous cycle by placing the economy on an upward spiral of growth. This was due to the multiplier effect of the initial investment made by the government.

The Classical theory of money in short states that an increase in the quantity of money is inflationary and the price level in an economy changes with any change in the quantity of money. Keynes replaced this with his revised theory of money, where he distinguished between situations of full employment and periods when unemployment prevailed. His revised theory stated, 'So long as there is unemployment, *employment* will change in the same proportion as the quantity of money; and when there is full employment, prices will change in the same proportion as the quantity of money'.[34] He reached this conclusion based on the logic that any increase in the money supply in an economy with unemployment would increase effective demand, thereby triggering fresh employment.

Turning to interest, the Classical theory, in the same vein as for employment and money, held that the interest rate in an economy is the result of demand for investment intersecting with savings, which is the source or supply for investment. Keynes brought into this equation the effect of income. He believed savings were much more influenced by income level changes than the rate of interest. He held that interest rates had little influence on the quantum of savings in an economy. Income level changes influenced the rate of savings through the mechanism of propensity to consume.

The Keynesian Era

John Maynard Keynes was born in a family of wealthy academicians. His father was the registrar of Cambridge University and after his own education at Cambridge, Keynes qualified for the civil services, working for two years before he returned to the academic world to teach economics. Right through his career, he successfully straddled the academic world and the corridors of power. Keynes played an active role in organizing finances for the British First World War efforts. Later, he was a member of the British delegation negotiating the peace treaty with Germans.

Keynes' first claim to fame was as the author of *The Economic Consequences of the Peace*. In this essay, he predicted the outcome of the ill-conceived reparation terms set for the Germans in the Treaty of Versailles. He foresaw the consequences of the social upheaval (which eventually led to the rise of Hitler) that ensued as Germany was pushed into an economic crisis by the impractical demands made by the victorious allies to compensate them for their war losses. With detailed workings he demonstrated that the terms of repayment set for Germany were beyond its existing productive capacity. After this maiden recognition, he was an active contributor on public debates. With a receptive audience, he was widely heard on issues ranging from monetary policy, funding strategies for war and the toughest economic challenge of his era – the unemployment thrown up by the Great Depression.

As the Second World War came to an end, Keynes was at the forefront of initiatives to create a new international monetary system. The 1944 meeting at Bretton Woods, New Hampshire, attended by delegates from forty-four nations, was the culmination of these efforts to install a new international monetary system. This meeting laid the foundation for four new global initiatives, and the three organizations conceived there survive till date – the International Monetary Fund, World Bank, and the General Agreement on Tariffs and Trade, which has now morphed into the World Trade Organization.

The fourth initiative[f] was not an organization but a well-defined system for regulating the relationships between the currencies of the participating countries.

The core principle behind these four initiatives was a spirit of cooperation among nations, where any country in distress would be helped back to normalcy by other nations. The objective was to achieve what was later outlined in Article 55 of the United Nations Charter: promoting 'higher standards of living, full employment, and conditions of economic and social progress and development.' Keynes, addressing the concluding plenary session of the Bretton Woods summit, wrapped up his address with optimism by highlighting the birth of a new era based on mutual cooperation. He noted that this was only the beginning and expressed his desire for more by concluding:

> Finally, we have perhaps accomplished here in Bretton Woods something more significant than what is embodied in this Final Act. We have shown that a concourse of forty-four nations are actually able to work together at a constructive

---

f   The Bretton Woods Agreement, as it is popularly called, was a mechanism for regulating the relationship between currencies of the participating countries. As most of the countries engaged in the war had resorted to deficit finance and printed money to provide liquidity, they could not return to the gold standard, as they did not have adequate gold reserves. In the gold standard, currencies issued by the governments are backed by gold reserves and any holder of the currency could redeem it for gold or give gold and get currency in return.

The Bretton Woods agreement provided only for US dollars to be convertible into gold and all the other countries were required to fix the exchange rate for their currencies with respect to US dollars. Once fixed, these exchange rates would remain unchanged, unless there was a crisis in that country, which led to a structural imbalance. The crisis-plagued country would then be permitted to revise its exchange rate in consultation with the IMF, the organization created to implement this system.

task in amity and unbroken concord. Few believed it possible. If we can continue in a larger task as we have begun in this limited task, there is hope for the world.[35]

This new agreement survived twenty-seven years before the United States of America unilaterally revoked their commitment to exchange gold for their currency on August 15, 1971.[g] This decision not only signaled the end of the Keynesian era, but also heralded the arrival of a philosophy advocated by the Austrian School and the Chicago School of Economics. At the core of this philosophy was individualism. It effectively triggered the rebirth of capitalism with its clarion call for unregulated markets.

Capitalism Reborn: The Foundation

The major opposition to Keynesian economics was because it allowed governments to decide major economic matters without market inputs. What added fuel to this spark of disagreement was the use of stimulus and subsidy packages, an 'excuse' for letting government spend more than their income, running fiscal deficits. The final missile that demolished Keynesian economics was the spectre of inflation that haunted

---

g   Robert Triffin in 1960 found a structural flaw in the Bretton Woods system that is popularly called Triffin's Paradox. Triffin pointed out that the faster this system is accepted, the sooner it would collapse. The logic for his observation was twofold. First, in this system, the exchange rate between the currency and gold is fixed in perpetuity. Secondly, while holding the currency earns interest, holding gold has no reward. This means that when the system gained acceptance, investors will prefer to hold currency which will grow in value. In contrast, the USA would be holding gold which remains fixed in value. Over time, the USA will need to redeem much more than what it initially received, forcing it to abandon this system when the investors want their dollars redeemed.

the globe in the 1970s, and which was popularly attributed to government excesses.[h] The philosophy of individualism was the launching pad from which this missile was propelled.

Individualism and Economic Order is an interesting philosophical book written in 1947 by Friedrich von Hayek, the Austrian economist, which articulates the foundation for this economic system. The first chapter in this book is titled 'Individualism: True and False'. In it Hayek set out to amplify the different nuances of individualism and identify the meaning that he personally attached to it. He traced his concept of individualism to a long list of English philosophers including John Locke, Bernard Mandeville, David Hume, Josiah Tucker, Adam Ferguson and Adam Smith. He concluded this chapter by presenting his version of individualism as an attitude and process for human achievement that is beyond the capacity and comprehension of any one individual, thereby needing every mind in the society to be free.[i] Therefore, for human society to thrive, he concluded, no individual mind should be subservient to any other human being. [36]

While this book laid the foundation for Hayek's economic system based on free unregulated markets, it was abstract and not intended 'for popular consumption.' Hayek had preceded

---

h   Inflation in the 1970s was a result of the collapse of the Bretton Woods system and the cartel formed by the Organization of Petroleum Exporting Countries (OPEC). OPEC increased oil prices from $3 per barrel to $11 in 1973, followed by another increase from $13 to $28 in 1980. Government budgetary deficits too played their part. The relative importance of each of these three factors is tough to quantify or rank.

i   In Hayek's own words, 'What individualism teaches us is that society is greater than the individual only in so far as it is free. In so far as it is controlled or directed, it is limited to the power of individual minds which can control or direct it.'

this book with a book for the masses that contained more concrete examples. Even its title, *The Road to Serfdom* was explicit. This book turned out to be a bestseller, despite the war-time rationing for paper. Writing it between 1940 and 1944 in Britain, while he volunteered for 'fire duty' i.e. looking out at nights from rooftops for German bombers, Hayek penned his motive in the preface to the book. Writing this book, he remarked, was a duty that he should not evade. He continued that he was voicing the apprehensions of many who could not express their views publicly about the growing political and economic ideas of central control seen in the Nazi movement in Germany and the socialist movement in the Soviet Union.[37] In this book, Hayek argued why socialism and collective decision making or central planning must be shunned and in its place a competitive system based on unregulated markets and individualism promoted. He saw the expanding role of government as the first step to providing a fillip for a socialistic government and a central planning framework. He believed that only in a competitive system could power be decentralized. While acknowledging that wealth could be concentrated in the competitive system, he drew the readers' attention to the limited powers that a millionaire employer had over his employees, contrasted to the overpowering authority of a minor bureaucrat in a centralized state to regulate an individual's work and lifestyle.[38]

In summary, Hayek equated any increase in the power of government over economic activities to a move that would end in totalitarianism and hence his deep conviction 'that the system of private property is the most important guarantee of freedom'.[39]

In 1950, Hayek moved from the London School of Economics to the University of Chicago, where Frank

Knight, who professed a similar view, had taught in the first half of the twentieth century. Together they, along with Milton Friedman and George Stigler, emerged as the nucleus for a new school of thought, the Chicago School of Economics that would take on Keynesian economics head-on and replace it as the dominant economic philosophy in the last quarter of the twentieth century and the beginning of the third millennium.

Markets and Equality

The free market is an environment in which individualism thrives. The proponents of free markets challenged Keynesian recommendations for government interventions as the method to solve macro-economic problems. Their idea was built on the belief that free individuals interacting with each other while choosing the best for them can realize a synergy that far exceeds individual expectations and gains. Not only was their solution at variance with Keynesian recommendations, even the social ideal that inspired it challenged the basic Keynesian concept of cooperation emanating from the desire to reduce income and wealth inequality in a society.

In contrast to Hayek, Ludwig von Mises, an important member of the Austrian School of Economics, built his system advocating free markets on the basis of inequality. Mises outlined the rationale for free markets in his composition *Human Action, A Treatise on Economics,* published in 1966. In this, he first highlighted the fact that inequality was a natural feature in our world. He came to this conclusion after noting the variance in the ability of individuals to perform different kinds of labour. This innate variance was compounded by the differing physical conditions prevailing across various parts of the world.[40] Given this, Mises believed that equality before law was a human construct that emerged from an acceptance of inequality among human beings. He advanced the logic that the champions of equality under law were aware of this natural inequality and therefore created this concept to promote civilization and cooperation. He felt that this concept was promoted not to eliminate the universal fact and make inequality disappear, but to derive the maximum benefit from this inequality.[41]

Mises only highlighted the inequality that existed in society. But it was his disciple, Murray Rothbard, who made it more explicit by giving this inequality a value, describing the strong and the weak. Rothbard claimed that free markets promote the interest of the weak. He elaborated on his conclusion by describing the voluntary exchange that takes place in a free market. He drew attention to the fact that the strong do not crush the weak. Instead, he noted that the strong benefit from exchanging with the weak.[42]

In a different context, at the beginning of the nineteenth century, the English economist David Ricardo forwarded a similar logic when he advanced the theory of comparative advantage. Ricardo argued that free international trade benefited both the efficient and the less efficient nation. He highlighted its benefits even in cases when a country is more efficient in producing all its needs. Taking the example of England and Portugal and two commodities, wine and cloth as illustrations, he showed how both England and Portugal would benefit, even if Portugal was more efficient in producing both the goods. Contrary to the obvious comparison made between prices prevailing for the same commodity in the two countries, he suggested making a more relevant comparison of the relative price ratios that prevail in the two countries.[j] This, he showed, was the rationale that propelled international trade in many instances. The same logic works in local trade too. As Murray Rothbard of the Austrian School of Economics pointed out, it pays a doctor to engage a secretary less efficient than himself to do his typing and filing chores, as it frees his time to do the more valuable job of treating patients. In fact, this principle is one of the drivers for division of labour, both nationally and internationally.

With a strong philosophical base and a sound economic rationale, the conquest of the world by the free-market ideology was both rapid and complete. The collapse of the Soviet Union in 1989 was its crowning moment. Incidentally, the same year also marked the translation of free-market philosophy into an operating economic policy: the Washington Consensus.

The Free Market Menu

The economic policy of laissez-faire in the eighteenth century was a result of the social restrictions and feudal codes that prevailed in European society. Initially a measure recommended

---

j   David Ricardo illustrated his theory of Comparative Advantage with an example using England and Portugal trading in wine and cloth, when Portugal had an absolute advantage in producing both goods. While the cost of producing a gallon of wine was 80 and a yard of cloth 90 in Portugal, the comparative costs in England were 120 and 100 respectively. In this example, it would benefit both the countries to trade, as comparatively wine was cheaper to produce in Portugal while in England cloth was cheaper to produce. Even though Portugal could produce both at a lower price, by selling wine in England it could obtain a higher realization as the prevailing ratio was 1.2 yards of cloth for a gallon of wine, while at home it commanded only 0.89 yards of cloth. Likewise, by selling cloth in Portugal England could get 1.125 gallons of wine in contrast to 0.83 gallons at home, thus benefiting both the countries.

by the physiocrates to free French labour, soon it was adopted by the English merchants who wanted the same 'freedom' that their prosperous Dutch counterparts enjoyed.[k] Though it had multiple motives, the end that both the French and the English intellectuals had was only one, an economy in which goods, labour and capital moved freely without constraints imposed or enforced by the government, which they believed would result in economic prosperity.

In contrast to the nineteenth century call for dissolving social restraints, the twentieth century call for free markets was triggered by the need to protect political freedom in the face of an expanding communist empire, coupled with a fear that ceding power to the government to regulate economic activities could result in complete totalitarianism. While there was complete consensus among the free market advocates at the philosophical level, in its implementation there emerged a wide range of options. The solutions varied mainly on the extent of government role that each one envisaged. At one extreme were the advocates of perfect competition who envisaged an active role for the government to maintain the competitive environment and at the other extreme were the sponsors of a minimalist government of the 'night watchman' variety. In between the two extremes, the vast majority of free market votaries forged together the 'Washington Consensus,' a programme feasible for global implementation.

All free-market advocates or liberalists as they called themselves, irrespective of their personal preference about the path adopted to realize a free market, believe that the government has a role to play in defining the rules of the game. At a minimum a free-market economy needs three prerequisites: a property

---

k   For details of the origin of laissez-faire, see Chapter 3 of this book.

rights definition, dispute resolution mechanisms and a contracts enforcement agency. A fourth feature was added by Henry Simons, a professor in the University of Chicago. He outlined it in his pamphlet, *A Positive Program for Laissez-faire: Some Proposals for a Liberal Economic Policy* written in 1934. At the peak of the Great Depression, the fourth factor that Simons felt that the government should concern itself with was the presence of monopolies that coerce individuals, which in his view were a threat to free markets. His fear of trade unions monopolizing the power of labour could have triggered this train of thought. Starting there, he identified monopolies in all other spheres by noting that they were the enemy of democracy.[43]

With this rationale, Simons advocated an expansion in the role of the minimal 'night watchman state' that the free-market advocates endorsed to prevent theft and enforce contracts. He believed his suggestion was the key to keeping the markets competitive. A monopolist in his view was an implicit thief as he extracts prices using coercion that do not reflect the market realities. He observed that in the past governments had failed to achieve economic goals as they sought to regulate the heart of free-markets, the market price, whereas they could have achieved better results by creating conditions for keeping markets competitive. He therefore recommended an active role for the government in proactively breaking up monopolies. Using the philosophical base of the free-market advocates for protecting freedom, he asked for monopolies to be broken up as they wielded huge power. Under monopolies he included all types of power concentration and listed among them, 'no leader, no faction, no party, no "class", no majority, no government, no church, no corporation, no trade association, no trade union, no grange, no professional association, no university, no large organization of any kind'.[44]

Simons, the true free market advocate, identified that in addition to breaking up monopolies, a government promoting free markets had the responsibility of 'facilitating new enterprise and multiplication of moderate-sized firms'.[45] Further, he recommended a progressive system of income tax to promote egalitarianism and price stabilization through monetary interventions during recession.[46] Seen in his time as an important member of the Chicago School, by the 1980s, Simons was disowned by his own school, when Ronald Coase, a Nobel Prize winning member of the Chicago school questioned his credentials as a liberalist for advocating a more active role for the government.

Of The Extreme and The Mean

In contrast to Henry Simons, who accepted the idea of a free market as beneficial to humanity and proposed whatever he thought was required to make it functional, Murray Rothbard, the Dean of the Austrian School of Economics and a prolific writer, started with the idea of authorizing only a minimalist government. In the third of his seminal works, *The Ethics of Liberty*, he equated individual liberty with the establishment 'of the rights of private property'.[47] He derived this profound conclusion by noting that in a free market, exchange takes place not of products or services but of 'the *rights of ownership* to them'.[48] He then defined free markets as 'a society of voluntary and consequently mutually beneficial exchange of ownership titles between specialized producers'.[49] To preserve free markets and thereby safeguard individual liberty, Rothbard placed the right to property as supreme, to be upheld under all circumstances, without exception; to be upheld even under extreme situations of life and death choice, as in the lifeboat illustration he put forward.

Describing a conflict between the right to property and the right to life that comes up in the extreme situation of a sinking ship with more passengers than lifeboats, Rothbard suggested various avenues to resolve it. After exhausting all the possible options for rationally allocating the lifeboats, he concluded that the owner using the lifeboat or giving it to a person of their choice is the only right solution. He conceded that this was not a 'humane or comforting' solution. But he observed that this cannot be a reason for negating the right to property. Drawing a parallel of a parent trying to save his two drowning children, Rothbard substantiated his logic. If in reality only one child can be saved, he pointed out that logic would advocate that we save that one child rather than abandon the thought of saving both the children. Likewise, in the lifeboat situation, even if all the passengers cannot be saved, the right to property should be upheld and not discarded. Taking a prophetic view, Rothbard saw the 'lifeboat kind' of events as a rarity. He then predicted that in a free-market economy that protected property rights, the standard of living would rise and situations of extreme shortage would also be a rarity.[50]

With this firm conviction, Rothbard went on to the other extreme of advocating free-markets even for property right protection and contract enforcement i.e. the police and the judiciary. Terming the state a criminal for the physical coercion used in obtaining its revenue in the form of taxation and the use of monopoly of force and decision-making that prohibits free competition, Rothbard called for the abolition of the state altogether. While making this call, he knew that it was not a goal that would be realized soon, but nevertheless, he believed it should be made. As he saw it, there is a clear distinction between goal-setting and formulating plans for realizing the goals, and sequentially, goal-setting comes first, pre-empting any moderation or feasibility validation.[51]

In between the two extreme ideological positions of Simons and Rothbard, there emerged the operating economic policy that translated the philosophy of free markets into action. A consensus emerged within two decades, evolving from the 1970s, following the exit of Keynesian policies from the global platform. It was crystallized in 1989 and articulated as the Washington Consensus, a policy that would define the contours of economies in Latin America, Africa and the Asian continent, a policy that withstood the onslaught of free-market opponents for the succeeding two decades. Just as it looked like it was gaining global acceptance, it was discarded on its home-ground, the USA, because of the financial crisis in 2008. What prompted this doubt? Would it, like Keynesian economics, make way for its successor or will it, like the phoenix, rise again from the ashes?

Box 5.2
The Washington Consensus

The Washington Consensus is a term coined by the economist John Williamson, of the Peterson Institute for International Economics. In the face of financial crisis in the Latin American countries, Williamson coined this term in 1989 to identify the policy recommendations made by the three organizations based in Washington DC: the International Monetary Fund, World Bank and the Treasury department of the USA. It contained ten policy recommendations that could be grouped under four broad categories – macro-economic discipline, a market economy, global free trade, and the basic belief that protecting property rights will propel human progress.

Macro-economic discipline

1. Fiscal discipline: Governments to run manageable budget deficits.
2. Reordering public expenditure priorities: To shift funds from pro-poor subsidies to essential services like elementary education, primary healthcare and basic infrastructure.
3. Tax reforms: Reduce marginal tax rates and broaden the net for tax-payers.

Market economy

4. Liberalize interest rates: Free financial markets and promote market-determined interest rates.
5. A competitive exchange rate: Promote market-influenced or market-determined exchange rates.
6. Deregulation of business: Discard regulations that prevent entry and exit of enterprises for reasons other than safety and environmental concerns.
7. Privatization of state-owned enterprises: To realize the benefits of market-promoted efficiency.

Global Free trade

8. Trade liberalization: To remove quantitative restrictions on imports and exports.
9. Liberalization of Inward Foreign Direct Investments: As a progress towards capital account convertibility, free inward foreign direct investments.

Basic Belief

10. Property Rights: Establish property rights as a concept enforceable by law.

Endnotes

1 Briggs, A., *The Age of Improvement 1783-1867*, Longman Group Limited, 1979, p162-3

2 Say, J. B., *A Treatise on Political Economy; Or the Production, Distribution and Consumption of Wealth*, Batoche Books, Kitchener, 2001, p7

3 Ibid, p29

4 Ibid, p26

5 Ibid, p56

6 Ibid, p56

7 Ibid, p56

8 Ibid, p56

9 Ibid, p57

10 Sismondi, J. C. L., *Political Economy and the Philosophy of Government*, 1847 edition, The Online Library of Liberty, p67

11 Ibid, p73

12 Ibid, p74

13 Ibid, p74

14 Ibid, p75

15 Ibid, p75

16 Ibid, p83

17 Ibid, p84

18 Ibid, p68

19 Ibid, p69

20 Malthus, T. R., *Principles of Political Economy*, London: W Pickering, 1836, he Online Library of Liberty, p278

21 Ibid, p220

22 Ibid, p221

23 Say, J. B., *A Treatise on Political Economy; Or the Production, Distribution and Consumption of Wealth*, Batoche Books, Kitchener, 2001, p217

24 Ibid, p217

25 Malthus, T. R., *Principles of Political Economy*, London: W Pickering, 1836, he Online Library of Liberty, p225

26 Ibid, p284

27 Taylor, O. H., *A History of Economic Thought*, McGraw Hill Book Company, 1960, p484

28 Pressman, S., *Fifty Great Economists*, Routledge, First Indian Reprint 2004, p99

29 Samuelson and Nordhaus, *Economics*, Tata Mcgraw-Hill, 18th edition, 2005, p 423

30 Keynes, J. M., *The General Theory of Employment, Interest and Money*, ISN ETH, Zurich, www.isn.ethz.ch, p24

31 Ibid, p25

32 Ibid, p68

33 Ibid, p12

34 Ibid, p147-8

35 Quoted in the article, Bretton Woods: Birth and Breakdown, by John Braithwaite and Peter Drahos, www.gpf.org

36 Hayek, F. A., *Individualism and Economic Order*, The University of Chicago Press, 1948, p32

37 Ibid, p11

38 Ibid, p33

39 Ibid, p33

40 Mises, L. V., *Human Action, A Treatise on Economics*, Fox & Wilkes, Fourth Edition, 1996, p158

41 Ibid, p841

42 Rothbard, M., *The Ethics of Liberty*, New York University Press, 1998, p79

43 Quoted in, *In Defense of Henry Simons Standing as A Classical Liberal*, by J. Bradford De Long, in Cato Journal Vol.9, No.3 (Winter 1990), p605

44 Rothbard, M. N., *The Ethics of Liberty*, New York University Press, 1998, p36

45 Quoted in, *In Defense Of Henry Simons Standing As A Classical Liberal*, by J. Bradford De Long, in Cato Journal Vol.9, No.3 (Winter 1990), p613

46 Rothbard, M. N., Milton Friedman Unraveled, *Journal of Libertarian Studies*, Fall 2002,

47 Rothbard, M. N., *The Ethics of Liberty*, New York University Press, 1998, p xlviii

48 Ibid, p36

49 Ibid, p40

50 Ibid, p149

51 Ibid, p259

Part III: Looking Ahead

The economic crisis triggered by the collapse of the investment banking giant Lehman Brothers in September 2008 raised a few questions. These questions could not be answered without challenging some of the basic premise on which economics is built. A good place to begin this examination is with the works of the 69 Nobel laureates in economics and how their ideas influenced the events of the 2008 economic crisis. A small but growing section of the population began to question the basic premise on which free-market based, capitalist economies are built. The logical fallout of this reasoning is to evaluate the most visible alternative – socialist economic principles – and assess its viability. Given that socialist economies are not the most viable alternative, at least in the near future, the three basic challenges of the free-market based economies are identified to examine how economics could evolve in the twenty-first century.

Chapter 6

A Nobel Science: The Decisive Edge

I confess that I prefer true but imperfect knowledge, even if it leaves much indetermined and unpredictable, to a pretence of exact knowledge that is likely to be false.

— **Friedrich Hayek**[1]

In 1969, the Swedish Central Bank instituted a prize for outstanding contributions in the field of economics. It took enormous pains to make this prize resemble the Nobel Prize, which had been awarded in other disciplines from 1901 onwards. Their intention was achieved, as with the passage of time the distinction between the two prizes has almost vanished in public perception. In an interesting interplay, the revival of classical free-market economics coincided with the institution of this prize. Free-market economics had drastically expanded its influence and by the beginning of the twenty-first century, it had assumed a near-hegemonic status, which was not meaningfully challenged till the 2008 financial freeze in the USA and Europe. In hindsight, it looks like a vicious cycle was at play in the last four decades, where economic theories advocating free markets were reinforced by the 'Nobel' Prize awards that went to the originators of these theories. The high regard in which the recipients of these awards were held in, in turn galvanized the political and social climate in favour of free markets, till they imploded in the USA and rapidly in the rest of the world, wreaking havoc in the process. This chapter examines the impact of what is popularly called the Nobel Prize in economics, and the influence it has had on the development of the subject, most specifically in how the theories championed by it contributed to the 2008 financial crisis. This analysis is restricted to the winners of this prize, in deference to their undue influence on the course of events, not just at policy formulation levels but also in shaping the global discourse on economic issues.

Anatomy of the Impersonator

In 1895, Alfred Nobel, the Swedish ammunition manufacturer, philanthropist and pacifist[a] willed a substantial portion of his fortune amounting to about £1,750,000 to a trust. The trust was assigned the task of disbursing the interest earned on this corpus to award annual prizes to 'those persons who during the pervious year have rendered the greatest services to mankind.' Five categories were identified in the will, with the first three being the most important discovery or invention in physics, chemistry and medicine. The remaining two categories were for person producing outstanding literary work 'in an ideal direction', and for the person who had most or best promoted the brotherhood of nations, the abolition or reduction of standing armies, and the holding and promotion of peace congresses. An important feature of the will was its mandate to find the worthiest recipient in the world without any regard to nationality.

The first of the Nobel Prizes were awarded in the year 1901. Over the decades, the Nobel Prize has had an unparalleled standing across the world, which could be a result of the three critical parameters defined. Firstly, it was a prize awarded to

---

a   Alfred Nobel, the ammunition manufacturer believed that as more destructive weapons were developed, they would act as a deterrent to war and prevent future armed conflicts between nations.

the worthiest recipient irrespective of nationality. Secondly, the selection criterion was about the greatest service to humanity, and finally, the third aspect pertained to the awards category: three of the five awards are in science where objective criteria are used to pick the winner and tangible benefits from their discoveries are visible for all to see. In contrast, the awards for literature and peace are subjective and have not been without controversy.

It is against this backdrop that the decision of the Swedish Central Bank, the Sveriges Riksbank should be seen. Celebrating its 300th anniversary in 1968, the bank instituted a prize for outstanding contributions in the field of economic sciences. It was modelled on the Nobel Prize, awarding identical prize money, and with the selection, too, following a two-stage process. The Royal Swedish Academy of Sciences was the first filter and a Nobel Prize committee was the final selector. This prize too was to be administered by the Nobel Foundation. To top it all, the bank made a financial contribution to the Nobel Foundation to have them include their prize for economics on the website, along with other Nobel Prizes and award it in a similar ceremony. This award was titled 'The Sveriges Riksbank Prize in Economic Sciences in Memory of Alfred Nobel'. However, in popular parlance it is known as the Nobel Prize in economics.

Box 6.1
The Nobel Prize Winners

Between 1969 and 2011, 69 individuals were awarded the 'Nobel' Prize in economics. Based on the award citation and an analysis of their work, the winners' contribution can be categorized thus:

Analysis of Winners*

Subject Matter	Nature of Contribution				
	Lifetime contribution	New Insights	New Hypothesis	New Model	Total
Macroeconomic modeling		6		11	17
Markets / Property Rights	1	3	10	3	17
Financial Markets		2	4	4	10
Economic Theory	1	4	1	2	8
New Techniques / Tools				6	6
Economic Growth		2	1	1	4
Poverty & Human welfare		3	1		4
International Trade		1	2		3
Total	2	21	19	27	69

An analysis of the table reveals that 25 per cent of the winners were recognized for their work on markets/property rights. Another 14 per cent of the winners focused on financial markets. In contrast, work on poverty or human welfare received only 6 per cent of the awards.

*The listing of the winners and the category into which they are grouped is given in the Annexure. In addition, a brief write-up on the contribution of all the laureates is given in the Appendix.

The 'Nobel' Prize in economics was not without controversy. In the initial days, the primary objection was against classifying economics as a science in line with other physical sciences. Friedrich Hayek, the winner in the year 1974, differentiated between the two in his prize lecture by noting that physical sciences have organized complexity, in contrast to social sciences like economics, that have unorganized complexity, making their conclusions subjective and therefore less predictable. As more awards were given, the ideological bias in interpreting this unorganized complexity was reflected in the subjective nature of the conclusions. Nikolay Gertchev, an economist with the European Commission analyzing the awards in 2010 remarked, 'The Prize Committee is mostly accused of ideological bias in favor of neo-classical, monetarist and free-market approaches developed primarily by American men, and against less mainstream and more socially-oriented paradigms, including post-Keynesianism, developed by male and female scholars from the developing world'.[2]

The seeds of this bias may have been planted in the first decade after the 'Nobel' Prize in economics was introduced. It coincided with the end of an era and the heart of the global economic order was changed drastically. Competition replaced cooperation as the primary driver. This shift brought the markets to the centre-stage and revived classical supply-side economics with its laissez-faire focus.

The First Decade: What Changed?

Fifteenth August, 1971 was an eventful day for the global economy, signaling a change in the world economic order. It was the day when the system of a fixed foreign exchange-rate[b] that had come into existence at the Bretton Woods meeting in 1944

---

b The system of fixed foreign exchange rate is described in detail in Chapter 5.

collapsed. On this day, the US government stopped converting its currency into gold at the predetermined exchange rate, as it had committed to do 27 years earlier. Over the course of time, the need to collaborate felt by most nations in the aftermath of the Second World War had considerably reduced. The glue of the war-scarred economies that had held the nations together had gradually lost its adhesiveness. The immediate challenges of post-war recovery had been successfully addressed and the short-term needs of the nations were now at variance, as they jostled to gain a competitive foothold in global markets. Supplementing national self-interest was the economic rationale of free markets that resurfaced around this time. The free-market belief in competition resulted in collaboration being looked down upon as an inefficient mode of exchange among the various participants in an economy. Free-market ideology, previously dethroned during the Great Depression of 1930s, saw in the collapse of the Bretton Woods agreement the opportunity to reclaim its past influence on public policy.

A quick recap of the economic environment that led to the birth of the collaboration-based Bretton Woods framework of fixed foreign exchange system is required in order to appreciate the economic ideas that gained momentum following its collapse. To summarize, John Maynard Keynes advocated government intervention in the economy through public spending to pull the economy out of the Great Depression. He overthrew the prevailing economic theory of the classical supply-side, free-market based economists, by focusing on its inability to explain involuntary or forced unemployment. The Classical theory held that involuntary unemployment could not exist. According to it, an increase in the supply of labour willing to work, would lead to lower wages. Lower wages in turn would create more employment opportunities, absorbing the excess labour. Noting the prevalence of large scale involuntary unemployment in the 1930s, Keynes explained it as the absence of effective demand in an economy. Effective demand, he pointed out, was the demand anticipated by the entrepreneur, which generated employment and not the prevailing wage levels. Low wages by themselves could not generate employment in the absence of strong demand expansion. This reasoning led Keynes to recommend that governments must increase public spending to create demand in the economy, whenever there was slack demand. This thinking was based on the belief that individual participants competing with each other cannot get themselves out of a depression.

A byproduct of increased public spending is inflation. In the decades following Keynes' death, the gist of his idea came to be encapsulated in the Phillips curve, named after the British economist William Phillips. Just as supply-side economics is crudely captured in Says' Law, Keynesian economics too was reduced by many free-market advocates to the Phillips curve, a graphic illustration, which captures the inverse relationship between unemployment rates and inflation rates in an economy.

William Phillips, a New Zealand-born economist with the London School of Economics published an important paper[c] in 1958 in the journal *Economica*. Studying the relationship between changes in nominal wage and unemployment in the United Kingdom, he came across a consistent co-relation that had been embedded for almost a hundred years. Between 1861 and 1957, Phillips found an inverse relationship between changes in nominal wages and unemployment levels. As

---

c The Relationship between Employment and The Rate of Change of Money Wages in the United Kingdom, 1861 - 1957

nominal wages increased, unemployment levels fell and as the nominal wage declined, the unemployment level rose.

Paul Samuelson (Nobel laureate, 1970) and Robert Solow (Nobel laureate, 1987) conducted a similar study using data from the USA in 1960. They too found an identical relationship. They extended the relationship from nominal wages to inflation and termed it the Phillips Curve. Thus, the Phillips Curve depicts the relationship between inflation and unemployment in an economy. Based on this curve, they inferred that as inflation levels fell, unemployment increased and as inflation levels increased, unemployment fell. This triggered a host of studies on the relationship between inflation and unemployment in the 1960s in different countries which all reaffirmed the inverse relationship between inflation and unemployment. The logical conclusion from these studies provided decision makers with a clear choice. A high inflation rate could be induced in an economy via government spending in order to reduce the level of unemployment. Therefore, the choice for the decision makers was between high inflation and high unemployment. Given this choice, it is no wonder that the economic wisdom of that time opted for a higher inflation rate.

Inflation in an economy does not affect the exchange rate in a fixed exchange rate system. Therefore increasing public spending (and thereby inflation) has little consequence on the economy's external trade, as the exchange rate is fixed. However, where the exchange rate is market determined, the domestic inflation rate has a significant impact on the exchange rates. The collapse of the Bretton Woods system of fixed foreign exchange in 1971 was followed by a period of economic flux, as the international trade and settlement system was left without an anchor. Adding further instability was the Arab-Israel war in October 1973. The Arabs lost their initial advantage from a pre-emptive strike on the Israeli air-force with the entry of the USA into the conflict, in support of Israel. The USA was significantly dependent on imported oil, so the Arabs retaliated with their most powerful economic weapon – control over the global oil supply. In the middle of the war, on October 16th, they cut oil production and simultaneously increased crude oil prices by 70 per cent to hurt their new foe. Soon, this was followed in December by a further price increase of 128 per cent. Within a period of three months, oil prices shot up by around 400 per cent from $3 per barrel to $12 per barrel. This triggered double-digit inflation across the globe.

Lulled into complacency by the Phillips curve, the decision makers initially did not act in the face of double-digit inflation. But, for the first time since the Phillips curve was constructed, contrary to the relationship it established, high inflation did not promote employment. Instead, high levels of unemployment persisted along with high inflation. On the production front, high inflation and a stagnant economy was the reality. Stagflation, a new term, was invented to describe this unusual condition. Stagflation persisted for the rest of 1970s, imploring the Keynesian economists for an explanation.

Just as Classical economists were asked to explain the forced unemployment of the 1930s, forty years later, the question before the Keynesian economists was: how to explain the coexistence of high inflation with high unemployment? This puzzle provided an opening for the free-market advocates to get back to business.

The Laureates Answer

The two decades of robust economic growth[d] preceding the 1970s provided Keynesian economics with excellent credibility. This, in turn, weakened the research findings that challenged Keynesian economics. The position changed in the 1970s. Persistent stagflation injected strength into what were initially perceived as feeble challenges. The Chicago School of Economics, which had been at the forefront of this assault on Keynesian economics, now gained in prominence. Many of its members were recognized by the Nobel Prize committee. Friedrich August von Hayek[e] (Nobel laureate, 1974) who provided the ideological foundation for free markets was the first[f] to be recognized. It was his comparative study of economic systems that highlighted a key lacuna in the central planning of the socialist economies, catching the attention of the Nobel Prize committee. Hayek pointed out that centrally-planned economies lacked the vital information flow that exists in a market economy, since this is contained in prices and their behaviour.

At a more 'technical' level, Milton Friedman (Nobel laureate, 1976) took the challenge head-on by questioning the Keynesian theory on three fronts. He challenged Keynes' theory of consumption, its prescription of increased

---

d The global GDP growth rate of the 1950s and 1960s was driven by strong performances in Japan and Western Europe which benefited from the reconstruction efforts after the Second World War

e The contribution of Friedrich von Hayek in developing a coherent ideology for free markets based on individual freedom, which opposed the Keynesian recommendations for a greater government role in the economy is detailed in Chapter 5.

f Prior to 1974, Nobel laureates in economics were recognized for building econometric models and their contributions to economic theory.

government spending to promote employment and the role it accorded governments in stimulating demand. Two decades later, Robert E. Lucas Jr. (Nobel laureate, 1995) another product of the Chicago School was recognized by the Nobel Prize community. He provided an explanation for forced unemployment during the Great Depression that had eluded free-market advocates forty years earlier, contributing to the birth of Keynesian economics.

Keynes had outlined his theory of consumption by linking it to income. An increase in income would lead to higher consumption he noted; only the level of consumption would vary depending on the propensity to consume. Due to this, Keynes believed that any increase in income would lead to higher consumption. But based on empirical data on income, consumption and savings for the USA, Friedman found Keynes' inference invalid. Instead, Friedman proposed the **Permanent Income hypothesis**. According to it, spending depends on future income expectations. He noted that small business owners sometimes saved large fractions of their income and in other instances were willing to dip into their savings to consume more. Analyzing this, he concluded that increase in consumption takes place only if there is a belief that 'permanent income' will go up, i.e. the future income will also be higher. He termed this the permanent income hypothesis. According to it, consumption would vary with permanent income and not merely with current income. This hypothesis had an important impact on the Keynesian recommendation for active fiscal intervention via government spending in order to stimulate demand in an economy.

Keynes believed that higher spending by the government would lead to higher consumption by individuals in an economy, as their incomes went up. This formed the rationale for his proposal to increase public spending during periods of recession. But Freidman extended the idea of the permanent income hypothesis to show that public spending during a recession would fail to generate additional consumption in the economy, as individuals would view this as a temporary increase in income. They would not spend the additional income, thereby not increasing their consumption. In contrast, he proposed monetary policy, which involves changing the money supply in an economy, as a short-term stimulus, while acknowledging that in the long run, neither monetary policy nor fiscal policy can have any economic impact. In the short term, an increase in the money supply would lead to higher economic activity within six to nine months. But after six to nine months, the impact would wear off and be felt only on prices and not on production, resulting in inflation. Friedman had outlined these arguments in the 1950s. However, it required the persistent stagflation of the 1970s to give it credibility and attract a wide enough audience to shake the foundation of Keynesian economics.

Following Friedman, another challenge to Keynesian economics came from Robert E. Lucas Jr. (Nobel laureate, 1995) who extended the concept of rational market expectations to macroeconomics, thereby conceptually demolishing the Phillips curve. His most famous contribution was the **Lucas Critique**, in which he stated that an individual's economic behaviour will change in response to a policy change due to their ability to look forward. According to Keynesian theory, a tax cut will lead to increased demand in the economy as consumers have more money to spend. But according to the Lucas Critique, an individual will realize that the deficit generated by tax cuts will need to be paid back in the future and therefore the government will levy higher taxes in the days ahead. Considering this, the rational individual will save more to meet the future tax burden and hence will not increase his consumption, as anticipated by Keynes.

Lucas linked the persistent stagflation in 1970s with his rational individual behaviour theory. He posited it as the reason why the relationship between inflation and employment depicted in the Phillips Curve failed. Lucas pointed out that the Phillips Curve assumed irrational individual behavior and for this reason was invalid. In another insightful study, Lucas explained labour supply in an economy as a conscious choice by each worker between work and leisure. He said that workers decide whether to work or abstain by comparing the real wage against benefits from leisure. Using this rationale, he explained unemployment in an economy as workers waiting for wage levels to rise.

Such was seen to be the impact of his contribution that while awarding him the Nobel Prize in 1995, the presenter remarked, 'Robert Lucas is the social scientist who has had the greatest influence on macroeconomic research since 1970'.[3] His work led to the development of the 'new classical school' in Economics, as macroeconomic theory for many returned to its pre-Keynesian conclusions. Demand-side economics after being dominant for over three decades, ceded the throne in favour of supply-side economics in the 1980s.

The Second Decade: Expanding the Economic Sphere

The 1970s provided two new economic concepts. The first was stagflation and the second was its derivative – the Misery Index. Arthur Okun, an American economist put together a new index to reflect the hardship faced by individuals in an economy in the aftermath of the oil crisis in 1973. He added together the two components of the Phillips curve – the unemployment rate and the inflation rate and termed it the Misery Index to reflect the hardship faced by individuals in an economy. The Misery Index was not just an economic indicator. It proved to be a potent electoral weapon in the USA. Jimmy Carter popularized the Misery Index by repeatedly referring to it in his 1976 victorious US presidential campaign. A high and increasing Misery index was a sure indicator for political change and more importantly, a change in the economic policy pursued. As the Index continued to surge during his rule, Carter lost the 1980 elections to Ronald Reagan. A year earlier, Margaret Thatcher had come to power in England without the aid of this index, as the ground reality of people suffering from unemployment and inflation was too harsh to miss.

The presence of Reagan and Thatcher at the helm of the two major economies provided the required patronage for supply-side economics to dominate the global scene once again. 'Reaganomics' and Thatcherism were the form in which supply-side economics manifested itself, gaining strength from the ideological foundation provided by Friedrich Hayek and Milton Friedman. These Nobel Prize-winning economists of the 1970s became the patron saints of the new economic era, setting the stage for this ideology to flourish.

In a very insightful extension of the economic concept of rational behavior, James M. Buchanan (Nobel laureate, 1986) brought politics into the economic domain by developing the concept of **public choice**. Widening the concept of self-interest used to analyze economic decisions, he suggested that rational economic man who seeks to maximize his utility doesn't only exist with respect to economic activities, but can also be in the political domain. Buchanan advocated that the politician and the bureaucrat should also be viewed through the same lens. Political exchanges, like economic exchanges will be made with the expectation of personal gain, he noted. This, in gist, is the concept of public choice and it was contrary to the popular belief of that time, which held politicians and bureaucrats to be driven by public interest. Based on this logic, he derived the important conclusion that politicians in a democracy work for re-election and not for public welfare. As re-election is enabled by large budgets that provide the politician with an opportunity to distribute largess, politicians will favour a bigger government, resulting in a larger budgetary deficit. To prevent this, he advocated a constitutional change that required governments to balance their budgets. Buchanan's study resulted in a movement across the globe to rein in budgetary deficits, with some governments even enacting Financial Responsibility legislations to limit public spending.

Buchanan shook the foundation of Keynesian economics by advancing the view that only individuals can know what is good for them and what benefits them. Any outside party or body cannot determine objectively what is good for the people. Hence, increasing the role of bureaucrats with bigger government spending can only result in reduced individual freedom and choice, thereby limiting their welfare. This view negated the Keynesian view that government intervention can further public welfare.

While Buchanan only extended the concept of self-interest and rationality to the political domain, Gary S. Becker (Nobel laureate, 1992) enlarged its scope outside the realm of traditional economic inquiry. He adapted the concept of self-interest and rationality used in economic analysis to a wider range of human activity, such as individual decisions regarding fertility, marriage, divorce, addiction, crime and punishment, and called it purposeful behaviour. Analyzing divorced couples in the USA, Becker found that marrying early was more likely to result in a divorce. He attributed it to the search time for the spouse being shorter, resulting in suboptimal decisions. Likewise, he viewed families as 'small factories' producing services for their members. The decision to have a child was similar to buying consumer goods like a car or taking a vacation, to be evaluated on a cost-benefit scale. Raising a child involves cost as the parents must pay for food, shelter, clothing, toys and education. The benefits came from the joy of having and raising children and the desire to be cared for in old age. Using the concept of purposeful behaviour, he attributed the falling fertility rates in Western societies to the higher costs of raising children and an increase in opportunity cost due to higher income earned by women. He also noted that old-age income guarantees by governments reduced the benefit of having children, thereby further depressing the fertility rates.

The works of Buchanan and Becker, along with anecdotal evidence to show the impact of self-interest and rational behaviour prevailing in multiple spheres of daily life, strengthened the case for supply-side economics and its call for free markets. However, the fear of monopolies and the desirability of a market economy for the general consumer were matters of concern. These concerns too were resolved 'scientifically' by Maurice Allais (Nobel laureate, 1988) who built a mathematical model to prove the superiority of market economies, even as George J. Stigler (Nobel laureate, 1982) sought to prove that monopolies were not commercially feasible.

Modelling the Markets

Adam Smith was among the first to advocate the merits of free markets in the eighteenth century. He outlined the conceptual model where both the consumers and producers pursuing their self-interest would optimize their combined utility. This was due to the fact that their interaction was moderated by the mechanism of price. Leon Walrus, the nineteenth-century French economist, built a mathematical model in which this descriptive conceptual model was validated. This resulted in the formulation of the General Equilibrium Theory, which showed how markets optimized total utility in an economy. The Walrus model required the use of an auctioneer and an iterative process for an economy to settle at an equilibrium level. While this model was a major advance in economics, and well appreciated at the time, it had a few drawbacks that came to light only in the twentieth century. For instance, it did not account for the sub-optimal trades that took place before the equilibrium level was reached. In addition, this mathematical model could produce both zero prices and negative prices, both of which do not prevail in the real world.

Maurice Allais addressed these shortfalls with a more rigorous model. He mathematically showed that at market equilibrium, a socially efficient solution is reached. This efficient solution, he proved, could not be improved without reallocating the initial resources in that society. The contributions of Buchanan, Becker and Allais placed the economic theory of free markets in an invincible position. The political patronage of Reagan and Thatcher only strengthened its impenetrable position. Further, the Soviet Union disintegrating in the same decade reinforced its standing as the sole dominant ideology for the twenty-first century. The only concern that remained in adopting a market economy was the harmful impact of monopolies. But even this concern had been dismissed in the 1980s.

George J. Stigler, who pioneered the study of the Economics of Information and the Economics of Regulation, advanced a new logic on why the fear of monopolies was unfounded. Studying the feasibility of price cartels in creating monopolistic situations, he found that the cost of enforcing these agreements far exceeded any gains that accrued to the participants. Hence, he ruled out collaborative price cartels. He also found that economic legislations enacted to prevent monopolies often protected the interests of the incumbents in the industry, who were better organized to lobby with the regulators, as opposed to the general public, who initiated the legislation.[g] With this, he made a strong case against enacting any anti-monopolistic legislation. The 1980s ended with the formulation of the Washington Consensus,[h] promoting policies that ushered in free trade and de-regulated financial markets, all necessary for establishing a free market economy.

The strong intellectual foundation laid for a rapid expansion of free market philosophy was a necessary prerequisite, but for this philosophy to be realized, two other essentials were needed. One, the need for lubricants to keep the engine of the capitalistic economy chugging along at a healthy pace and the

---

g   The example often quoted to substantiate the relative powers of consumer and providers of goods and services is the system of licensing for taxis in a metropolis. In 1991, New York City taxi medallions were being sold for $150,000, reflecting the high profits earned by the incumbent taxi operators. Without licensing, the number of taxis would have increased, contributing to reducing the consumer fare due to higher competition, thereby benefiting the consumers.

h   For more details on Washington Consensus please refer to Chapter 5.

other, evolved market institutions to meet the increased volume of voluntary economic exchanges.

The Third Decade: Financial Markets Come of Age

Tribology is the science and engineering of interacting surfaces in motion. Etymologically derived from the Greek word *tribo* meaning 'I rub', tribology studies friction. An important contribution from this science is the use of lubricants to increase the pace of motion and reduce wear and tear. Though in existence for a few thousand years, this science came to prominence during the nineteenth century, when the Industrial Revolution made automation possible. Automation significantly accelerated the pace of movement. Knowledge of lubricants was essential to make fast and durable machinery that could stand up to the pace. Likewise, in the market economy driven by independent agents transacting as producers, distributors, brokers and consumers, frequent interaction is an essential feature. These interactions too produce friction and need lubricants to increase transactional efficiency and the relationship durability.

Economic tribology produced superior financial lubricants as money evolved from commodities of daily use to fiat money.[i] The next major change was towards the end of the twentieth century, when the quality of lubricants increased multifold as derivatives[j] came in to supplement investment

---

i   Fiat money currency is made legal tender by the government and is not backed or convertible into gold or silver. For a more detailed analysis of its emergence see Chapter 4.

j   Derivatives are financial contracts executed in the present to fix the price of a commodity or an asset for a given date in the future. They are used both for hedging the risk of price fluctuations and for speculative gains.

instruments. The increased volume of derivative transactions fueled economic growth. The Nobel endorsement received by financial market theorists and analysts played a key role in popularizing derivatives as their public acceptability went up with each endorsement.

Box 6.2
The Five Phases of Capitalism

Hyman Minsky, an American economist, identified five phases in the evolution of capitalist economies. He painted a vivid picture of this evolution by identifying the triggers for change and the power wielders in different eras. He traced the origin of capitalism to sea trade in 1600 CE and identified the merchants as its primary drivers. The advent of the Industrial Revolution shifted the power from the merchants to the industrialists, marking the second phase. The third phase saw the rise of the bankers, who usurped power from the industrialists by financing mergers and acquisitions to build big businesses. The Great Depression in 1930s brought to the forefront the importance of management in running big businesses, placing power in the professional managers' hands. This marked the fourth phase. The fifth and the final phase identified by Minsky was the advent of institutional investors who shaped the economy, with equity markets acting as the barometer of economic climate.

Minsky identified the fifth phase as money manager capitalism. In this phase he saw economic power wielded by institutional fund managers, with expertise in finance being the key type of knowledge in an economy. His analysis was validated by the growing importance of capital markets in the 1980s, which accelerated in the 90s and galloped into the

> twenty-first century. As capital markets assumed prominence, research into the valuation of companies, financial instruments and optimum investment techniques gained in status.
>
> The research of the earlier decades in these theories and techniques and in derivative instruments suddenly assumed increasing importance. This was reflected in the awards of the Nobel Prize committee, when six laureates[k] were recognized for their work in financial markets in a short period starting from 1985.

Franco Modigliani (Nobel laureate, 1985) was the first among the 'financial scientists' recognized. He along with Miller (Nobel laureate, 1990) developed the Modigliani-Miller theorem. In short, they concluded that in a theoretical world without transaction costs and taxes, which has perfectly functioning markets, the enterprise value[l] of a company would be constant and not change with different debt-equity levels. They reasoned that an increase in debt level would increase the risk of equity[m] and hence reduce its value correspondingly. They later extended this concept to dividend declaration by a company, and held that its payout decision would not impact its market valuation. In the real world however, due to the presence of taxes and transaction

---

k   Franco Modigliani, Harry Markowitz, Merton Miller, William Sharpe, Robert Merton and Myron Scholes

l   Enterprise value is the sum total of the debt outstanding of a firm and its market capitalization

m   In the capital structuring of a company, debt is a contracted obligation and equity is the residuary obligation. Both for income distribution on an ongoing basis, and for redemption on liquidation, the claim of debt holders is for a defined sum and has a priority over the claim of equity holders. Hence any increase in debt level in a company increases the risk element of an equity holder.

costs, their theory had a major impact on a different front. It segregated the operating efficiencies of a business from its financial structuring gains. Modigliani-Miller, with their theory on optimal capital structures, provided a basic platform for corporate finance to emerge as a distinct value-creating discipline. This in essence translated to the Corporate Finance function being viewed not as a staff function, but as a line function on par with 'real' ones like research, development, manufacturing and marketing.

In 1990, the Nobel Prize committee formally acknowledged the emergence of 'a new field of Financial Economics and Corporate Finance', when they awarded the prize to three contributors working in distinct but related areas of this new field. Markowitz (Nobel laureate, 1990) was recognized for his theory of optimum portfolio selection. In summary, he translated the popular idiom 'don't put all your eggs in one basket' into a mathematical model. In the process, he showed that the risk of investing in a particular security could be reduced by holding significantly diversified portfolios. While market fluctuations could not be eliminated, their impact could be increased or reduced depending on the investor's risk appetite. William Sharpe (Nobel laureate, 1990) was recognized for conceptualizing the Capital Asset Pricing Model. He showed how an investor could vary his return using the capital markets by changing the risk of his portfolio by developing 'beta', a measure that quantified risk. Merton Miller (Nobel laureate, 1990) was belatedly recognized for his contribution to the Modigliani-Miller theory of optimal capital structures, five years after his partner Modigliani received the prize. In their theory of optimal capital structures they showed that in a theoretical world where transaction costs and corporate tax do not exist, the risk levels of an enterprise cannot be altered.

However, in the practical world, as transaction cost and taxes are present, risk levels in a firm could be increased or reduced by the varying the combination of debt and equity used to finance the enterprise.

With financial markets gaining in importance through the 1980s, the second boost to growth came in the form of derivatives. The collapse of the Bretton Woods system in the year 1971 gave place to market-determined exchange rates for different currencies. With a fluctuating domestic currency, their interest rates too began to swing, increasing the risk of businesses, especially international businesses. In response to this volatility, for the first time, derivatives – financial instruments primarily intended to insulate the buyer from price fluctuations, in the form of currency futures – were introduced in 1972 by the Chicago Mercantile Exchange. Three years later, interest rate futures too followed.[4] Soon these instruments were introduced in other large financial markets creating a new segment – the exchange traded derivatives. The advent of currency swaps in 1980s, a different form of financial derivative for use by larger players, led to the 'Over The Counter', or OTC, markets. For a long time, derivatives remained an exotic instrument traded only among the professional elite. The credit for demystifying derivatives and bringing them to the general investors goes to Fischer Black, Myron Scholes (Nobel laureate, 1997) and Robert Merton (Nobel laureate, 1997), when they developed a model for pricing options[n], the exotic variant of derivatives.

---

n   See 'The Pricing of Options and Corporate Liabilities' by Fischer Black and Myron Scholes in *The Journal of Political Economy*, 81, 1973 and 'The Theory of Rational Option Pricing' by Robert Merton in *Bell Journal of Economics and Management Science*, 1973

The Nobel Prize committee in 1997, honoured Robert Merton and Myron Scholes for independently discovering a new method of valuing options, a distinct type of derivatives. Fischer Black, the co-founder of the model with Scholes, had died two years earlier, becoming ineligible for the prize, as the Nobel Prize is granted only to candidates living at the time of the prize announcement. Experts considered this discovery the equivalent of the Holy Grail in derivative pricing, reflecting its importance to the field.[5]

In short what the Nobel Laureates had done was to quantify risk. In their quantification of risk, most users had missed out on a critical assumption that Fischer Black highlighted. The assumption was that their mathematical models, with many decimal points, communicated a false sense of precision, a misleading idea, when the information the models conveyed was inexact.[6] By the time the derivatives market realized the grave implications of this fallacy, the world would pay a heavy price, running to trillions of dollars of bailout packages for banks and other financial institutions, the major participants in the derivatives markets. This large loss was due to the scorching pace of growth in the use of derivatives between 1998 and 2008. The nominal value[o] of derivatives outstanding grew from $94 trillion or about twice the size of global GDP in December 1998 to $650 trillion or about ten times the size of global GDP by December 2008.[7] This meant a compounded annual growth rate of 21 per cent per annum, in an economy growing at around

---

o   Derivatives are like insurance policies. The nominal value of the derivatives are the equivalent of the sum insured, while the actual money that changes hand on entering into a derivative contract is the equivalent of the premium paid on that insurance policy.

4 per cent per annum. This growth itself was tempered by the Lehman Brothers bankruptcy in September 2008, for in June 2008, prior to their crash, the nominal value of derivatives outstanding was actually $766 trillions. What led to this multi-fold increase in derivatives?

New Light on Market Institutions

The growth of financial markets in the 1980s reflected their increased importance in the economy. As the pace of economic growth accelerated, financial market institutions were also better understood and appreciated. This was reflected in the Nobel Prizes awarded. James Tobin (Nobel laureate, 1981) analyzed the factors promoting the creation of assets in contrast to asset purchase in an economy, thereby throwing new light on the importance of stock markets in promoting capital mobilization. Ronald Coase (Nobel laureate 1991) provided new insights into issues involving property rights and the rationale for a firm's existence. George Akerlof (Nobel laureate, 2001) explained the logic for market institutions and how they enhanced exchange efficiency.

James Tobin provided the conceptual bridge between the financial markets and the real or physical markets, when he formulated the Risk Theory of Asset Allocation. He noted that individuals make their investment decisions by trading off yield and risk. Calculating the cumulative effect of these individual decisions in an economy enabled him to explain the prices for various financial assets like bonds and shares. Using this base, he arrived at a transmission mechanism to connect fiscal policy and foreign exchange-rate changes to consumption and investment decisions in an economy. A practical application of his research allowed for computing the 'q' ratio, which explains fresh investment in assets. The 'q' ratio is computed by dividing the market value of an asset by its replacement cost. He found that where this number was less than one, it is more profitable for firms to buy other firms rather than invest in building new assets. His research provided a leading insight into the role of stock markets in the capital formation of an economy.

Over the years, a constant and clearly visible phenomenon has been the growing size of commercial firms. This was looked upon with mixed feelings by both regulators and consumers. Their apprehension about the growing power of the firms on one hand conflicted with the benefits derived from their economies of scale. Ronald Coase, the 1991 Nobel laureate, provided a convincing logic for the existence of firms and what limits their size. Coase noted that while inter-firm transactions of sales and purchases were determined by market price, intra-firm transactions of inter-departmental exchanges, in the nature of goods and services provided by one department to another, were not decided based on market prices, even though they formed a sizeable portion of the overall exchanges in a business. He explored the question, that if markets are so efficient why do they exclude inter-departmental transactions within a firm? After analysis, he found that traditional economic theory did not consider transaction costs and hence it could not explain the reason for the existence of inter-departmental transactions within a firm. Viewed through the lens of transaction cost, the economic rationale for the firms' existence became very clear. Market transactions involve a transaction cost in the form of time and resources incurred on contracts.[p] Where the

---

p Time spent on contracting to define the obligations of each party is a factor of the trust levels between them. A lower trust level means that the need for watertight contracts is going to be higher. This is essential for trading in markets.

benefits of exchange exceed the transaction cost of contracting, the market is the ideal choice. Hence market transactions are feasible only in instances where the responsibilities of each party can be clearly defined. Where there is lack of clarity in the role of the contracting parties, either due to the evolving nature of the relationship between them or due to the relative low value of goods or services transacted in relation to the cost of defining the roles, administered or centrally-decreed prices prevail, justifying the existence of firm. Based on this analysis, Coase concluded that in a world without transaction costs, individuals would deal among themselves and firms would be redundant. On the other hand, the inefficiency of bureaucracy in fixing administered prices would render large firms commercially unviable, thereby limiting their size. Coase's Nobel Prize provided some reassurance that the size of the firms would not exceed their economic benefits.

Further, Coase posited that property rights are not a right over goods and other resources but the right to dispose of those goods and resources. With this view, he advanced the theory that in an economy with zero transaction costs, legislation and court decisions would be immaterial as an individual who could derive better value from an asset, would buy it from the holder by parting with a portion of his or her incremental benefit. In contrast, where transaction costs exist, it could be more than the incremental benefit the buyer gets. With this insight, Coase converted all goods and resources from being objects of use value or 'natural use' as defined by Aristotle to objects of 'unnatural use' or exchange value.[q] This provided the basis

---

q   Aristotle illustrated his idea of natural use and unnatural use with the example of a shoe. Using a shoe as footwear was its natural use, while selling a shoe to buy some other goods was unnatural use, according to him. Please refer to Chapter 2 for a full exploration of this idea.

for looking at all the goods and services through the lens of exchange value, i.e. with regard to the price they commanded in the marketplace.

A decade after Coase was awarded the Nobel Prize, George Akerlof (Nobel laureate 2001) was recognized for his insights into the need for market institutions. Akerlof noted that the real markets differed from the markets studied by theoretical economists in a very critical respect. The information available to the contracting parties in the market was not equal as presumed in theory. Studying the trade practices in pre-owned automobiles he observed that often the sellers were better informed than the buyers. He also noted that at any given price, a seller of high quality goods would be more reluctant to sell as a rational buyer would suspect all the willing sellers in the market of offering inferior quality goods and thus stay away from the market, further depressing the price. He called this process by which the market is pushed into a downward quality spiral the adverse selection bias. He observed similar bias in sale of medical insurance where any elderly person wanting insurance was treated as a suspect. In this scenario, he noted that free markets would not work. It was to overcome this limitation, he concluded, that many market institutions, like performance guarantees, licenses or certifications and brands, had emerged.

The justification provided for stock markets and large firms, and the rationale for the existing market institutions, validated by the awarding of Nobel Prizes, created a strong belief in the infallibility of market economies. Markets were seen to be the philosopher's stone that could transform any economy into a prosperous one with a sole touch. The absence of any credible alternative only enhanced their attractiveness. At the beginning of the third millennium, the primary focus of the major global economies was to make the markets work. The USA did not just have the largest economy in the world, but for many, if not all, it was also a role model to be emulated.

Fourth Decade: The Growth Fetish

The birth of the third millennium was marked by euphoria. Y2K, a feared technological challenge that had haunted the digital world, passed off without a hitch. In response, stock markets globally touched record highs in the first quarter of the year 2000. The unprecedented boom in the last decade of the twentieth century had seen the creation of millionaires and billionaires overnight. But these gains accrued only to those participating in the stock markets. Employees in financial services and senior management teams in the 'new economy' companies became the new 'white collar' workforce. In contrast, all the other 'old economy' participants were pushed into the 'blue collar' category, as young students and experienced professionals of science, technology and engineering gave up their core professions in exchange for jobs in the financial sector.

The desire among the 'old economy' constituents was to emulate their new economy counterparts. This is perhaps what seeded the concept of financialization of economies, an outlook in which the real world was viewed through the lens of financial markets.[r] And more importantly, higher profits accrued to those in the financial domain. It led to a world in which any

---

[r] Financialization has multiple meanings. It is measured by the contribution of the financial sector to GDP, the ratio of employment in the financial sector to overall employment and the proportion of profits accruing to the financial sector. In this section, this term is used as the proportion of profits accruing to the financial sector.

risk could be quantified and traded off against its returns; where individuals borrowed to trade, businesses financed their customers and the commercial banks opted to insure their credit risk in lieu of diligent credit checks.

Despite multiple adverse events in the form of the dotcom burst which led to a stock market collapse, a terrorist attack that shook the roots of globalization by putting up security barriers between nations, and a spate of accounting scandals[s] that raised the spectre of recession, the US economy continued its impressive march in the first two years of the twenty-first century. This performance was built on the broad principles identified in the Washington Consensus.[t] Particular emphasis was laid on promoting the market economy and global free trade based on a basic belief in free markets. This in essence boiled down to low interest rates as a stimulus, deregulation to promote financial innovation and employee incentives used to fuel a credit-fed growth.

Stemming from the free-market belief, at the first sign of US economic slowdown in the twenty-first century, monetary policy was used to rev up growth. For the first time in forty-five years, the US Federal Reserve cut its interest rate down to 1 per cent in June 2003. What made it more decisive was the drastic drop from the 2001 levels of 6.25 per cent. Alan Greenspan, the Chairman of the US Federal Reserve Board, talking

---

s   A large number of insider trading cases that came to light probably prompted the Nobel Prize Committee to recognize in 2001 Akerlof, Spenser and Stiglitz (laureates 2001) for their study on asymmetric information in markets. In addition, the findings of Herbert A. Simons (laureate 1978) on decision-making in large firms being motivated by arriving at an acceptable solution to all stakeholders and not driven by profit maximization put these cases in perspective.

t   For details on the Washington Consensus refer to Chapter 5.

about this decision to reduce interest rates in his memoirs remarked,

> At the FOMC meeting in late June, where we voted to reduce rates still further, to 1 per cent, deflation was Topic A. We agreed on the reduction despite our consensus that the economy probably did not need yet another rate cut.… We wanted to shut down the possibility of corrosive deflation; we are willing to chance that by cutting rates we might foster a bubble, an inflationary boom of some sort, which we would subsequently have to address. I was pleased at the way we'd weighted the contending factors. Time would tell if it was the right decision, but it was a decision doing right.[8]

By itself, this decision to reduce interest rates to 1 per cent and keep them there for a year may not have had much impact. But in hindsight, what is clear is that this low interest rate worked in conjunction with a more powerful stimulus: deregulation. Deregulation in bits and pieces, over the past three decades had built up to a tipping point and the low interest rate was just the final straw required to fuel growth.

In the past, the regulation mandated after the 1929 stock market crash in the USA was the Banking Act of 1933 in the USA, more popularly known as the Glass-Steagall Act, meant to control speculation, which is believed to have led to the crash. A key provision of this Act prohibited a bank-holding company from owning other financial services companies, as it was felt that the resource of public deposit should not be leveraged for speculative purposes. The Act also mandated regulated interest rates on savings bank accounts to ensure prudent borrowing and lending in banks. However, this Act was dismantled bit by bit beginning in 1980, when the safeguards against speculation were set aside, to accommodate the new engine of finance to power economic growth.

In 1980, the Depository Institutions Deregulation and Monetary Control Act was enacted in the USA to provide control to Federal Reserves over non-bank members like credit unions and savings & loan companies. This act allowed banks to merge, increased deposit insurance from $40,000 to $100,000 and allowed credit unions and savings & loans companies to offer checkable deposits. In a critical provision, interest rates on savings accounts, hitherto regulated by the Banking Act of 1933, were set free. In tandem with this move, interest rates on loans too were liberated. This, in effect, removed the cap on interest rates and provided a backdoor entry for usury, a hotly-debated topic in earlier centuries. Prior to this mandate, lending to less creditworthy borrowers was not entertained as the maximum interest rate was capped. The banks therefore could not take a higher risk to earn a higher return.

On November 12, 1999, the second and the most critical provision of the Glass-Steagall Act was repealed. The prohibition against a bank-holding company owning other financial-services companies was revoked. This prompted commercial banks to once again leverage investment banks to grow their own business, in the process fueling growth in the economy. The logic used to reverse this decision was the absence of such legislation in other parts of the world.

Low interest rates and unregulated financial markets were only the fuel for growth. The spark that ignited this combustible material was self-interest, i.e. the individual incentive to accumulate private property, which is the primary driver in market economies. As sparks go, the presence of this in the financial-services sector was uniquely positioned to create a large blaze. The compensation structure in the financial-services sector, especially in investment banks and senior management in commercial banks had a unique composition:

the base salary was relatively low, with a very large proportion of annual compensation given as a performance bonus. This incentive was sufficient to produce innovation on a scale rarely seen before. It was as if a new 'industrial' revolution had begun, only this time confined to financial products.

The 'Financial Revolution'

In a very short period at the beginning of the twenty-first century, there was both the invention of a new business model and innovation of financial products. The combination of commercial banking with investment banking led to the creation of a new business model in housing mortgages. Mortgages that were traditionally 'lend and hold' products evolved into an 'originate and distribute' product. This transformation saw a wave of product innovation as mortgage originators sought to increase the flow of transactions and collect their profits. Products like NINJA (No Income No Job or Assets) loans, ARMs (Adjustable Rate Mortgages), teaser rate loans, interest-only mortgages, negative amortization mortgages etc multiplied like rabbits. The primary driver for new buyer was the lure of capital appreciation, as evidenced by the interest-only mortgages, where the borrower was only required to pay the interest, in the belief that the underlying asset covering the principal would appreciate over time. Going further, in negative amortization mortgages, only a fraction of the interest accrued was recovered, as both the parties to the transaction were confident of rising home prices that would give both the lender and the borrower with a profit to share after paying off the unrecovered interest.

The housing boom led by mortgage finance helped in turning around the US economy. As Alan Greenspan noted, analysts estimated that 3 to 5 per cent of the annual increase in housing wealth translates as incremental demand for all other goods and services.[9] This played its part in the US economy accelerating from an abysmally low GDP growth rate of 0.76 per cent in 2001, to 1.61 per cent growth in 2002, 2.52 per cent in 2003 and touching 3.65 per cent in 2004; almost the level of growth that was witnessed in the year 2000. This revival was a resounding success for the advocates of a free-market economy, who saw their faith vindicated by the US economy's strong performance; and a green signal for pushing Washington Consensus policies the world over.

Box 6.3
The Tales the Numbers Tell

The period of the Bretton Woods agreement, with its emphasis on international collaboration was termed by some as the Golden Age of Capitalism. Robert Skidelsky in his book, *The Return of the Master: Keynes*, captured the global economic performance during this period and contrasted it with the subsequent period of the Washington Consensus. Between 1951 and 1973, which he termed the Golden Age, average annual GDP growth rate was 4.8 per cent. In contrast, the period between 1980 and 2009, the Washington Consensus era, averaged a growth rate which was a third lower at 3.2 per cent. Similar performance was seen in unemployment levels too. Unemployment during the Golden Age averaged 4.8 per cent in USA, 1.2 per cent in Germany and 3.1 per cent in France. In contrast, in the period between 1980 and 2009 it was significantly worse off, recording 6.1 per cent, 9.5 per cent and 7.5 per cent respectively. In the most telling of statistics on financial stability, the number of financial crises too was lower in the Golden Age: 38 episodes in contrast to 139 episodes in the Washington Consensus era.

Is it possible that the resounding success of the free market policies, seen in the strong growth witnessed in the USA, after what looked like a stutter, was one of the influencing factors in the Nobel Prize committee's recognition of Finn E. Kydland and Edward C. Prescott as the winners for 2004? In contrast the Keynesian school had failed to correct the stagflation of 1970s. Both the winners, working together, had studied the stagflation of 1970s and why the economy did not respond to government initiatives. They concluded that the ineffectiveness was due to the low credibility of governments, who could change their action in addressing the situation. This they called the 'time consistency problem'. As a remedy they pointed out that government policy initiatives would be more effective if there was prior commitment to a stated policy line, which was both feasible and credible. In addition, their study also discarded the Keynesian view that business cycles were caused by demand fluctuations. In its place they proposed a supply-side explanation for economic cycles, i.e. shortage in crude oil supplies for the downturn in the 1970s and information technology for the boom in the 1990s.

Two years later, as the US economic growth rates hovered around the 3 per cent mark, Edmund S. Phelps was recognized in 2006 by the Nobel Prize committee, again for explaining the stagflation of the 1970s. Phelps, studying the ineffectiveness of the Philips curve during that decade, noted that inflation expectation plays a critical role. When the inflation expectation in the economy becomes predictable, the relationship between inflation and unemployment breaks. Hence, he contended inflation can only influence employment in the short run.

As the healthy economic growth in the US continued for the fifth continuous year, there were growing concerns about its sustainability. Beginning in 2007, mortgage companies began filing for bankruptcy, with their numbers increasing with every passing month. What was initially seen as a minor sub-sector problem in housing gradually began to take a stranglehold on the US economy. The historical lessons of Charles Kindleberger who studied economic crashes over centuries were being revisited. The failure of Lehman Brothers on September 16, 2008, marked a decisive point in global economic history.

Does History Repeat Itself?

Economic downturns are not a new phenomenon. They have occurred repeatedly over the centuries. In the nineteenth century they were called panics in the USA. Over time euphemism was practiced by calling economic downturns 'depressions' in the twentieth century and 'recessions' in the first decade of the twenty-first century. It took all of a few trillion dollars and four quarters of economic decline to free the global economy from its 'death-grip'. 'Death-grip' literally translates to mortgage in French; etymologically it comes from the two French words *Mort* as in death and *Gage* as in grip. While the sub-prime mortgage excesses are identified as the most proximate cause for the Great Recession, the primary factors that led to this crisis are more varied and have deeper roots.

Historically, panics, crisis, depressions or recessions, irrespective of what they were called followed a common pattern. Charles Kindleberger, an authority on this subject, captured the history of financial crisis in his classic, *Manias, Panics, and Crashes*, first published in 1978. He classified the anatomy of a crisis into three parts elaborated in the book title. In the first phase or the maniac zone, people blindly chase the asset in fashion; not for the income earned by holding it, but in the quest for large profits on resale. They not only liquidate their other assets to fund this purchase, but also liberally borrow to chase the proverbial 'two birds in the bush'. In the second phase, the trend is reversed as panic sets in. The trigger for this is often an innocuous event that suddenly makes people realize their illogical assumptions for future price rise. People now abandon the 'asset in fashion'; some on their own, to limit losses and the others, who have borrowed money, forced by their lenders to repay their loans. This rush to sell results in a crash in the price of 'assets in fashion', heralding the third and concluding phase of the crisis.

Unfortunately, the cost of these speculative excesses is not paid for by the greedy investors alone. The innocent population too pays a heavy price. Following the crash that marks the end of all economic excesses, as the overall credit in the economy shrinks, genuine businesses too suffer. In addition, job loss, home foreclosures and destruction of safety nets, i.e. the loss of contingency funds set aside for a rainy day all cause huge human suffering. Given these dire consequences, what can be done to eliminate them?

The Postmortem Report

A year after the Great Recession, popular opinion converged to the view that the downturn was a result of misplaced belief in promoting free-markets to achieve economic growth. Deregulation was pursued to promote innovation. A by-product of this innovation was the concept of 'financialization' which accelerated global economic growth. As hindsight revealed, financialization moved the risk levels a notch higher among all participants in the economy. Individuals behaved like businesses, businesses like banks and banks like hedge funds. Ample and easy credit in a globally-integrated world promoted financial leverage. In contrast to 'debt' that had a negative tone to it, 'financial leverage' was seen in a positive light and considered desirable. This concoction, in the opinion of many experts, created the events that led up to the Great Recession as explained later in this chapter in detail. However three decades earlier, an American economist, Hyman Minsky, had foreseen the consequence of this potent combination and warned the world; a warning that fell on deaf ears.

Box 6.4
What the Laureates Missed

In 1972, Hyman Minsky, an American economist from the Keynesian school, proposed the '**Financial Instability Hypothesis**' after inductively analyzing the capitalistic economy. Within four decades of his outlining the theory, the first economic crisis of the twenty-first century played out as if Minsky had written a case study to illustrate it.

Minsky in his hypothesis defined capital deployment in a capitalistic economy as 'exchange of present money for the future'. While the present money exchanged was real and definite, future money was only a conjuncture. In addition, capitalistic enterprises used loans that had fixed repayment, leaving only the variable residue to the owners of equity. Elaborating the debt-income relationship, he identified three strands – hedge, speculative and the Ponzi finance variety. Hedge financing was when the contracted debt could be repaid along with interest by the cash-flow generated. When only the interest could be repaid from income but not the principal, it was termed speculative financing, as it needed a 'roll over', i.e. fresh loans to fund the principal repayments. The third category, which required fresh loans to repay both the interest and principal repayments, was termed Ponzi finance.[u]

Minsky noted that when hedge financing prevails, the economy will be equilibrium-seeking. But when speculative and Ponzi finance dominate, the economy will amplify the underlying deviations and become increasingly unstable as it moves towards disequilibrium. Based on this analysis, he arrived at the Financial Instability Hypothesis, consisting of two theorems:

Theorem 1:

'The economy has financing regimes under which it is stable and financing regimes under which it is unstable.'

Theorem 2:

'Over periods of prolonged prosperity, the economy transits from financial relations that make for a stable system to financial relations that makes for an unstable system.'[10]

Minsky further noted that if inflation prevails in an economy and the authorities act to contain it, speculative financing models will turn into Ponzi financing and Ponzi financed units will become insolvent, thereby resulting in forced asset sales and an asset price collapse.

The United Nations Conference on Trade and Commerce put out a report titled '*The Global Economic Crisis: Systemic Failures and Multilateral Remedies*' in 2009, where they summarized the crisis and recommended four national and multilateral

---

u   Ponzi schemes refer to the 1920 modus operandi followed by Charles Ponzi in a Boston fraud, where he promised investors 50 per cent return in 45 days. He collected $9.5 million in less than eight months by paying the initial investors their returns from the collection received from the subsequent investors. This bubble burst in July 1920, when the Boston Police got the wind of it and shut him down. For the sheer audacity of it, all such financing schemes are called Ponzi schemes or Ponzi finance.

remedies. These remedies were linked to the factors that contributed to the crisis, which were:

1. **Cause:** Market fundamentalist laissez faire policies of the last 20 years have dramatically failed the test by promoting financial deregulation that pushed the global economy into debt deflation. **Remedy:** Regulatory reforms to systematically weed out financial sophistication which have no social returns.

2. **Cause:** Blind faith in the efficiency of deregulated financial markets and the absence of a cooperative financial and monetary system created an illusion of risk-free profits and licensed profligacy through speculative finance in many areas. **Remedy:** Comprehensive reform and reregulation that enable governments to intervene whenever major disequilibrium looms.

3. **Cause:** The growing role and weight of large scale financial investors on commodities futures markets affected commodity prices and their volatility. **Remedy:** Regulatory interventions to monitor OTC markets to prevent excessive speculation.

4. **Cause:** The absence of a cooperative international system to manage exchange rate fluctuations facilitated rampant currency speculations and increased the global imbalance. **Remedy:** Multilateral or even global exchange rate arrangements needed to avoid the collapse of the international trading system.[11]

Similar thoughts were echoed in *e-journal USA,* a publication of the US Department of State, Bureau of International Information Programs. In one of the articles in the issue devoted to the Global Financial System, author Mark Blyth, a professor of political science identifying the reasons for the crisis noted, another ideology has failed. The beliefs [that] markets are good and self-regulating entities, while the states are always and everywhere bad and overregulating monstrosities, is a recurring nightmare in the history of capitalism.[12]

This brings us to a much larger question: is it the ideology that failed or was it improper implementation which caused this failure? This question needs serious contemplation as the Great Recession has a global cost that extends beyond money. Financially, the banking sector was the epicentre and consequently the worst hit. The IMF estimated that between the year 2007 and the first half of 2009, $1.5 trillion were written off as bad debts by banks. In addition, another $1.3 trillion loss was expected to be written off in the next few years. Of the total $2.8 trillion, USA would account for $1 trillion and the European banks for $1.6 trillion. In addition, in the fourth quarter of 2008, when the crisis hit the peak, Central Banks globally provided liquidity of $2.5 trillion to banks by buying their assets, as well as providing fresh capital of $1.5 trillion.[13]

While the financial impact of the global economic crisis is staggering, it pales into insignificance when compared with the human costs. The International Labour Organization in their *World of Work Report 2012* estimated that about 50 million jobs are missing at the end of 2011 compared to the pre-crisis level.[14] In addition, the Food and Agricultural Organization in their 2010 report estimated that the number of undernourished people had increased by 11 per cent in 2009, as a direct result of the financial crisis.[15] The end result, one in every seven humans on this planet is undernourished, with the total number of sufferers exceeding a billion. This grim situation calls for a serious evaluation of the alternatives available to the market economy, despite their poor track record.

Endnotes

1 Hayek, F., Prize Lecture, Lecture to the memory of Alfred Nobel, December 11, 1974

2 Gertchev, N., The Economic Nobel Prize, *Libertarian Papers,* 3, 9, (2011), p4 online at www.libertarianpapers.org

3 Presentation speech by Professor Lars E.O. Svensson of the Royal Swedish Academy of Sciences

4 *City Business Series, 2002, Derivatives,* International Financial Services London, June 2002, p3

5 Das, S., *Traders, Guns and Money, Knowns and Unknowns in the Dazzling World of Derivatives,* Pearson Power, 2007, pp189-90

6 Ibid, p160

7 *Derivatives 2009,* IFSL Research, June 2009, p1

8 Greenspan, A., *The Age of Turbulence,* Allen Lane, 2007, p229

9 Ibid, p230

10 Minksy, H. P., *The Financial Instability Hypothesis,* Working Paper No.74, May 1992, Prepared for Handbook of Radical Political Economy, edited by Philip Arestis and Malcolm Sawyer, Edward Elgar, Aldershot, 1993, pp8-9

11 UNCTCE., *The Global Economic Crisis: Systemic Failures and Multilateral Remedies,* 2009, p iii

12 Blyth, M., The End of American Capitalism? Mark Twain, Lake Wobegon, and the Current Crisis, *ejournal USA, The Global Financial System,* US Department of State/ Bureau of International Information Programs, p8

13 IFSL Research, *Banking 2010,* February 2010, p2

14 ILO, *World of Work Report 2012, Better jobs for a better economy,* International Labor Organization, 2012, p1

15 FAO, *The State of Food Unsecurity in the World, 2010, Addressing Food Security in Protracted Crisis,* FAO of United Nations, Rome, 2010, p 8

Chapter 7

A Steadying Anchor: Value-based or Value-neutral?

Value in the larger sense, as I understood it, means that power of an object to influence behaviour and pertains to all objects that are of importance to us.

– Charles H. Cooley, founder member, American Sociological Association[1]

Attempts to develop value-neutral economics on the lines of the physical sciences ran in parallel with the attempts to construct economic policies for realizing an egalitarian society. A prominent trigger for these developments was the advent of the Industrial Revolution, which coincided with the emergence of a market-based economy in which the factors of production — land, labour and capital were bought and sold in the marketplace. As labour became a market-traded commodity, government-sponsored poor-relief policies increased the labour cost, resulting in many employers calling for their abolition. Simultaneously the Socialist school emerged, calling for the abolition of private property, the first prerequisite of economics. The Socialists wanted to develop society on the principle of family, where every member contributes according to their ability and consumes according to their needs. Three prominent schools of socialistic thought, i.e. Communism, Gandhian economic ideas and Fabian Socialism are explored here. In the last two centuries, these ideas have only remained in the realm of thought and have not been fully realized. Given this, we explore the hurdles they faced and their future prospects.

Of Facts and Opinions

Jean-Baptiste Say was among the earliest writers to view economics as a science. In his most popular work, *A Treatise on Political Economy, or The Production, Distribution and Consumption of Wealth,* published in 1803, Say used the word science in its fourteen-page introduction, no less than seventy-one times with reference to the subject of political economy. This is in stark contrast to Adam Smith, who just a few decades earlier, writing his magnum opus, *The Wealth of Nations,* did not mention the word science even once to describe economics. The motive for Say to take a 'scientific' view was the desire to develop an objective set of principles that could be considered absolute truths. He believed that both moral and political science can also through logical and scientific analysis 'present truth equally indisputable'.[2]

Say, the founding father of supply-side economics, provided his followers in addition to their ideology, with the lens of objectivity.[a] What was initially an interesting approach to social science gradually began to acquire larger dimensions. With each passing decade, supply-side economists began to develop a science of economics. This science attempted to uncover truths and state the 'universal' laws governing economic phenomena. However, these truths and laws were not unanimously accepted by all. The

---

a Please refer to Chapter 5 to trace the influence of Jean Baptise Say on free-market advocates.

dissenting school of economists who saw their discipline as a means to an end, shaped by human values, strongly opposed these value-neutral developments. The dissenters' influence however waxed and waned with the changing tides of the economic cycle. During periods of crisis when economics came under intense scrutiny, they emerged in popular forums as viable alternatives and as the prosperous phase reappeared, they quickly faded into obscurity; but interestingly, they did not die out. Milton Friedman, the high priest of free-market advocates a century later, built on the original idea expounded by Say, in the face of this periodic opposition:

> Positive economics is in principle independent of any particular ethical position or normative judgment.... Its task is to provide a system of generalization that can be used to make correct predictions about the consequences of any change in circumstances. Its performance is to be judged by the precision, scope and conformity with experience of the predictions it yields. In short, positive economics is, or can be, an "objective" science, in precisely the same sense as any of the physical sciences.[3]

The steadily expanding influence of 'objective economics' led to the search for the trigger that pushed this social science to adopt the methods of a natural science. Philip Mirowski, who investigated this aspect, saw a parallel in the development of physics, especially in the field of energetics that developed in the second half of the nineteenth century. The economists of this period aped the methods of their physical science counterparts. In this insightful study, Mirowski noted that the marginal utility theory, which emerged during this period, had a few parallels with new discoveries in physics of the same era. Quoting Stanley

Jevons, one of the four concurrent discoverers[b] of the marginal utility theory, Mirowski highlighted the similarity seen between utility and gravity. To quote Jevons, 'Just as the gravitating force of a material body depends not alone on the mass of that body, but upon the masses and relative positions and distances of the surrounding material bodies, so utility is an attraction between a wanting being and what is wanted.'[4]

The marginal utility 'revolution' was also the period around which mathematics and mathematical models entered the domain of a till-then purely descriptive subject. Comparing economics with physics was the direct result of some economists viewing physics as nature's economics. Use of mathematics and mathematical models with their precision and repeatability brought in the element of objectivity to physics. At that point, economics was a purely descriptive discipline, lacking such objectivity. Mathematics plays a key role in promoting and shaping 'scientific' economics as the physics of humans. Mirowski quoting Francis Ysidro Edgeworth, an economist of that period, highlights three critical comparisons used to justify the use of mathematics by comparing its role in physics:

1. Every psychical phenomenon has a corresponding physical phenomenon.
2. Pleasure in the psychical side is the concomitant of energy in the physical side.
3. Maximizing energy is the objective of all investigations in physics, and maximizing pleasure would be the objective of all investigations in economics.

---

b For more information on the origin of the marginal utility theory, refer to Chapter 4.

Based on this rationale, mathematics slowly but surely entered the domain of economics. With it, the science of economics began to take deep roots, despite protests from the dissenting school. As the move to develop a value-agnostic, objective science gained momentum, their opponents – economists who believed in a value-based discipline – searched for the latent value hidden in the work of free-market advocates. What could be the latent value that guides 'positive economics'?

The Latent Value

Paul Hayne, a divinity student turned economist who, after five decades in this field as a scholar, prolific writer and professor, described himself as 'an economist with an interest in ethics rather than an ethicist with an interest in economics' answered this question succinctly. His knowledge of both the fields helped him observe that it was not possible 'even in principle' to construct a science of economics devoid of any particular ethical position. He went on to remark,

> Economic theory is a set of special spectacles through which economists filter experience in order to manufacture facts. If economists cannot see that they are wearing spectacles, or cannot recognize any of the ways in which political and ethical values have grounded their lenses, they had better at least recognize that many others have noticed. Moral theologians have definitely noticed.[5]

On deeper analysis, it becomes clear that while professing value neutrality, free-market advocates were tacitly endorsing the value of efficiency. The concepts of private property and self-orientation that were their foundation contributed in no small measure towards choosing this value subconsciously. Efficiency is a measure of the ratio between inputs and outputs.

It is in this measure that the value proponents saw an inherent value judgment. Even an individual with a mere acquaintance with physics knows that matter can neither be created nor destroyed; it can only be transformed. Therefore, efficiency only measures the quantity of 'valued' output to the total 'valued' inputs used in the process. Due to this selective lens used, the computation ignores any 'free' inputs. Likewise, the value-less output termed 'waste' is also ignored in computing efficiency. In the contemporary language of free-market advocates, this translates to their sole preference for economic growth, ignoring the 'waste', which includes, among others, the ill-effects of environmental degradation and the economic inequality it breeds with its latent trigger for social unrest.

The proponents of value-based economics are quick to point out that, unlike gravity which operates universally, free-market economics requires a favourable setting to flourish. Nailing this need, the neo-conservative thinker Francis Fukuyama remarked, 'A decade that began with the so-called "Washington consensus" neo-liberal approach to development emphasizing the markets ended with a realization that in the absence of effective state institutions, no development would be possible'.[6] This realization resulted in the emergence of governance for commercial enterprises and the rule of law in political economies, as essential prerequisite for free-markets to function.

In contrast to the tacit value preference of free-market advocates, the value proponents choose a social vision first, based on human values. Subsequently they developed their economic theory to realize this social vision. Family, the basic social unit in every community, was the overarching ideal example for the value proponents. Ideally, in a family, members contribute according to their ability and consume based on their need, without any conscious attempt to correlate the two. The value proponents wanted to enlarge this idea to the entire community, especially as social developments were moving in the direction of diluting not only family and social ties, but also the government's initiatives to help the poor, which had evolved out of a deeply-felt need over the centuries.

Box 7.1
The Origin of Government Funded Poor-relief

Ever since civilization began, the rich and the poor have been a feature of every human society. In each society, the rich provided the poorest with alms to survive, in most cases because this was mandated by religion. It was in England, in the aftermath of the Black Plague, which led to a severe labour shortage, that alms giving was first legally banned. This ban on alms was to ensure that every able-bodied labourer was available for work. A byproduct of the alms ban was that specific provisions were legislated, in order to care for the 'impotent' poor, which included the sick, the invalid, the aged and single women with children. Over the centuries, the material success of England provided the rest of the world an economic model to adopt for replicating their material success. This, in turn, influenced the approach to poor-relief in other parts of the world too.

The word poor is derived from the word *pauperes*. In ninth- and tenth-century Europe, *pauperes* were commoners who did not carry weapons and hence needed protection from other weapon-bearing members of the society. While they were not economically affluent, by no means were they socially despised; on the contrary, a section of the poor was placed on a moral pedestal. It followed from the divine social order held forth in the Bible[c], that the poor were considered superior, especially if they had voluntarily renounced wealth. A prevailing social practice was for noble and wealthy persons to wash the feet of the voluntarily poor and invite them to dine at their homes, as they represented a path to divinity. The practice of giving alms too was encouraged by many religions as it benefited both the receiver and the giver.

In England, the situation changed dramatically around 1348 as the Black Plague had wiped out a large section of the working population, threatening the material wellbeing of their 'masters' as the surviving workers demanded higher wages. This situation resulted in the enactment of the First Statute of Labourers in 1349. The preamble identified that there was a shortage of servants, with those willing to work demanding higher wages, while others preferring to beg rather than work.[7] To remedy the situation, this Act ordained compulsory work for wages at pre-epidemic rates. Every healthy man or woman below the age of sixty, who did not have a job or their own home, was bound to work for anyone who requisitioned for their labour. If individuals refused to serve, they would be imprisoned. In addition, any employer offering or promising higher wages was penalized with a fine.

This Act defined the poor as people without their 'own home'. It enslaved the poor to work; not to a single master, but to masters in general. Prior to this Act, people without homes, a section of which included the wandering vagabonds

---

c   Poverty, chastity and obedience were the three Counsels of Perfection recognized by the Church and mandated for the evangelical class. These three practices enabled an individual to focus their full attention to serving God. Similar concepts existed in most other religions where voluntary renouncement of wealth was prized. Ascetic, fakir, hermit, monk and sanyasi are favourable names for all those who practiced voluntary poverty and were honoured for their chosen path.

who voluntarily renounced wealth, were able to live on alms. A specific provision of this Act, formulated to ensure that all available hands worked, made the giving of alms to able-bodied workers punishable. In short, this Act reflected the changing attitudes of society towards the homeless and halted alms-giving.[d]

Soon after this enactment, realization dawned on the implementers that the poor were not all the same. Some who did not work simply could not work. This realization resulted in the enactment of new provisions in 1388 to treat women with children and sick individuals, who begged for alms, with leniency. Over time, this list expanded as the legislators confronted social reality. They also made alternative arrangements for the indigent and incapable, instead of letting them beg for their livelihoods. Funds for this poor relief came from the local population. Preachers, pastors, vicars and curates were encouraged to sermonize and collect funds. Initially a voluntary contribution, it soon became a local levy collected by force.[8]

The Poor Law of 1601 made a big difference. This Act provided for relief to the poor under three categories – the poor by impotence, the poor by casualty and the thriftless poor.[9] To the impotent poor, i.e. those who could not help themselves, direct assistance was provided. To the poor by casualty, i.e. the unemployed, work was provided. The thriftless poor, i.e. poor by choice, were imprisoned in the houses of correction. Gradually the government assumed the cost of providing this relief. Over time, the workhouse and the poorhouse became common social institutions in England.

---

d A second Act was passed in 1350 to strengthen the provisions of wage control by fixing specific wages for various categories and plugging some leaks in the earlier Act.

Initially the workhouse housed the unemployed who were put to work to defray at least a portion of their costs. Unpleasant conditions were intentionally created and social restrictions imposed on the inmates to ensure that the workhouse did not become an attractive substitute to working for a livelihood. In contrast, poorhouses were primarily intended for the sick, the aged and the invalid. Though the inmates of the poorhouse did not have to work, their living conditions were made equally unattractive.

Triggers for Change

The Industrial Revolution of the eighteenth and nineteenth century in England produced material success on a scale unprecedented in human history. At the centre of this revolution was the factory that produced not only material wealth, but also an equally impactful social byproduct on a colossal scale – human misery. For the first time, labour was engaged in large numbers in a tightly-monitored work environment: the factory. In the factory, the relationship between the employer and the employed was only economic. In contrast, in the earlier agricultural setup, when labour was used by the feudal lord it was seen as a multifaceted relationship, with enormous social implications. The labourer and his family had a place to live, with access to some land that could house their possessions (such as a cow, sheep, few hens and a kitchen garden or some elements of it). The entire family toiled for their feudal overlord, thereby earning a livelihood, with the children too lending a hand. Viewed from the present perspective, this is not the desired form of relationship as it has strong feudal overtones that impinge on individual freedom and human rights. At the same time, contrasted with the factory, there is an element of economic security. In the factory, not only is economic security lost, but with it even the basic means for existence, which are a prerequisite for freedom. The end result is that human rights are also taken away in the factory environment.

For the first time, in factories the employer-worker relationship turned purely economic. Karl Polanyi, the economic philosopher, identified this change brought on by the Industrial Revolution, in his classic, *The Great Transformation.* He remarked, 'Man under the name of labour, nature under the name of land, were made available for sale; the use of labour power could be universally bought and sold at a price called wages, and the use of land could be negotiated for a price called rent.' With it, a market for labour and land was established, where the prevailing wages and rent determined the quantity demanded. All other factors faded into oblivion.

Box 7.2
1834: The Birth of Modern Capitalism

The last decade of the eighteenth century saw increased distress in British society. The conditions of wage earners deteriorated as for the first time inflation[e] began to take its toll. Fixed wage earners could not meet their essential needs as prices of essential commodities galloped. Moved by poverty and the struggle of wage earners to balance budgets, in a unique action, the justices of peace in the county of Berkshire linked wages to the price of bread and the number of members in a family. Wages were now linked not just to the work done but also to family needs. Workers were entitled to receive this assured wage that met their basic family needs. If the employer did not pay it,

---

e   In 1793, a war with France resulted in the English Government resorting to deficit financing resulting in inflation.

the shortfall was to be made good under publicly-funded poor relief. This unique system was called the Speenhamland Act[f], after the town in which it was first initiated.

The Speenhamland Act of 1796 had multifold implications. It moved poor relief from indoor, as in a workhouse or a poorhouse, to outdoor relief, at the place of the family's residence, by supplementing the wages paid. This outdoor relief assumed four distinct forms – first, an allowance to supplement wages to those already working at below the designated wage; second, payment to the unemployed over what they could earn though partial employment; third, employers forced to hire the unemployed or pay a tax in lieu of doing so; and finally, public employment via building roads and gravel pits. Karl Polanyi commenting on this act remarked, 'it introduced no less a social and economic innovation than the "right to live." and until abolished in 1834, it effectively prevented the establishment of a competitive labour market'.[10]

Karl Polanyi identified the year 1834 and the ending of the Speenhamland allowances as the birth of modern capitalism. The labour market is an essential component of capitalist economy, as labour is one of the four factors of production. The prevalence of Speenhamland allowances made a free labour market untenable, as the wage level lost all meaning in influencing the demand for labour. It assured the worker of a guaranteed subsistence. Employers could induce labour to work only if they offered a wage higher than the minimum amount assured by the Speenhamland act. With its revocation, for the first time a labour market emerged in England, where labour could be hired and fired, influenced only by the wage offered.

---

f   The Speenhamland Act has many similarities to the National Rural Employment Guarantee Scheme in place in India today.

This new labour market driven purely by money exchange had a dramatic impact on working conditions. Earlier, labour worked with limited supervision. In factories not only did the level of supervision increase, but also the working conditions were minutely regulated. In the labour market, children and women were valued at a premium due to the lower wages at which they could be hired. In addition, demand for them increased as for many delicate operations, their dexterity was more productive, making their employment more profitable. It was not unusual for children aged seven years and above to work a fifteen-hour workday. They began at 5 a.m. and ended only at 8 p.m. with two half-hour breaks for breakfast and dinner.[11] After work, these children were housed in 'prentice-houses' located next to the factories, where the conditions were equally inhumane.

The plight of these children is what moved Robert Owen, the first among the social visionaries of that period, to develop an alternative economic system. He outlined a concrete action plan for an alternative model to address the new challenges posed by the industrial economy. His plan envisaged a society that would combine filial empathy with industrial production. Many philosophers over the ages had speculated on utopias and articulated their thoughts on different modes of organizing society to increase the welfare of the less fortunate. The prevailing labour conditions, especially those of the children, forced Robert Owen and his contemporaries to not only voice their vision, but also to act and realize it. These visionaries seeded an alternative to classical economic thoughts based on private property and self-interest. They wanted to build a new society on the tripod of collective ownership, cooperation and altruism.

Banning Private Property

The nineteenth century saw multiple variations of a socialistic vision emerge, based on collective ownership, cooperation and altruism. This cluttered space covered both theorists and practitioners. Yves Guyot, a free-market advocate, not only captured the prevailing landscape of socialist thinkers but also provided the historical context to appreciate their inspiration in his book, *Socialist Fallacies*. Covering ideas from the time of Plato, he organized them into practitioner and theorist in the first two parts. The remaining book discussed at length the idea of scientific socialism propounded by Karl Marx and Frederick Engels, reflecting their relative importance among other socialist thinkers, even before the birth of the twentieth century. Two decades into the twentieth century, after the Russian Revolution in 1919, their stature grew exponentially as for the majority across the globe their vision represented the only viable alternative to free-market economy.

Das Capital was Marx's magnum opus. In its three volumes[g], he analyzed the capitalist economy and identified both its strengths and weaknesses. His analysis built on the thoughts of the earlier economists. Among others, Ibn Khaldun and Adam Smith, living centuries earlier, had recognized labour as the primary source of value. Answering the question, how can one accumulate wealth disproportionate to their individual labour, Ibn Khaldun identified the role of rank in society. He remarked, rank made other individuals part with their wealth voluntarily to either gain undue benefit or avoid harm from the rank-holder. With a keen sense of observation he

---

g   The first volume was published during Marx's lifetime. The second and the third were published after his death, by Engels, who edited the final version based on the multiple manuscripts left behind by Marx.

noted that the higher the rank, the greater the accumulation; for they touched more people and had a larger influence, commanding greater gifts. But, Ibn Khaldun lived in the pre free-labour market era, where the wage was not set by demand and supply of labour.

Living in the age of the 'free' labour market, Marx traced the accumulated wealth of the capitalist to the surplus labour value, i.e. the value created by the labourer but denied to him. In the words of Marx and Engels, 'The rate of surplus value is therefore an exact expression for the degree of exploitation of labour-power by capital, or of the labourer by the capitalist'.[12] *Das Capital* in all its three volumes provided a comprehensive and valid critique of the capitalist economy. However, in terms of ideas or plan to realize an alternative social system it did not offer anything concrete. For specific solutions, the *Communist Manifesto* of 1847 remains the primary document. Additionally, in this Manifesto, the position of the communists is identified with respect to the other socialist actors, by describing their specific role, which is as a movement to attain the immediate aim of enforcing the momentary interests of the working class and also caring for the future of that movement.[13]

The *Communist Manifesto* was the first joint publication where Marx and Engels spelt out their alternative to the free-market economy. Striking at the roots, they wrote, 'In this sense, the theory of the Communists may be summed up in the single sentence: Abolition of private property.'[14] Further, commenting on the predominantly economic nature of the relationships in capitalistic society, they noted that personal worth was now equated to a monetary count. Honoured professionals like doctors, lawyers, poets and scientists were evaluated as paid labourers. On another level, they noted that the multi-dimensional concept of freedom was turned into a mono-dimensional call for free trade, which by focusing only on the economic sphere, ignored elements of oppression and coercion present in other aspects of life. Turning to family, the most personal of relationships in society, and ideally untainted by economic factors, they noted that with the advent of factories and their form of child labour, 'The bourgeoisie has torn away from the family its sentimental veil and has reduced the family relations to a mere money relation'.[15]

The *Communist Manifesto* began with a ferocious attack on the free-market economy, which was followed by a comprehensive ten-point action plan to establish a Communist society. The main focus of the plan was to abolish private property and inheritance rights, introduce progressive income tax, provide free education for all children in public schools and make it a duty for every individual to work.

Reflecting these ideas, Communism at its most visible level translated to the negation of private property and state control over all channels of production. As the owners of private property and channels of production do not voluntarily give up their rights, violence in the form of revolution was an inherent feature of Communism. The *Manifesto* acknowledges this by noting that 'despotic inroads on the rights of property' were 'unavoidable'.[16]

In the twentieth century, the global influence of Communism gained momentum starting with the Russian revolution of 1919. With every passing decade the Red revolution spread to all parts of the world from the USSR and China. However, this movement was dramatically halted in the 1980s. It is possible that the lack of freedom for its citizens was a critical element in making the system unstable and unviable. The disintegration of the USSR in 1989, the collapse of the Berlin Wall and the tacit adoption of capitalist methods in China, all around the same time, rendered this ideology all but a relic. What are now left behind are the broad principles on which it was conceived. The Ten Point programme found in the *Communist Manifesto* is a good pointer to the residue of this ideology.

Box 7.3

Ten Point Programme of *The Communist Manifesto*

1. Abolition of property in land and application of all rents of land to public purposes.
2. A heavy progressive or graduated income tax.
3. Abolition of all rights of inheritance.
4. Confiscation of the property of all emigrants and rebels.
5. Centralization of credit in the hands of the state, by means of a national bank with State capital and an exclusive monopoly.
6. Centralization of the means of communication and transport in the hands of the state.
7. Extension of factories and instruments of production owned by the State; the bringing into cultivation of wastelands, and the improvement of the soil generally in accordance with a common plan.
8. Equal liability of all to work. Establishment of industrial armies, especially for agriculture.
9. Combination of agriculture with manufacturing industries; gradual abolition of the distinction between town and country by a more equitable distribution of the population.

> 10. Free education for all children in public schools. Abolition of children's factory labour in its present form. Combination of education with industrial production.
>
> Extract from *The Communist Manifesto*

After its dismal performance in the twentieth century, both the critiques and the supporters of Communism held one view – its implementation was disastrous to say the least. John Burdon Sanderson Haldane, the famous British biologist and the proponent of the modern theory of evolution[h], best explained the reasons why centrally-planned socialist economies fail. More importantly, his view can be considered impartial and objective, as he was a socialist – a member of the Communist Party and a weekly columnist for the *Daily Worker*, the party publication in Britain. Examining the feasibility of a centrally-planned socialist society in the context of his biological investigations, he pondered on its practicality. The biologist in him, who saw functionality reflected in the sizes and shapes of various organisms, wondered how socialism could be adapted to a large society. Writing in 1920s, he conceded the feasibility of implementing socialism in small countries like Andorra or Luxembourg, but could not find parallels in biology of the functionality socialism sought to implant in larger countries. Illustrating with a visually appealing analogy, he described the futility of implementing socialism in large countries, 'I find it no easier to picture a completely socialized British Empire or United States than an elephant turning somersaults or a hippopotamus jumping a hedge'.[17]

---

h   Haldane combined the Darwin's theory of survival of the fittest and Mendel's theory of genetics to formulate the modern theory of evolution.

While the critics argued that an idea is only as good as its implementation, its ardent supporters clutched the idea that better means would help them realize their vision in the days ahead.

Sharing Private Property

Social inequalities high and low, prince and peasant, colour and race?

Economic differences of rich and poor, the exploiter and the exploited, the owner, labour and slave?

Famines, pestilence and oppression?

Traffic in goods harmful to the body such as narcotics and strong drinks?

One nation lording it over the other – imperialism?

Nations warring against nation?[18]

The above is not an extract from *The Communist Manifesto*, though it could be for its thoughts and style.[i] The extract is from the writings of Joseph Cornelius Kumarappa, a Gandhian disciple, who lived with the Mahatma in the twentieth century and expressed his economic ideas. Just as *The Communist Manifesto* laid out ten points to usher in a communist society, in his second book on economics, *Economy of Permanence*, the Gandhian economist Kumarappa too identified suggestions that would guide the planning of an economy embodying the principles dear to the Mahatma.

---

i 'Freeman and slave, patrician and plebeian, lord and serf, guild-master and journeyman, in a word, oppressor and oppressed, stood in constant opposition to one another, carried on an uninterrupted, now hidden, now open fight, a fight that each time ended, either in a revolutionary reconstitution of society at large, or in the common ruin of the contending class.' This extract is from the second chapter of *The Communist Manifesto*.

He identified eight principles (listed below) [j] as the corner-stone for his economic system:

1. Planning should benefit the life of every living person in the society.
2. Self-sufficiency in food and shelter is the first priority.
3. In agriculture, first prioritize food for consumption and raw materials for village and cottage industries. Where production, distribution and consumption take place in the village, it is a village industry. Where only production takes place in the village, it is a cottage industry. Use taxation to achieve this objective.
4. Adopt labour intensive production, do not ape the English, who were capital-rich in the eighteenth century or the USA which is short of labour.
5. Production of luxuries to be taken up only after necessities for all people are met.
6. Commence production for export markets only after the domestic requirements are met.
7. Co-operative institutions would promote self-sufficiency.
8. Economic dictatorship and political democracy cannot co-exist. Economic decentralization is the only solution for a meaningful and functioning democracy.

Summing up the similarities between Marxist and the Gandhian thoughts crisply, Kumarappa wrote 'At its best and when superficially looked at, Communism does not appear to aim at anything less than what Gandhism does'.[19] He went on to add that they differ with regard to the means adopted.

---

j These principles have been extracted and rearranged from what is contained in the narrative of the original text to provide it a logical flow in its summarized form.

A deeper analysis reveals that there are many more features in common between the two ways of thought. At the same time, the contrast between the two in achieving the end objective could also not be more glaring.

Mahatma Gandhi enunciated a comprehensive way of life, without dividing it into social, religious or economic spheres. It was his trusted disciple, a professionally qualified accountant, who articulated Gandhian economic thoughts. Kumarappa was not just a theoretical economist. He was also a practioner who implemented his economic model. As the head of the All India Village Industries Association, he chose to implement the Gandhian economic model. However, ill health after Indian independence and an early death in 1960 prevented much more of the Gandhian economy from being realized in his lifetime.

Over a period of two decades, Kumarappa wrote three books that had predominantly economic content. The first of these books, titled *Why The Village Movement,* was published in 1936. In the preface, Kumarappa gave his reason for writing this book: 'Among the thinking people the world over there is a growing dissatisfaction as to the efficacy of capitalism as a cure for the poverty that faces us'.[20]

Nine years later, Kumarappa wrote his second book on economics, titled *Economy of Permanence.* In the preface he identified its link to his first book by noting that while the first book compared the status in India with leading western countries, in the second, he outlined a positive prescription suited to the Indian people. In his third book, *Gandhian Economic Thought,* published after Gandhi's death, Kumarappa summarized and interpreted Gandhian economic thought. In these three books, Kumarappa extracted the essence of economic thought embedded in the Gandhian way of life.

Kumarappa joined hands with the socialists in viewing

economics as a fascinating psychological study. He was critical of the Western classical economists who wanted to view economics as a physical science. He noted that English scholars like Marshall and Pigou had studied economics as a physical science like laws of gravity and missed the 'fascinating psychological study of human nature.'[21] Further, in sharp contrast to Adam Smith, who in his *Wealth of Nations* identified and made respectable the pursuit of self-interest, Kumarappa laid as his foundation the twin values of truth and non-violence. Writing on these two principles that shape Gandhian economics, he reasoned that economics is an integral part of life and cannot be separated from it.[22]

In all his three books, Kumarappa took an evolutionary approach to arrive at Gandhian economics. He did concede that the prevailing capitalist economy was based on self-interest and at variance with Gandhian thoughts. He saw Gandhian economics as the next stage in economic evolution; a stage in human society where duties would prevail, dethroning the reigning deities: rights born of self-interest, as the primary human motives in an economy. Noting that this change would not happen by itself, he looked at education as a means to usher it in. Optimistically, he felt that when this stage is reached, it would be easy to recognize, as duties would prevail and the concept of rights would fade into oblivion.

Around the Corner or The Brand New World

Marxist and Gandhian proponents both viewed the capitalistic economic system as transitory, with a socialistic form succeeding it. Kumarappa laid out an insightful analysis of the evolution of economic systems in human history. He viewed it from the multiple angles of dominant instincts, inter-relationship between production and consumption, representation in nature, forms of society, economic systems and the different stages of evolution in human society. In this evolutionary path, he saw the Gandhian economy succeeding the centralized socialist economies like the one practiced in the USSR.

Table 7.1: Gandhian View of the Evolution of Economic Systems as posited by J C Kumarappa

Description	Stage1	Stage2	Stage3	Stage4	Stage5
Dominant Instinct	**Parasitic**	**Predatory**	**Enterprising**	**Gregarious**	**Service**
Relationship between production and consumption	Only consumption, no production		Production & Consumption	Production exceeds consumption	Production without any thought to personal consumption
Representation					
in nature	Tiger#	Monkey#	Bird	Honey-bee	Mother
in human Society	Robbers & thieves	Pickpockets	Farmers	Hindu Joint family	Mother-child relationship
in economic system	Imperialism	Global dominance by USA through markets	Self-sufficient agricultural economy	Soviet Russia & Nazi Germany	Yet to be realized
Dominated by	**Animal pleasures**		**Material needs**	**Altruist feelings**	**Ideals**
Stage in human evolution	Tribal Groups		Capitalism	Socialism	Gandhian society
Reflecting the human ability of	Imitation	Adoption	Material creation	Social innovation	Sublimation

 # Kumarappa identifies the tiger's relationship with food as parasitic, as it kills its prey; and in the case of monkey, only as predatory, as its method is not fatal to its victims.

Using the lens of truth and non-violence, Kumarappa measured violence in an economy by its dependence on non-renewable resources. Terming non-renewable resources as reservoirs, he noted that due to their finite availability, dependence on them would lead to violence. On the contrary, the use of renewable resources, he noted is non-violent. Further, he saw in his five-stage evolutionary path a movement away from violence towards non-violence. The parasitic instinct in Stage 1 represented by the violent tiger which kills its prey evolves into a less violent monkey that lives by plundering, though violent but not fatal to its victims. Likewise, altruism replaces individualism (which is dominant in the first three stages), with cooperation replacing competition, a more violent form of interaction. Acknowledging that a gregarious ideal drove Soviet Russia and Nazi Germany, he noted they had adopted violent means to enforce their ideas, which was their shortcoming. In contrast, the Gandhian economy he visualized would fuse altruism with non-violence to attain sublimation.

Turning to human organizations, Kumarappa saw them divided into two distinct groups separated by the use of violence: carnivorous, food-hunting, self-centred packs of animals like wolves versus the herbivorous, security-oriented, and herd-focused animals like cattle. He highlighted this line of thought, probably comparing highly-centralized communism with the decentralized Gandhian economy, when he elaborated on the difference between these two types of organizations on multiple fronts. Reflecting dispassionately on the table, it looks as if Kumarrapa may have attributed some qualities to these types of animals based on his perceptions, which may not be borne out by actual facts.

Table 7.2 Contrast between Pack type Organizations and Herd type Organizations: Kumarappa's View

Pack type or Individualistic Organizations	Herd type or Social organizations
Central control and organization of power	Social control, decentralization and distribution of power
Short-term thinking	Long-term outlook
Rigorous discipline	Rule of conduct and social regulatory mechanism
Disregard of the welfare of the actual workers or contributors to the success	Safeguard the weak and the helpless
Suppression of individuality of workers	Encouragement given to individual growth and tolerance
Prospect for gain the motive for all activities	Activities directed by a set of ideals and social movement
Concentration of benefits obtained and the sharing of them amongst a limited few	Distribution of gains as wide as possible according to the needs of the individuals
To gather as much without reference to altruistic value	The object is to satisfy the needs judged from an altruistic view

Kumarappa did not leave his economic thoughts at an abstract level, suitable only for deliberations and debate. He outlined a role for each individual in bringing about a Gandhian economy by being a responsible consumer. The need to know how goods were produced was his logic for advocating the local production of goods. Just as a responsible individual would not buy a necklace from a robber who has murdered a child to get it, even if offered at a substantial discount, Kumarappa believed that each consumer had a responsibility to answer these specific questions related to production before they consume:

a.   Where does the article come from?

b.   Who makes the article?

c.   From what material?

d.   Under what conditions do the workers live and work?

e.   What proportion of the final price do they get as wages?

f.   How is the rest of the money distributed?

g.   How is the article produced?

h.   How does the industry fit into the national economy?

i.   What relation has it to the other nations?

Kumarappa believed that the consumer could only answer these questions if production took place near the place of consumption. The idea of promoting local production is seen in the inadequacy of price to reflect all dimensions of value, as it captures only the economic aspect.

Though not explicitly identified by Kumarappa, the increasing gestation period for satisfying a need is what becomes visible in the evolutionary path identified by him. In the first two stages (parasitic and predatory mode), the gap between a need arising and its satisfaction is almost negligible, though a critic may say there is an element of planning involved in both that defers gratification. In the third stage of enterprise, the gap expands and is measurable in terms of months and years, but still within the perceivable horizon. As we move to the gregarious state, driven by a sense of altruism, the gratification period can be extended significantly, though still there is a need to see the results within a lifetime. When idealism dominates, as in the Gandhian society, the focus is on means. The focus is belief-driven: the belief that pursuing the right path will lead to the desired goal, even if it is beyond their lifetime. At the centre of this belief is the idea that human nature is malleable.

The Basis for Optimism

The study of human nature and its evolution has been at the fringe of mainstream economics. A century before in 1914, Wesley C. Mitchell wrote an article in *The Quarterly Journal of Economics*, titled 'Human Behaviour and Economics: A Survey of Literature'. In this article, he argued that human nature should be a subject of study in economics. An interesting point he noted was the divide between the mainstream economists who believed in a reasonably stable human nature and the socialists who believe that human nature evolves. Exploring the literature on behaviour study, he outlined an interesting evolutionary path. Tracing the source of behaviour from unicellular organisms to multi-cellular organisms and from there to the development of the brain and the ability to access extra-somatic knowledge he outlined its implications, as tabulated here:

Table 7.3 Evolution of Human Behaviour

Stage	1	2	3	4
Basis for behaviour	Tropism	Reflex	Instinct	Intelligence
Found in Organisms	Unicellular	Multi-cellular, with nervous system	With a central repository, brain	With evolved memory
Basis of behaviour	Act	React	Respond	Adapt

Two factors emerge from this evolutionary path. The first is a growing ability to delay gratification. As organisms evolved, their lifespan grew from a few hours to a few years, eventually spanning decades. The growth in size and lifespan exposed these organisms to more varied environments, where survival required tailor-made responses. Options too varied from a singular response in unicellular organisms to a choice between responding or abstaining in multi-cellular organisms. The addition of a central repository brain brought with it a wider range of options. These options can be placed on a scale where time is measured by the gap between opportunity to satisfy a desire and the exercise of that option, indicating an ability to delay gratification.

The second aspect of this evolutionary path is in the expanding concept of self. The evolution from a unicellular organism to a multi-cellular organism results in an expanded concept of self from single cell to multiple cells. As we move to the third stage, we see the concept of self expand to a family, with the maternal instinct developing into the most potent of all instincts. In the fourth stage, experience plays a key role in shaping the intelligence of individuals. These experiences need not be personal. The process of education enables vicarious experiences to be as effective in influencing human memory. The development of intelligence has expanded the concept of self beyond blood relationships to an entity spanning political bodies like nations. For a small but hopefully fast-expanding minority, it has extended to encompass the entirety of humanity.

In the last two centuries of human history, a relatively short period, we have seen slavery abolished but not eliminated, discrimination towards females outlawed but not eradicated and racial bias globally censured but sporadically erupting. For millennia slavery, gender bias and racial bigotry were integral parts of human societies. Many even believed that they are hard-wired into our genes. Education and introspection are seeing these practices gradually fade into history books. In the same way, individualism, selfishness and greed too, need not be accorded the status of genetic hard code.

For the diehard socialist, there is a glimmer of hope on the distant horizon that the primary human motive could be altruism and with it, the advent of a socialistic society could be a reality. Matt Ridley in his book *The Origin of Virtue* provides an explanation for why cooperation and altruism could emerge victorious. After discarding the 'individualistic self-centred' explanations for altruism like kinship, reciprocity and moral restraints, he notes that evolutionary selection could be made, not at the level of individuals, but at the social group level. Explaining this he wrote, 'cooperative groups thrive and selfish ones do not, so cooperative societies have survived at the expense of others.'[23]

Despite these positive explanations, the realization of socialistic ideal societies in the near future seems to be a long odds punt. But a group of English intellectuals in the nineteenth century started an incremental approach to getting there.

The Fabian Approach[24]

As the revolutionary approach to abolishing private property was being organized elsewhere and the evolutionary approach yet to kick in, a group of English intellectuals in 1884 sought to take the democratic route and place the idea of socialism in the domain of political debate. Realizing the strength of the well-entrenched incumbent position enjoyed by private property in society, they opted to play a patient, waiting game. The Roman General Fabius Maximus was their inspiration. Fabius avoided the better-armed, larger, well-entrenched Carthaginian army led by Hannibal in the Second Punic War in direct battle. This denied the stronger army a victory, which enabled Fabius to keep the morale of his allies high. Instead, he engaged the Carthaginian army in irritating skirmishes to weaken it. Inspired by the Roman General, these intellectuals named their group the Fabian Society. In their first tract published in April 1884 titled, '*Why are the many poor?*' they printed two mottoes[k] on the title page, the second of which read:

> For the right movement you must wait, as Fabius did patiently, when warring against Hannibal, though many censured his delays; but when the time comes you must strike hard, as Fabius did, or your waiting will be in vain and fruitless.[25]

Inspired by the ideas of Henry George as articulated in his book, *Poverty and Progress,* published around the same time in the United States of America, the Fabian Society recognized that in a democratic society, change could be achieved by political methods. A Bill drafted by a competent lawyer could be enacted into law by a majority of the voters acting through their elected representatives. They also realized that to introduce total socialism, revolution was not essential: it could be brought about piecemeal.[26] While the approach was gradual, their intention was not. Reflected in their Manifesto drafted by George Bernard Shaw, an early member, is their clear intent, which among other things stated, 'Nationalization of Land in some form is a public duty'.[27]

Based on the belief that a socialistic society could be achieved by educating individuals, the Fabian Society started

---

k   The first motto of the Fabian socialists was 'Wherefore it may not be gainsaid that the fruits of this man's long talking of counsel—and (by the many so deemed) untimeous delays—was the safe-holding for all men, his fellow citizens, of the Common Weal.'

a multi-pronged programme. Their activities included, among others, publishing tracts to popularize socialist ideas, organizing lectures, establishing libraries and actively canvassing for legislative change. To give an idea of the magnitude of their efforts, in the year 1890-91, ten tracts were published and 335,000 copies printed. In the following year, 3,339 lectures were organized. George Bernard Shaw and Annie Besant were among the prominent speakers. Libraries were started with books on socialism, economics, history and social problems. Boxes, each containing around twenty books, were lent to cooperative societies at 10 shillings per year. In addition to one-off lectures, regular education programmes were organized in the Liberal and Radical Working Men's Club of London every Sunday for eight months in a year. For the more interested students, a correspondence course was offered with textbooks containing questions at the end for the students to answer. The Fabian Society evaluated the answer scripts too.

On the legislative front, the Fabian Society canvassed among other issues, for an eight-hour workday, fair-wage policy and mid-day meals for schoolchildren. A year after they started their advocacy, in 1906 the mid-day meal scheme was enacted into law, showing the power of a democratic movement to influence economic outlays.

Prominent members of the Fabian Society also played a role in the establishment of the London School of Economics and Political Science. Henry Hutchinson, a generous member of Fabian Society who financed the initial lecture series, died in 1894, leaving an estate of around £9000 to be spent within the next ten years, after naming a few select members of the Fabian Society as trustees. They resolved that this fund would be used for a special work, and initiated the London School of Economics and Political Science. The objective of establishing this school was the realization that a knowledge of economic and political science was a necessity in social reconstruction and it was essential for public officials to be provided with an opportunity to learn the modern line of thought in these domains.[28]

To ensure that the School they established was independent of their own bias, the trustees did not retain any control over it. They reasoned that the best science should be taught. Confident that their own ideas were right, they concluded the School would only endorse them after evaluation and if they were wrong, they concluded that it is better for the School to discredit them.[29]

Among all these significant contributions, the most critical one of the Fabian Society, as identified by Edward R. Pease, its secretary for the first twenty-five years, was in filling the gap left by Karl Marx, who had identified and highlighted the shortcomings of the capitalist society and also identified an alternative. However, as Pease noted,

> 'His [Marx's] followers did not notice that he had indicated no method, and devised no political machinery for the transition; or if they noticed it they passed over the omission as a negligible detail. If German Socialism would not suit, English Socialism had to be formulated to take its place.'[30]

The English socialists by proposing nationalization of land, railways, healthcare, mines and electric utilities by publishing Fabian Tracts made the private property debate an integral part of the democratic political process.

Global events over the last fifty years in general, and in particular, the developments over the last twenty years in India, the homeland of Mahatma Gandhi, are not very encouraging for the establishment of a socialistic Gandhian economy in the near future. To paraphrase Haldane, it looks as if the elephants will turn somersaults and the hippopotamus jump the hedges only when the intensity of the gravitational force of self-interest is significantly reduced. Until then, the only influence of the socialist thinkers seems to be in tempering the existing free-market economy with social concerns. Humane capitalism is the result of this influence.

Endnotes

1 Cooley, C.H., The Progress of Pecuniary Valuation, *The Quarterly Journal of Economics,* November, 1915

2 Say, J.B., *A Treatise on Political Economy; Or the Production, Distribution and Consumption of Wealth,* translated from French by C. R. Prinsep, Batoche Books, Kitchener, 2001, p21

3 Friedman, M., The Methodology of Positive Economics, *In Positive Economics,* Chicago, University of Chicago Press, 1966,p 4

4 Mirowshi, P., Physics and the 'marginal revolution', *Cambridge Journal of Economics*, 1984, 8,p 363

5 Hayne, P., *"Are Economists Basically Immoral ? and Other Essays on Economics, Ethics and Religion,* The Online Library of Liberty, 2008, p86

6 Fukuyama, F., 'Still Disenchanted? The Modernity of Postindustrial Capitalism' CSES Working Paper Series Paper #3, February 2003, p15

7 Quoted in the article, *Five Hundred Years of the English Poor Laws, 1349-1834: Regulating The Working and Non Working Poor,* by William P. Quigley, p6

8 Oakesshott, J. F., *The Humanizing of the Poor Law,* Fabian Tract No.54, The Humanitarian League, 1987, p4

9 Ibid, p4

10 Polanyi, K., *The Great Transformation,* Beacon Press, Boston, Ninth Print, 1968, Chapter 7

11 Gordon, P., Robert Owen, Published in *Prospectus*, a quarterly review of education by UNESCO, vol.24, no.1/2, 1994, p279

12 Marx, K., *Capital: A Critique of Political Economy,* Volume 1, Progress Publishers, Moscow, Based on First English Edition, 1887, p143

13 Marx, K., and F. Engels, *Communist Manifesto,* Marxist Internet Archive, Marxist.org, p34

14 Ibid, p22

15 Ibid, p16

16 Ibid, p26

17 Haldane, J.B.S., *On Being the Right Size,* Collection of Essays, edited by John Maynard Smith, p9

18 Kumarappa, J. C., *Practices and Precepts of Jesus,* Navajivan Press, 1952

19 Kumarappa, J.C, *Gandhian Economic Thought,* Vora & Co., Publishers Ltd, 1951, p62

20 Kumarappa, J.C., *Why The Village Movement,* A. B. Serva Seva Sangh Prakashan, 1936, Seventh Edition, p5

21 Ibid, p70

22 Kumarappa, J.C, *Gandhian Economic Thought,* Vora & Co., Publishers Ltd, 1951, p9

23 Ridley, M., *The Origin of Virtue,* Penguin Books, 1996, p175

24 Information for this section is taken from Pease, E. R., *The History of the Fabian Society,* E. P. Dutton & Company, Publishers, New York. Mr. Pease was the secretary of the Fabian society for twenty-five years.

25 Ibid, p24

26 Ibid, p49

27 Ibid, p25

28 Ibid, p75

29 Ibid, p76

30 Ibid, p140

Chapter 8

The Last Horizon: Economic Democracy

Above all things, good policy is to be used that the treasure and moneys in a state be not gathered into few hands. Otherwise a state may have a great stock, and yet starve. And money is like muck, not good except it be spread.

— **Francis Bacon in *Of Sedations and Troubles***

Economic democracy can be defined as a society in which all individuals and groups participate in choosing how natural and social resources are utilized to realize the human potential of all individuals in society. Over the last hundred years, it is very evident that economic democracy is yet to be realized in most parts of the world where political democracy is accepted, although there is significant progress in some pockets.

A historical examination of how economic resources have become concentrated in the hands of a few individuals and the impact of this concentration is a good place to start our examination of why economic democracy is so elusive. When we differentiate between intra-generational and inter-generational wealth accumulation, we can see the benefits from the former in the form of promoting greater individual efforts, while seeing the inefficiencies inter-generational wealth transfers promote by providing inheritors with unearned luxuries. It is through this lens that the prevailing global inequality in wealth needs to be scrutinized and attempts made to correct it in the capitalist economies.

The impact of the purchasing power commanded by individuals and its influence on political and social decisions in an economy is the second aspect we will examine. The lack of a voice for a large number of vulnerable members of society, who do not command adequate purchasing power, and the implications of such a set-up are also considered. Nordic societies seem to be an exception in substantially reducing this vulnerable group, if not eliminating it. The ideas behind the Nordic economic model are studied to see its if it is adaptable elsewhere in the world.

Finally the popular management axiom, what is measured is managed, holds true in economics too. Economic policy is increasingly targeted to achieve GDP growth, an economic parameter of activity that is easy to measure. Often this growth is and could be at the cost of human welfare, as it ignores the impact of unequal income distribution and natural resource degradation.

Attempts to address these three challenges over human history are analysed and some suggestions are offered to resolve them.

A Unique Human Attribute

Jean-Jacques Rousseau wrote an interesting discourse in 1754 titled, *What Is The Origin of Inequality Among Men, And Is It Authorized by Natural Law?* In this, he examined the nature of inequality and the probable reasons for its continued existence. Rousseau noted two kinds of inequality: natural or physical inequality as a result of age, health, bodily strength and qualities of mind and soul; and moral or political inequality, which he sourced to wealth, honour and power, all of which depend on social convention for their existence. In short, we can term this second type economic inequality, or the divide between the rich and the poor. In all other species, only natural inequality separates the strong from the weak; humans are subject to natural inequalities as well, but they are not the only determinant of inequality. Rousseau, in this discourse, wanted to uncover the origin of socially-created economic inequality, which is a unique human attribute.

Rousseau began his enquiry with humans in their natural state. With what is at best conjuncture, as he himself admitted, he detailed a scenario where economic inequality in the state of nature was non-existent or in his words, 'hardly felt'. From this stage, he went on to trace the origin of this socially-created economic inequality. He reasoned that it could have arisen only when mutual dependence among the members of a society had taken firm roots. For in its absence, each individual would meet his or her own needs without giving any room for economic inequality to arise. Mutual dependence, he argued, led to exchange, and in exchange was embedded the concept of property which gave birth to this economic divide:

> But from the moment one man began to stand in need of the help of another; from the moment it appeared advantageous to any one man to have enough provisions for two, equality disappeared and property was introduced, work became indispensable, and vast forests became smiling fields, which man had to water with the sweat of his brow, and where slavery and misery were soon to germinate and grow up with the crops.[1]

After identifying the origin of economic inequality to the advent of private property, he went on to trace its growth to an increase in the division of labour in society and its consequent effect — the promotion of higher interdependence among individuals. In this interdependent society, he observed a unique relationship between the value placed by the society on a particular skill and its wider need. Identifying agriculture as the most essential of services in a society, he noted that the price commanded by agricultural products will be the least profitable of all other products as the poorest people must be able to afford it.[2]

From this observation, Rousseau extracted an interesting paradox, '*that arts in general are more lucrative in proportion as they are less useful*'. This belief is not unique to Rousseau but has a large following, stemming from the view that inequality in opportunities is unnatural, though many other reasons like economic efficiency and social costs are also advanced to eliminate it.

Box 8.1

The Contours of Economic Inequality

Economic inequality is visible in three primary dimensions today:

- between societies located in different geographies,
- in a given geography between the urban and rural sections, and
- within a given section between the numerous poor and a handful of the rich.

Looking at human history, the earliest advent of the three inequalities looks to have been the third one: in a given society, between the rich and the poor. Gordon Childe, the famous archaeologist writing in 1940s, identified the shift away from savagery[a] to 'an economic and scientific revolution that made the participants active partners with nature instead of parasites on nature.'[3] In the state of savagery, as among other mammals,

---

a   At the time Gordon Childe wrote in 1940s, savagery was an accepted term which defined the stage in human evolution when humans used fire, bows and pottery but had not learnt domestication of animals and agriculture.

there would have been inequality between human beings too. But this inequality would be of the natural kind, a result of age, health, mental and bodily strength. To collaborate with nature, humans needed to create and use tools and techniques. Individuals who mastered this art would have been placed in an advantageous position, creating the foundation for the first economic divide in a society. With the increasing use of tools and techniques, income too would have varied widely, depending on the tools available and the ability to use them, deepening the economic divide.

As the division of labour increased in society, towns and cities became more distinct. Although size and population density are the most visible aspect of the urban-rural divide, dependence on land for livelihood is the less-visible separator. Land dependence brings with it a fluctuating fortune, dependent on the vagaries of the weather. By producing the essentials to human life, rural fortunes can at best have only a sustenance-level existence, their productivity making no difference to their well-being. An abundant production results in low prices due to the market reality of excess supply driving down prices. Even sparse production does not bring in better prices, as price caps and anti-hoarding regulations are introduced to protect urban life which depends on rural production. In contrast, the urban section with its desirable but optional skills, mainly in the technical and intellectual spheres, oscillates between the sustenance mode and a prosperous state, amplifying the urban-rural divide.

While the rich-poor divide has existed since the birth of civilization, and the urban-rural divide emerged soon thereafter, the vast economic divide between different countries is of recent origin. Even about two hundred and fifty years ago, the difference in the average per capita consumption between the richest and the poorest country was in the order of five to one, but in recent times it has exponentially moved to a factor of four hundred and is still growing.[4] In short, the contrast between the extremes – a rural poor person, living in a tropical or semi-tropical geographical area and the urban rich resident of the temperate zone – will be in the magnitude of a few thousands, if not more.

Based on multi-decade-long meta research,[b] with data from around the world, Henry Tam, an author and professor at Birbeck College, London, shows that power inequalities in any form – wealth, decision-making authority or hierarchical status, are directly correlated with a higher incidence of violence, poorer levels of average health, lower degrees of interpersonal trust, and more illiberal behaviour.[5] David Landes, the Harvard-based economic historian, calls the rich-poor divide the greatest single problem facing the world of the third millennium.[6] In line with similar practices in socialist democracies, in India too, the importance of economic equality in sustaining democracy is recognized and reflected in the directive principles of the Indian constitution, which direct the state to eliminate economic inequality.[c]

---

b Meta research is the method of synthesizing research results by using various statistical techniques to select, retrieve and combine results from previous separate but related studies.

c 'The State shall, in particular, strive to minimize the inequalities in income, and endeavour to eliminate inequalities in status, facilities and opportunities, not only amongst individuals but also among groups of people residing in different areas or engaged in different vocations.' Directive Principle 38 (2) of the Indian Constitution

Of Good and Bad Cholesterol

The concept of *Manna,*[d] the idea that all the earth's resources are a gift from God to humanity, to be enjoyed by all equally, is one of the reasons why individuals believe inequality in opportunities is unnatural. Their opponents think that the quest for economic equality stems from a lack of appreciation for wealth creation. Contrary to the Manna idea, they consider wealth to be the result of individual initiative, risk and efforts with little to do with 'God's gift'. The very presence of inequality in its multiple hues: among countries (the north-south divide), within countries (the rural-urban divide), and within a society (the rich-poor divide), supports their view. Also supplementing this view is the fact that many countries rich in natural resources are economically poor, while the converse is not always true. The proponents of 'nature endorsed inequality' believe that 'the dream of an egalitarian society will never be realized, and attempts to impose it produce only poverty, stagnation, and oppression'.[7] Given these divergent views, is economic inequality good or bad?

Francisco Ferreira of the World Bank compared inequality in society to cholesterol in human blood.[8] Like good and bad cholesterol, inequality too can be similarly bifurcated. Low density lipoproteins can clog up blood vessels leading to fatal blocks, while high density lipoproteins remove fat from the tissues and organs and take it back to the liver for recycling, cleaning up the arteries in the process. As lipoproteins are classified based on their density, inequality too can be classified, based on its generational impact. Good inequality, Ferreira noted is that which arises within a generation, while

---

d   Manna here is used to denote divine or spiritual nourishment, inspired by the Biblical reference to it.

bad inequality accumulates over generations. The logic for this reasoning is not difficult to see. The primary benefit in promoting inequality is to provide an incentive for higher risk taking, showing more initiative and expending higher efforts, when all of these result in increased wealth. Precisely for the same reason, inter-generational inequality is classified as bad, since inherited wealth is seen to reduce the need for risk taking, initiative and effort by the inheriting generation, as it provides them with their needs and more on a silver platter.

The impact of inter-generational correlation between the income of the parents and their offspring is available for the United States of America. This data shows that the probability of an person with parents in the lowest decile of income moving to the highest decile is only 1.3 per cent, whereas the probability of their remaining in the last decile is 31.2 per cent. In contrast, the probability of a person with parents in the highest decile of income reaching the lowest decile is at 2.4 per cent, while the probability of their remaining in the highest decile is as high as 22.9 per cent.[9] Considering the lack of economic mobility reflected in the data for the USA and making a considered judgment to extend this conclusion to the rest of the world, an important question to explore is the reasons for this inertia. What could be the primary reason and how entrenched is it?

Technology the Accelerator

Economic growth moved in tandem with population growth for long periods in human history. It is only in the last few centuries that economic growth accelerated, breaking this link. Its impact is visible in the quantity, quality and variety of goods and services available today. The first of such shifts began around the fifteenth century in Europe.[e] However, the second and the more decisive breaks were in the eighteenth century, which spilt over to the nineteenth and twentieth centuries and are continuing their impact into the twenty-first century. Technology that significantly enhanced human capability is at the centre of this accelerated economic growth.

Technology at its core is knowledge, the knowledge of how to use resources uniquely to meet a human need. Unlike physical goods, it can be used for multiple simultaneous applications without additional resources. With artifacts like machinery, this dilution is substantially reduced if not eliminated by using some additional resources. Charles Babbage, credited with the idea of conceiving computers, was among the first few to articulate crisply the benefits of machines – a form of technology. In 1832, Babbage wrote a book titled *The Economy of Machinery and Manufactures,* in which he outlined the avenues by which human capability is expanded:

> The advantages which are derived from machinery and manufactures seem to arise primarily from three sources: The addition which they make to human power. The economy they produce of human time. The conversion of substance apparently common and worthless into valuable products.[10]

The power of water, wind and steam were the three additions to muscle power that Babbage identified. In addition, he argued that improved work techniques to reduce friction resulted in cutting down human effort. Illustrating this with the example of moving a large stone block, he noted a reduction in effort by a factor of fifty when rollers are used on smooth greased surfaces, (utilizing the technology of wheels and lubricants). Turning to time-saving devices, he highlighted the example of gunpowder

---

e   For details of this change look at Chapter 3

used to blast rocks and diamonds to cut glass. Producing potash from the hoofs and horns of cattle was the third example he gave, for the dimension of converting worthless materials into valuable products.[11]

The three principles identified by Babbage are visible even today in the harnessing of nuclear energy to supplement human power, telecommunications and television to save commute time (by enhancing the ability to communicate over distance without travel), and the conversion of sand into silicon and bio-waste into energy. However, the use of technology is not unique to human beings. Nor were humans the first organisms to transmit knowledge from generation to generation, non-genetically. Most mammals and birds teach their young ones. The amount the young ones can learn is limited only by their brain size. In humans, such learning increased exponentially, separating them from other mammals.

The link between evolution, learning and technology is quite intricate. Richard Wrangham, a professor of biology and anthropology at Harvard University proposed a new idea on how humans rapidly evolved by cooking their food – another form of technology – in his book *Catching Fire: How Cooking Made Us Human*. Studying the chimpanzees, Wrangham noted that their average caloric consumption per hour was around 400 calories.[12] For an average human who daily needs around 2,400 calories, this would translate to an eating time of about six hours using only raw food. These six hours exclude the time taken to hunt or gather the food. He then noted that cooking is a unique skill mastered only by humans among all other species. It offers unique advantages too. Cooking first softens the thick skin or husk, then it makes the inner cells tender, and converts molecules of protein and starch into more digestible forms. In addition, cooking makes the indigestible portion more easily fermentable and reduces its toxin levels.[13] Cooking, in short, provided the human species with calorie-rich food, the first beneficiary of which are the brain cells, which consume a disproportionate amount of energy. To quantify, in human beings, the brain constitutes only about 2 per cent of the body weight but consumes approximately 20 per cent of the metabolic resources.[14] Since the time humans mastered the use of fire, the resource essential to cooking, the human brain size too began to increase, separating them from other mammals. A direct result of the increased brain size is the ability to access, store and transmit knowledge non-genetically. Starting with pictographs, books and libraries, the transmission mechanism has today graduated into radio broadcasting, television transmission and the internet. With the increase in knowledge, technologies too multiplied.

Technology reflected in inventions like steam power, electricity and the internet among others, significantly accelerated material prosperity. With technology embedded in assets, individuals who commanded these assets gained from the technology. The result was that technology-led prosperity did not benefit everyone as it accrued only to individuals with wealth. This led to a concentration of income and wealth in the hands of a few. Higher income and wealth in turn gave the holders a competitive advantage by providing them better access to newer technologies. This in turn set in motion the vicious cycle of increasing inequality. Its flipside was accelerating prosperity for the select group who harnessed the latest technologies. As a consequence, some had luxuries at their command, while the life of a significant portion of the human population remained in abysmal poverty.

Just as the control of fire separated humans from other mammals, is the growing concentration of wealth in a small section of the population a surrogate for technology like fire, dividing humans into the rich and the poor? If yes, what is this wealth, and what is its magnitude?

Sizing the Economic Monarchy

Personal wealth means an individual's net worth, which is the claim an individual can make on society without undertaking any concurrent or future obligations, and is represented by physical and financial assets. This is in contrast to income, where the individual undertakes current obligations. In an economy, the sum total of physical assets and financial assets owned by all individuals who constitute a household reduced by the amount of debt they have incurred, represents **household wealth**. While household wealth is easy to define and list conceptually, its computation at the global level is only an estimate and multiple methods are used to try to quantify it. OECD[f] countries and a few other economies use Personal Balance Sheets[g] to quantify it, while the income multiplier method is adopted in countries that lack this statistical sophistication.

---

f   The Organization of Economic Cooperation and Development consists of 34 countries representing those with per capita incomes at the higher end of the scale.

g   The Personal Balance Sheet method for computing household wealth in an economy is the quantification of all assets and liabilities owned by the household sector.

Global household wealth in the year 2010 is estimated at $200 trillion,[15] in contrast to the global GDP[h] estimate of $62.6 trillion.[i] Geographically, more than half of this wealth is owned by the residents of the USA, Japan, China, France, and the United Kingdom. Even within these five geographies, the distribution is uneven, with the USA contributing $54.6 trillion or more than a fourth of the total. Global household wealth can also be converted into a per capita measure. Per capita wealth can be expressed using multiple denominators – households, families, or adult individuals. As only adults are permitted by law to control assets in most societies, this is the commonly used measure. By this yardstick, $69.2 trillion (or 34.6 per cent) of the wealth is owned by 0.5 per cent of adults, with each of the households in this segment owning more than a million US dollars. At the bottom of the pyramid, 68.4 per cent or approximately 3 billion adults owned just 4.2 per cent of the wealth, i.e. $8.2 trillion, each owning less than US$10,000.

The Gini Index is a frequently used technical measure of wealth and income concentration. This index has scores in the range of 0 to 1. At zero, the index reflects an equal distribution of wealth or income among all its members and at one, it indicates one individual in the group owning or earning all the wealth or income to the exclusion of all others. A study

---

h GDP is an estimate of the market throughput of all goods and services produced and traded in a defined period within an economy. It is the sum total of the nation's personal consumption expenditure, government expenditure, net exports, (i.e. exports less imports from the country), and increase in the value of capital goods in the economy. GDP measures all activities within the economy based on location.

i Global GDP figures for 2008 extrapolated based on growth estimates contained in the World Economic Outlook, October 2010.

on 'The Global Distribution of Household Wealth' by the United Nations University, World Institute for Development Economic Research, noted that, 'Typical Gini Coefficients for wealth lie in the range 0.65-0.75, and some are above 0.8. In contrast, the mid-range income Gini is 0.35-0.45.'[16] While these distributions are at a country level, aggregating them at the global level reveals that the Gini index is much more skewed as it is estimated at 0.89. To illustrate this, imagine if $100 were to be distributed among 100 individuals: at the current wealth concentration level, one individual would own close to $90 and the remaining 99 would share the balance $10.

Box 8.2
The Treasures of Wealth

Human beings are distinguished from other mammals by a long period of childhood and youth, during which they only consume without producing. This long period of dependence is one of the primary reasons, if not the sole reason for human progress. Household wealth plays a critical role in making humans, 'human' by funding this period.

Wealth has both an enabling and a disabling role. When a family faces illness, unemployment, old age or death of the bread-earners, its critical role is visible. By supplementing and substituting household income, it keeps the family away from destitution. In societies that lack a publicly-financed social security net, absence of household wealth propels many individuals into a life of poverty, creating a class of helpless poor people consisting of the orphaned, the sick, the widowed and the aged.

The enabling role of household wealth is vital in supporting the longer period of dependence for an individual.

> On the statute books of most countries, primary education is universal and free, but secondary and tertiary education are both optional and expensive. This education has a direct impact on increasing the individual's income. It is in making this investment that the enabling role of wealth in promoting and amplifying economic inequality is magnified. Post education, wealth also provides a softer cushion for risk-takers by limiting the price entrepreneurs pay for their failures. Household wealth thus plays an accelerating role in making the rich richer and the poor poorer.

Given the powerful impact of wealth as an economic segregator in society, its lopsided distribution only compounds with time. The experience of the last few decades shows that a primary focus on economic growth does not reverse this trend; in fact it only amplifies income and wealth inequalities.[j] This raises a vital question, should economic power be inherited in societies which pride themselves on their democratic political culture?

Dethroning Economic Monarchy

The belief that all men are created equal was first articulated in religious scripture.[k] Thereafter, it took a long time for this

---

j   The United Nations Conference on the World Financial and Economic Crisis and Its Impact on Development, New York, 24-26, June 2009, highlighted growing inequality as a source of the 2008 financial crisis.

k   'O mankind! Be careful of your duty to your Lord Who created you from a single soul and from it created its mate and from them twain hath spread abroad a multitude of men and women. Be careful of your duty towards Allah in Whom ye claim (your rights) of one another, and towards the wombs (that bare you). Lo! Allah hath been a Watcher over you.' Quran, IV:1

belief to emerge in the political sphere. Two eighteenth-century events – The American Declaration of Independence, followed closely by the French Revolution[1], unequivocally attempted to translate this belief into practice. Around the same time, the idea of equality spread from the political sphere into the economic domain. Realization dawned that political equality would be rendered meaningless if economic inequality thrived, as plutocrats would rule in the guise of democracy. In the eighteenth century itself, plans were formulated to reduce economic inequality and create a fertile ground for political democracy to flourish. Thomas Paine in the United States of America was at the forefront of this advocacy.

'Personal property is *the effect of society;* and it is as impossible for an individual to acquire personal property without the aid of society, as it is for him to make land originally,'[17] wrote Paine in his essay *Agrarian Justice.* This very short and insightful essay was written in the shadow of the French Revolution, which brought the rights of man to the forefront. Paine analyzed the implications of human civilization and concluded that poverty was its byproduct. He noted that an individual living in isolation like Robinson Crusoe could not get rich. It is only in a society where property rights exist that wealth accumulation is feasible. He then argued that a man born in a 'civilized' society should not be worse off than a man born in the natural state.

---

1 American Declaration of Independence in 1776 CE: 'We hold these beliefs to be self-evident, that all men are created equal, that they are endowed by their creator with certain unalienable Rights, that among these are Life, Liberty, and the pursuit of happiness.' The French declaration of the Right of Man and Citizen in 1789 CE: 'Men are born and remain free, equal and free in rights; social distinctions may be based only upon general usefulness.'

Paine outlined a plan of action to remedy the situation arising from economic inequality in society. He sought to provide each individual their rightful 'natural' inheritance on reaching the age of twenty-one. To this he added two humanitarian provisions for old-age pension for individuals on reaching the age of fifty and a monthly allowance for the physically handicapped. To fund these outflows, he identified a novel source of income for society, which was in his view the best as it was 'the least troublesome and the most effectual'. This he identified as a tax on the property of the dead before it passed on to their heirs, noting 'In this case, the bequeather gives nothing: the receiver pays nothing.'[18] Believing that an individual does not have the right of inheritance, he remarked that a generous person would not wish it to continue and a just man will rejoice to see it abolished.

The Renouncing Monarchs

A century after Thomas Paine, another American, this time a successful industrialist named Andrew Carnegie concluded that inter-generational inequality was inefficient. However, he used a very different approach and provided an alternative solution. Carnegie too began by noting that civilization significantly increased the inequality between rich and poor. To illustrate, he noted that the difference between the comforts available to an American Indian Chief and the other members of his tribe was minimal and contrasted it with the widely differing living conditions of the millionaire industrialist and their common workers. But, he saw nothing wrong in this disparity. On the contrary, he welcomed it as beneficial. He concluded that inequality was the price paid by society for acquiring luxuries and comforts cheaply. In balance, he found this trade-off beneficial for human progress.

While Thomas Paine approached the problem of inequality from a political angle, Carnegie the industrialist used an economic lens, with efficiency as the principal criterion. In an economy operating on the principles of competition, such as the free-market economy, he saw the accumulation of wealth in the hands of a few as its inevitable consequence. The question that he addressed in his popular essay *The Gospel of Wealth* was how to use this accumulated wealth efficiently. He identified three alternate avenues: leaving it to the family of the deceased, bequeathing it to some public purpose on death, or the owner administering it during his or her lifetime for public purposes. Evaluating the three options using the efficiency criteria, he ranked the first option of leaving wealth to the family the lowest. Looking at the situation in Europe where the practice of inheritance by family had prevailed for a long time, he remarked, 'I would as soon leave to my son a curse as the almighty dollar.'[19] He arrived at this conclusion based on his observation of the property-inheriting aristocratic class, who were self-indulgent and lacked enterprise. The option of bequeathing wealth for a public purpose he ranked the second as the individual would have no control over when it would occur or how their objectives would be realized after their death. Moreover, he noted 'It is well to remember that it requires the exercise of not less ability than that which acquires it, to use wealth so as to be really beneficial to the community.' After eliminating these two alternatives, he applauded the option of the owner administering the surplus wealth during his or her lifetime, as this creates harmony in society by reconciling the temporary unequal distribution of wealth in a peaceful evolutionary mode rather than through a communist revolution.[20]

Andrew Carnegie's view has significant support among the 'super rich' billionaires today. The large number of foundations and trusts set up to promote charitable purposes is clear evidence. However, Thomas Paine had anticipated Andrew Carnegie's recommendation for voluntary redistribution of wealth a century earlier, and discarded it as an insignificant initiative in the face of human misery. He remarked that voluntary initiatives may satisfy the conscience of the giver but will have little impact on relieving human misery.[21]

In the two hundred years since Thomas Paine advocated the vehicle of inheritance tax to dethrone economic monarchy, it has been used sparingly and sporadically. In the nineteenth century, it was used primarily to mobilize revenue to fund war expenditure and withdrawn when the war ended. For the majority of the twentieth century, estate duty or inheritance tax formed a part of the statute books in most democracies. This time, though the intention was to reduce economic inequalities, it was inadequate, as enough loopholes were left to prevent its effective operation. In the last three decades, this source of redressing economic inequality has completely lost its potency. Concurrently, even the most accepted form of direct tax – income tax – too has also been used primarily to mobilize revenue rather than to reduce economic inequality, as can be seen reflected in the steadily declining direct tax rates.

While there could be some justification for the reluctance to making the rich poorer, what is the agenda behind the failure to invest in social safety nets that would make the poor safe and place them on the path to riches? 'Lack of resources' is a hollow excuse, given the firm action that countries across the world undertook when faced with the financial crisis in September 2008. Long prevailing notions of financial propriety about budget deficits were abandoned when property rights were threatened. Bailouts and economic stimulus packages totaling trillions of dollars were announced and funds released overnight to protect property values. So, what could be the reason for this indifference towards promoting universal human welfare?

Invisible Hand or the Clenched Fist?

Free markets permit individuals to pursue their own agenda in the belief that the common good is enabled through an invisible hand. The history of the last two centuries shows that this invisible hand only enables the realization of some parts of the common good. After a review of the performance of business entities, the primary engine in free markets, the King Committee on Governance came out with the *Draft Code of Governance Principles for South Africa* in 2009. They observed a critical shortfall in managing business when they remarked that 'Nature, society and business are interconnected in complex ways that decision makers need to understand'.[22] While this report is addressed to business leaders, its implications are equally relevant, if not more applicable, to the economist. Arising from this insightful observation is a basic question for economists to answer: 'What is the relationship between a society and an economy?' Are they two independent and unrelated systems? If not, what is the nature of this relationship?

Society consists of all connected individuals within a given geography, whereas an economy only counts the participants in the economic process. Their participation is either as a buyer or a seller of economic goods and services. In short an economy is a subset of society. Members of society who do not command purchasing power are excluded from the economy. Moreover in the economy, the voices of society members are only as audible as the purchasing power they command. While a society is counted by the number of members, an economy is measured by its purchasing power. Given the difference between the two, what is the nature of their relationship?

Box 8.3
The Society-Economy Relationship

Relationships between organisms that interact are classified under the broad umbrella of symbiotic relationships. These can be of four distinct types, based on the benefits derived from interaction. Where one party gains without any cost to the other, the relationship is termed commensalism. When the two parties compete, gain for one translates into a loss for the other. In a parasitic relationship only one party gains every time, but it is always at the cost of another. The fourth type of relationship is mutualism, where both parties gain. Given this range, where can we place the relationship between a society and its economy?

The emergence of an economy from society can be traced to the acceleration in material consumption. Gordon Childe, the anthropologist, identified this acceleration as humans partnering with nature, a change from living off nature. This initial relationship is visible in the coexistence of a subsistence economy with an exchange-based economy during the agricultural phase. The exchange-based economy promoted economic growth, but not at the cost of society as no individual was disadvantaged from their existing state. Those who did not participate in the exchange-based economy could still exist, reflecting the commensal relationship between the economy and the rest of society. When the focus on the economy intensified, goods in the public domain gradually became private or economic goods, starting with land. As more goods moved into the economic domain, the relationship began to turn competitive, as existence in the subsistence economy was threatened. But it was the advent of the Industrial Revolution in the nineteenth century, which turned a majority of society's members into merely labour, a solely economic relationship, that marked its entry into the parasitic phase.

In this phase, the economy grew, but at the cost of society, for it did not admit all society's members, especially the urban poor, into its fold. The onus now shifted onto the individual to graduate into the ranks of the economic players by participating in the exchange economy – and the need to do so was dire as members of society could not survive without being active economic participants. Parasites realize that they can live only if the host survives. In the absence of a robust host, a parasite's days too are numbered. A host stripped of its vitality to feed the parasite, weakens both. Only when the host recoups, can its parasites recover. Could this be the reason why free-market economies frequently collapse into recession after periods of strong growth necessitating stimulus packages to get back on the path to recovery?

Compared to societies in which the free-market model dominates, Nordic societies (consisting of Denmark, Finland, Iceland, Norway and Sweden) have integrated markets within society to evolve a new form of mutualism in the relationship between society and the economy. They have created an environment where the economy with its wealth creation activities thrives side-by-side with the public sector focused exclusively on creating a strong safety net to enable effective wealth distribution.

If we use the lens of symbiotic relationships for viewing the interconnections between a society and an economy, we see that a free-market arrangement aims to maximize the benefits to an economy, even if it is at a cost to the rest of society. The bottom line is higher efficiency even though some are left behind. This cost is acceptable to the free-market advocates who believe that in the long run all members of a society will become participants of its economy. On the other hand, the socialist ideology looks to maximize the benefits to society as a whole, even if it means a less efficient economy. The socialists consider the idea of leaving anyone behind to be cruel and not justified due to its impact on human life. Given this understanding, is it possible to balance the two interests and construct a mutually beneficial relationship between society and its economy?

Adam Smith, the founding father of modern economics, believed free markets are the most optimal avenue for wealth creation in a society. His advocacy was based on the belief that an invisible hand[m] will align the pursuit of private interests into socially-beneficial results. For the most part, his insight held true as economies based on free markets grew faster and provided more goods and services to the members of society. However, this success holds true only if aggregate consumption measures are used. The invisible hand that aligns the interest of the buyers and sellers recognizes only the desires of individuals who command purchasing power. In the world of free markets, buyers are heard more often than sellers. For the rest of the society who do not command purchasing power or do command inadequate amounts to live a dignified life, free markets turn into a visible fist that boxes them into an inexplicable void, making them a non-entity in the market place.

This clenched fist can be unclenched into the invisible hand. A prerequisite for this to happen is to make all members of

---

m   Adam Smith believed that explicit promotion of public welfare was neither feasible nor desirable. But public welfare could be realized by each individual pursuing their own welfare. He saw an 'invisible hand' at work when 'every prudent master of a family never attempts to make at home what it will cost him more to make than to buy' in the process promoting efficiency and increased output.

the society a participant of its economy as active consumers of goods and services. However, due to their inherent limitations a few identified groups cannot participate in this economy. They consist of children, the aged, the sick, the unemployable and those temporarily unemployed. In addition, as the voice of participants in an economy is only as audible as the purchasing power they command, it is imperative to provide each participant with an opportunity to control enough purchasing power to be heard. Providing the basic needs for a dignified existence like food security, healthcare and universal education – in short, a strong social safety net that enrolls all the members of the society as active participants of its economy by making them valued consumers of services and not charity recipients – is a prerequisite. Given this, is there a model that integrates all members of the society into its economy and thereby builds a mutually beneficially relationship? If yes, what could be the economic rationale for it?

The Secrets of the Bumblebee's Flight

A popular myth holds that bumblebees should not be able to fly if aerodynamic principles hold true. However in reality, they do. Likewise, in classical economics there is a belief that high taxes and a dominant public sector providing a strong safety net that promotes an egalitarian society cannot coexist with a thriving free-market economy. The rationale is that the individual incentive to exert, which fuels the free market, is dampened by high taxes and the presence of a strong safety net. In addition, the public sector is believed to be an inefficient substitute for the private sector. However, like the bumblebee in flight, the economic model of a dominant public sector contributing to about half of the national GDP, and high taxes of around fifty per cent funding a strong social security net, coexist with a thriving free-market economy in the Nordic countries.

Box 8.4
Sweden: An Illustration of the Nordic Economic Model

Sweden is a prime example of the Nordic economic model. It has characteristically high tax rates, a dominant public sector and a strong safety net for its citizens, coexisting with a thriving free market, home to some of the leading transnational corporations like ABB, Alfa-Laval, Electrolux, Ericsson, Saab, SKF and Volvo. To an individual living in the Nordic economies, these attributes translate to a secure economic life, in an egalitarian society with guaranteed personal liberty.

The most distinctive aspect of this model is its strong social net that protects all its residents. The social net consists of three elements: publicly produced and universally[n] accessible services for healthcare, education, childcare and eldercare; universal flat-rate benefits such as child allowance and old-age pension tied to citizenship; and mandatory social insurance for sickness, and earnings-related pension for all its labour.[23]

The logical consequence of this strong social security net is large public expenditure, accounting for around half of the national GDP. The conventional state functions of law and order, justice and national defense contribute to only a third of the public expenditure. The remaining two-thirds are contributed by social welfare expenses. For instance, in Sweden, public expenditure on education was 8 per cent,

---

n   Universal access means coverage of the entire population without consideration of their ability to pay. Services like law and order, national defense, justice system and public infrastructure are some examples of universal services provided in most economies across the world today.

on healthcare 9 per cent and on social security 17 per cent, totaling 34 per cent of the GDP in 2002[24], which is reflective of this model.

While the contours outlined till now look possible, their feasibility lies in balancing the books. A large public expenditure needs to be funded either by taxes or deficit financing. In Sweden, taxes fund the public expenditure. Taxes hovered at around 50 per cent of GDP for the most part and were at 46.6 per cent in 2009.[25] Who pays these high taxes? Does it not dampen their enthusiasm for working hard? How can they maintain their growth rates on par with other free-market economies?

A pro-welfare state hypothesis[o] explains this apparent paradox of high taxes and strong economic growth. This hypothesis quantifies the benefits from greater economic freedom and globalization, and shows that they exceed the cost of high taxes. Conventional wisdom holds that high tax rates act as a disincentive to economic transactions, thereby dampening growth rates. However, when the fabric of free trade is protected, high taxes only increase the transaction's costs but not its inherent profitability. The higher transaction cost can be offset by well-defined property rights, a functioning legal system and a stable domestic currency – all results of tax money well spent by the state – which more than offset this disadvantage, leaving a positive result.

Another option available to a welfare state in the global economy is in promoting the division of labour between

---

o   Andreas Bergh expands on this paradox and offers an explanation for the success of the Nordic Model in his paper, 'Explaining Welfare State Survival: The Role of Economic Freedom and Globalization', Ratio Working Paper 101, Ratio Institute, Stockholm (2006)

countries. Countries with stronger welfare systems export low-productivity jobs, while simultaneously importing the higher-productivity jobs due to their rich human capital. This could probably explain why the Nordic economic model has survived over most of the last century, despite much apprehension. This theory holds that the pulse of their survival is in maintaining a high level of economic freedom and furthering globalization.

The initial conclusion in the bumblebee case was based on steady-state aerodynamics, which took into account the wing size and beats-per-second and compared it with the body weight. Subsequent developments in aerodynamics showed that a combination of dynamic stall and vortex, a whirlwind-like action creating vacuum, helps a bumblebee lift its much heavier body weight. What is the equivalent of the dynamic stall and vortex in the Nordic economic model? Can it be uncovered by tracing the origin and development of the Nordic economic model?

After the introduction of agriculture, which marked the birth of civilization, most economies across the globe evolved on similar lines, the differences being only in form rather than in substance. It is only with the advent of industrialization that economies developed differently. These differences were primarily in countering the adverse social effects of the employer-employee relationship and urbanization. Both these features resulted in a landless working class without any alternative means of sustenance to their employment. In Sweden, industrialization brought with it labour unions and a political party to represent the landless working class. In 1889, the Social Democratic Workers Party came into existence. Four decades later in 1931, this party formed the government, which crafted the Nordic economic model, in conditions favourable for the model to flourish.

Sweden has a cherished and long history of promoting universal education. The first attempt to promote universal literacy is traced back to 1686, where the priests were entrusted with the responsibility for educating all their parish members to read the Bible.[26] A few decades later, in 1723, the responsibility for literacy among children was entrusted to their parents. A century later, in 1842, compulsory general education for children was mandated. However, this did not translate to compulsory schooling, as it was realized that knowledge and skills could be acquired at home too.[27] To supplement parental effort, each municipality or parish was required to set up at least one school with one teacher. A visible impact was seen in reading, writing and arithmetic skills across the country. Within decades, at the dawn of the twentieth century, Sweden had an almost fully literate population.[28] Literacy being seen as a sign of education is a hotly contested idea. But even its staunchest opponents will concede that literacy could promote education. Among other benefits, an educated view will show a range of options where earlier a single path existed. The 'dynamic stall' for the Nordic model to takeoff could be this educated view of seeing the long-term benefits of providing a universal social security system in their society.

As in most countries, Sweden's political thought too was divided between left and right wing ideology. The left was represented by the Social Democratic Party and the right by the Moderate Party, with the Agrarian Party playing a moderating role. Due to its geographical proximity, the Russian revolution in 1919 had a major psychological impact on Swedish politics. The dramatic change in Russia made the right and the left wing collaborate rather than take a confrontational stance against each other. The resultant synthesis is captured in the 1921 electoral speech of Per Albin Hanson, the Prime Ministerial candidate of the Social Democratic Party who discarded working-class dictatorship in favour of democracy and forwarded the view that,

> We are advancing in order, on the firm foundations of democracy, with the support of the majority of the people, to raise in equality of status the social classes which have hitherto been held back, in order to abolish classes, in order to make Sweden a good home for all Swedes.... In this great home there will be no stepchildren and favourites... class distinction must go, Sweden for all Swedes! [29]

In short, they defined a new system that maintained the core interests of the collaborators — capitalist ideology driving wealth creation, with socialist ideas shaping wealth distribution. Highlighting the value of universal suffrage[p] which had been recently introduced, Per Albin Hanson remarked, that it was an instrument for peacefully accomplishing a classless society which would one day become a good home for people.[30] This aim also defined the basics of the social security net. In a good home, the child is looked after and educated, the sick and the injured provided for and the aged live a life of dignity. Replicating this ideal, social welfare schemes in Sweden grant parental allowance to provide for children's needs, free compulsory education, mandatory insurance against sickness and accidents and state-financed old-age pension and healthcare for all. In addition special care was provided for the aged and the specially challenged. A key factor underlying all these welfare measures is universality – the sole eligibility criterion

---

p   Universal suffrage for men was introduced in 1909, with women getting the right to vote in 1919 which they exercised in the 1921 elections.

for accessing these services is need. No other filters in the form of income or wealth are defined.

In contrast to other selective models where only a specific section of the population is provided with the free publicly-funded services, under the universal model all members of society are entitled to it. A benefit of the universal model is in reducing the administrative costs of filtering the beneficiaries, which can be substantial. More importantly, it improves the quality of service as it also caters to tax-paying members who by right demand effective services. On the human front, by removing the social stigma of charity-beneficiaries, it restores dignity to the children, the aged, the sick and the unemployed who need these services. Tax-collection expenses for the incremental revenue required to expand services universally are the only additional cost incurred, as the higher cost of services provided to the 'non-deserving' beneficiaries is indirectly paid by them through higher tax rates imposed. Could universality be the 'vortex' that keeps the Nordic economic model stay afloat by ensuring the quality of services and removing the tag of charity-beneficiaries to those availing these services?

These explain to some extent the reason why the Nordic economic model exists and thrives. But what were the factors that triggered the birth and growth of this model in Sweden?

A Threat of Human Extinction?

The social welfare structure of safety nets was not innovated in Sweden. It was Germany under Otto von Bismarck that first introduced these measures. Explaining the logic for German national health insurance, a pension, a minimum wage and work place regulation provisions introduced in 1880s, Bismarck is said to have remarked, 'My idea was to bribe the working classes, or shall I say, to win them over, to regard the state as a social institution existing for their sake and interested in their welfare.'[31] However, in Sweden the motive for universal social safety nets was very different. The triggers relate to two phenomena of the 1930s – the apprehension of a dwindling population and an all encompassing, voluntary, collective bargaining agreement that provided the basis for dividing the responsibilities of the state, the employers and the trade unions.

The first quarter of the twentieth century in Sweden saw declining fertility. As concerns over the declining population gained momentum, in 1910 a law was enacted to ban public information being made available on the sale of contraceptives.[32] By the 1930s the problem had been exacerbated as total fertility rates dropped from four children per woman at the turn of the century to less than two.[33] As the prospects of a decline in the population looked real, it became a political issue. *The Crisis of the Population Question* written in 1934 by Gunnar Myrdal and Alva Myrdal, both Social Democrats addressed this challenge head on. They advocated a number of measures aimed at improving the quality of life for women by helping them combine family life with work to promote higher rates of child birth. The Social Democrats, who had come to power in 1931, acted on their advice. Their reforms included universal antenatal and child healthcare. Simultaneously, the ban on contraceptives was lifted and instead, family planning services offered.[34] The reasoning for this was to promote childbirth as a conscious choice rather than as an accident, as captured in the popular phrase of that time, 'love without children is better than children without love'. This epitomized the value Swedes placed on each human life, irrespective of where the person is born.

A strong start cannot explain continued momentum. The social welfare reforms introduced by the Social Democrats in the early 1930s needed to be sustained. The impetus for their sustained progress came in the form of a collective bargaining agreement between the Swedish Employers Association and the Swedish Confederation of Trade Unions in 1938. Following decades of industrial unrest marked by strikes and lockouts, the Social Democrats in the government wanted to intervene and provide a legal framework to usher in industrial peace. To prevent the government from taking a dominant role in their identified sphere of influence, the employers and the unions entered into a voluntary and binding agreement on December 10, 1938. Known as the Saltsjobad Agreement, it provided a unique cooperative climate by defining the role of all the three major players – the state, the employers and the employees.

The Saltsjobad Agreement defined processes to resolve disputes between employers and employees. A critical factor for everyone involved was that the state should be kept out of this negotiation process. The defined role for the state was to implement the welfare system to protect its citizens with a strong safety net. Secured by this safety net, the trade union took on a more constructive role by accepting wage negotiations against the backdrop of economic growth and stability.[35] The principle of increasing the living standards of labour by linking them to productivity levels was accepted. A well-defined mechanism to implement this principle evolved as well. As one third of Sweden's GDP came from its export sector, the importance of this sector was realized in providing employment and sustaining a robust economy. So, first, productivity levels in the export-oriented and highly-competitive domestic industries were set to meet the national objectives of full employment and a sustainable balance of payments. These productivity factors were taken as the ceiling for other, less-competitive domestic businesses segments.[36] In return, the employers agreed to real wage protection and a share of the productivity gains.

In another dimension of the agreement, equal pay for equal work was accepted by the employers' federation, regardless of a company's ability to pay. At the same time, the rights of the employer to hire and fire employees, allocate work and direct workers were ceded. These principles helped weed out low productivity firms and industries by encouraging them to migrate to higher productivity terrain, as they were no longer constrained to run non-profitable low productivity firms to simply provide employment to workers. Retrenched workers were Swedish society's problem. This required a conscious effort by the state to retrain workers, provide mobility assistance to help them move and provide temporary relief work.[37] In summary, the principles of free markets and free trade were assured for the employers, who in turn paid a higher tax that permitted the state to administer a universal social welfare state. The trade union, on their part, negotiated real wage protection and a share of the productivity increase. In short, it was a win-win agreement. This arrangement, with some modifications, remained in force for most of the twentieth century, providing support to the Nordic economic model.

The success of the Nordic economic model is not accepted by all. A large number of disbelievers, mainly from the free-market school question its sustainability. Even its limited durability in the Nordic region is seen as non-replicable elsewhere in the globe, due to the absence of sparse and homogenous populations, combined with large natural resources. But similar logic is ignored when economies across the globe are induced to ape the resource-rich American model.

Despite these reservations, some limited aspects of the Nordic model are gaining acceptability across the globe.

Livelihood support programmes to break the poverty cycle among the unemployed and the needy, like the Mexican *Oportunidades programme,* followed by the Brazilian *Bolsa Familla* and the Indian National Rural Employment Guarantee Scheme are a few well-known examples. The idea behind these schemes is to supplement the income of the vulnerable sections of population. Along with these schemes, the state's responsibility for the education and health of its members is also being increasingly acknowledged. 'Right to Education' and 'Right to Health' programmes are at varying stages of implementation or on the drawing boards of many developing countries. Could they be the sugar-coated pills that make universal safety nets an acceptable feature in our societies, promising all members of the society a dignified existence commensurate with the prosperity levels of the societies they live in? In implementing these schemes, will we see universality and comprehensiveness as a principle, with state funding on the same footing as for defense and other police state functions? What could be the hurdles in realizing it?

Free-market economists approve of spending on the basic state functions[q] of maintaining law and order as they enable higher GDP growth. On the other hand, building social security nets do not get the same endorsement as it is seen to dampen the growth environment in the short run. Only when the biological existence of its members is threatened by natural disasters, is the expenditure on social security nets grudgingly conceded as the alternative is a vitiated environment for pursuing economic growth. Given

---

q These state functions consist of maintaining internal law and order, enforcing the rule of law and protecting the country from external aggressors.

the prime position occupied by GDP in macroeconomic decision making, it is important to trace how GDP became the sole measure of economic performance despite its well-acknowledged inadequacies.

What the Numbers Count

Measurement is often at the centre of human thinking. In economics too, it is no different. Lord Shang, the Chinese economic thinker of the third century BCE, identified thirteen[r] parameters to measure the strength of a kingdom which includes many elements of both society and economy. Since then, the quest to quantify the size of an economy has been sporadic and based on individual interest. A possible reason for the absence of sustained interest could be the slow pace of economic growth. Angus Maddison, the noted economic historian, computed the annual compounded growth rate for the first millennium at 0.01 per cent and in the second phase of 1000-1820 CE at 0.22 per cent in his global GDP estimates.[38] With the onset of the Industrial Revolution in the nineteenth century, growth rates accelerated. With this, the interest in sizing an economy too gathered momentum. Initially these measures too were individual initiatives, but in contrast to the earlier efforts they were continuous. The US stock market crash of 1929 radically changed this position. For the first time in

---

r   He suggested that the number of granaries, able-bodied men and women, useful people i.e. those engaged in agriculture, oxen and horses, straw and fodder in a society were a measure of its prosperity. The remaining five categories measured the number of old and weak people, officials, officers, those who make a living by talking e.g. traders and scholars, all which reduced prosperity, according to him.

the 1930s, the US government got interested. The trigger for this was the dramatic collapse in economic activity following the stock market crash. As unemployment levels reached unprecedented highs, a measure to assess the real-time response to new policy initiative was felt. In short, an economic famine had descended. The health of the economy was failing and a quick cure needed. Equally important was the need to find a way to measure and mark its recovery.

In the year 1932, a quarter of the workers in the US were unemployed. Even amongst the employed, many were only partially engaged. Asset values had evaporated significantly. The banking system was collapsing. Farming income had halved.[39] In this situation, information on economic activity and the size of the economy was not available to assist in decision-making. In response to this vacuum, a resolution was passed in the US Senate requesting the National Bureau of Economic Research to compile and report data on National Income. The first report was received in January 1934. It showed that between 1929 and 1932, the US national income had declined by about 50 per cent.[s] Manufacturing income fell about 70 per cent and the construction segment's income declined by about 80 per cent.[40] Two reports were presented: the National Income Produced and the National Income Paid out. Measured by payment, wages had declined by 60 per cent, while salaries had fallen by 40 per cent. Given this specific and precise description, national income was a critical economic indicator to measure economic activity.

---

s   This reduction is in nominal terms. As the price levels too had declined, at constant prices the reduction in national income was lower. In real terms the decline was in the range of 30 - 40 per cent.

The first national income report illuminated the stark position of the US economy. Requests for periodic updates on national income followed, as a path to recovery was being charted. Soon thereafter, these reports were produced with regularity. Franklin D. Roosevelt, the US President at the time, began citing national income statistics to justify new policy initiatives. With the passage of time, national income morphed into Gross National Product to measure production in the economy and then with increased international trade into Gross Domestic Product. The end of World War II and the resultant need to reconstruct economies across the world led to the formation of the International Bank for Reconstruction and Development, now better known as the World Bank. Again, the need to measure the progress of this reconstruction surfaced. A single measure was ideal, and GDP emerged as the answer. Since then the World Bank has been using GDP growth rates to measure the success of its many initiatives. Over time, GDP growth has become synonymous with economic progress. The World Bank continues to popularize this concept by providing quarterly updates and forecasts of global GDP growth rates, reinforcing this basic belief that it is a measure of economic progress.

Simon Kuntz, the author of the first national income report in 1934 to the US Senate recognized the inadequacy of GDP as a measure of economic progress. He noted that the initial objective of the report was only to measure economic activity. Recognizing its handicap with great foresight, he remarked while presenting the first report that the simplicity and precision of presenting a single number for measuring economic progress would lend itself to the illusion of a complete measure, and to reporting abuse, especially as a complex matter was being communicated by oversimplification.[41]

Of Calories and Nutritious Diet

An analogy best exemplifies the shortcoming of oversimplification. In this context GDP numbers can be compared to caloric values. In nutritional terms, calories are an important measure of food quality. Especially during times of famine, caloric intake becomes a primary measure of health. To stop the body from cannibalizing its muscles during starvation, energy needs to be restored quickly so a calorie-rich diet takes priority. However, soon after the body gains the lost weight, the focus shifts away from a calorie-rich diet to a nutritious diet. What is true for the starving human body is equally true for an economy in distress, whether depression-induced or in the post-war reconstruction mode.

This analogy of the relationship between types of nutrition and the human body can be further extended to the types of economic welfare and the economy. In the first case, nutrition from fat provides the largest number of calories, while nutrition from carbohydrates and proteins of equal weight provide about half the caloric value. For good health, a combination of all three is required: fat for building an energy reserve for contingencies, carbohydrates for rapidly fueling the current energy needs and protein to repair and build muscles. Likewise in an economy, the GDP growth only measures the caloric value. A 'nutritious' measure of economic performance needs to consider income distribution, which plays the role of protein in building a strong society. Just as excessive caloric consumption turns into obesity in human beings, exclusive focus on economic growth results in highly unequal societies and depleted natural resources. Just as obesity is at the root of diabetes and coronary diseases in human beings, inequality is seen to be the main cause of social unrest and terrorism in the world. While the shortcomings of a calorie-rich diet are realized in humans, the negative implications of predominantly focusing on GDP growth are yet to register among many policy makers, especially from the free-market school.

In 2008, the World Bank, along with other economic institutions, commissioned a report on Growth and Development. This report, more popularly known as the Growth Report, was prepared by a team of twenty-one global leaders. The team included nineteen influential policy makers from across the globe including China and India and two Nobel Prize-winning economists. The report studied thirteen economies that had sustained high growth rates since the 1950s to analyze and provide guidance for other economies to emulate. The focus of the report is clear and its emphasis on GDP growth undiluted. It recognizes the limitations of GDP growth but still acknowledges its primary role by noting, 'Growth is, above all the surest way to free society from poverty'.[42] This statement reflects the inability of this group to look beyond the numbers indicating a calorie-rich meal to the other factors that determine whether it is part of a nutritious diet.

In contrast to this singular focus on GDP growth, in 2008 another team of economists, commissioned by the French President Sarkozy, looked at the shortcomings of GDP and explored an alternative measure of economic welfare. After a detailed study, they concluded that no single indicator can capture something as complex as our society and, given the importance of such measures, to have an open and public discussion on such metrics. As a caricature of the contrast between what GDP measures and actual human welfare, they quoted an interesting contrast,

> One is a happily-married woman (man) who goes home after work to her husband (his wife). Both may go home after a working day. They get pleasure from cooking their

gourmet meal together, using ingredients grown in their garden, after which they follow by a quiet evening reading together. The net contribution to GDP is the value of the few ingredients in their meal that they had to purchase and the cost of the books. By contrast, a lonely bachelor eats an unhealthy meal at a fast-food restaurant, then goes to a bar and drinks excessively as solace for his loneliness, visits a prostitute, and then wrecks his car while driving back, taking a taxi the remaining distance. This unhappy individual has, by contrast, contributed greatly to the GDP—the cost of preparation and serving of meal and drinks, the sexual services, the repair costs of the automobile, and the taxi home all enter into GDP accounting.[43]

The global financial meltdown in 2008 and its aftermath provide a prominent platform for this debate between the pro-GDP and the pro-welfare economists. It marks a significant milestone in a controversy that began more than fifty years ago and is still simmering, awaiting a definitive turn. But where did this debate start and why?

The Wealth and Welfare disconnect

Two decades after Adam Smith wrote *The Wealth of Nations*, Thomas Malthus raised a pertinent question in his best known work, *An Essay on the Principle of Population*. While Smith enquired into the causes of the wealth of nations, Malthus wondered if it was the same as enquiring into the causes that affect the happiness of nations. He went on to remark that while wealth and welfare were connected and generally moved in the same direction, there were also occasions where the two diverged and wondered, 'perhaps Dr. Adam Smith has considered these two inquires as still more nearly connected than they really are'.[44] Extending his analysis further, Malthus identified what he considered the two universally-acknowledged ingredients of happiness – health and a command of the necessities and conveniences of life.

In 1972, about four decades after the Great Depression, William Nordhaus and James Tobin reopened this debate in an aptly-titled article 'Is Growth Obsolete?' As global economies moved beyond the starvation phase of the Great Depression, they questioned the utility of a calorie-based measure of diets. The key question they asked were, Did GNP[t] measure *growing at all in a meaningful senses*?[45] They began by asking the question, what does GNP measure? Noting that it only measured economic activity and was an index of production, they went on to construct a new Measure of Economic Welfare (MEW). The idea behind this measure was to segregate the sort of consumption which enhances economic welfare. To quantify consumption, they classified GNP into consumption, investment and intermediate goods (those that are 'not directly sources of utility themselves but are regrettably necessary inputs to activities that may yield utility' e.g.: the cost of commuting to employment for individuals and defense expenditure for a country). They noted that the difference between consumption and investment is reasonably clear, while classifying goods as intermediate goods can be quite controversial. Notwithstanding this, they excluded services like national defense from consumption,

---

t   GNP is not used today, having been replaced with GDP. GDP measures all activities within the economy based on location. In contrast, GNP measures all activities of the residents of an economy by including activities outside its physical boundaries while it excludes the activities of foreigners within its physical location.

providing the rationale that the though the US national defense expenditure had increased from $0.5 billion in 1929 to $50 billion in 1965, it did not represent a hundredfold increase in national security. Defense expenditure, they concluded, was only an input to maintaining welfare rather than an output that enhanced welfare. Following the same logic of measuring only outputs that enhanced welfare, they excluded expenditure on health and education. They saw these as inputs or investments that will enable future welfare rather than promote current welfare.

In another significant departure from the 'blindly materialistic' economists, Nordhaus and Tobin added the monetary value of non-market activities like leisure and work performed for own consumption. Of the two, adding the value of leisure at its opportunity cost of the wage rate for the time spent was a sizeable addition. Between the period 1929 and 1965, they quantified the dollar value of leisure at a maximum of around 2.5 times the GNP. Even at its minimum, it was more than equal to the GNP. However, valuing leisure significantly contributed to increasing resistance from others in accepting the Measure of Economic Welfare as a substitute to GDP measures.

All in all, quantifying the Measure of Economic Welfare brought the divergence between GDP and economic welfare into public debate. But the authors did not push for making GDP measures obsolete. They answered to their own question 'Is Growth Obsolete?' with 'We think not'. They noted that the measurement of GDP, with some corrections, still communicated secular progress. But, what were these corrections? Did they identify all the modifications required or leave anything significant for their successors to find?

Nordhaus and Tobin, in addition to the aggregate, also looked at a per capita Measure of Economic Welfare. They realized that for economic welfare in a society to improve, per capita measures need to rise, not just the aggregate numbers, as aggregates do not account for rising populations. While they acknowledged the impact of this, they themselves did not account for skewed income distributions within society. Two decades later, a more evolved measure, the Index of Sustainable Economic Welfare (ISEW) was proposed by Daly and Cobb in 1989. In a short time, this morphed into the Genuine Progress Indicator. This measure factored in unequal income distribution in an economy by adjusting the aggregate consumption for inequality. To illustrate, in an economy where income is equally distributed, the entire consumption would be considered. However, purely hypothetically, if the total income in an economy is fully concentrated in the hands of one individual, for the purpose of Genuine Progress Indicator, the entire consumption would be disregarded and counted as zero to reflect the degree of inequality involved.

The attempt to quantify economic welfare that began with MEW in the 1970s has now mushroomed into multiple initiatives with an equally large number of measures. Many of these measures vary only in degree, though not in substance. Major differences between GDP and measures of economic welfare can be classified into adjustments for the impact of unequal income distribution, value of non-paid work, value of leisure time, cost of pollution, cost of natural resource depletion and defensive expenditures that are essential for earning an income (such as commuting costs) that do not add to the overall welfare of the worker. Another prominent initiative is to combine non-economic parameters along with the GDP measures to arrive at a composite index to measure human welfare. The most prominent example of this is the Human Development Index, which combines life expectancy, literacy achievements and per capita consumption to measure welfare.

While a large number of economists concur that GDP does not measure economic welfare, they are not in a position to agree on an acceptable alternative. In this context, it is inevitable that GDP continues to rule the roost. 'GDP is not wrong, but it is wrongly used' noted the team of economists commissioned by President Sarkozy in 2008. While a consensus on the ideal measure is not reached, is there any reason for us to continue to use a measure that we know does not measure economic welfare? What is the way ahead?

The Challenge Ahead

Alfred Marshall highlighted a critical idea in his *Principles of Economics*:

> Though economic analysis and general reasoning are of wide application, yet every age and every country has its own problems; and every change in social conditions is likely to require a new development of economic doctrines.[46]

The third millennium, with its enormous material wealth and the humungous challenge of global warming and economic inequality, needs new economic analysis and reasoning. A good place to start is by questioning the basic prerequisites of the second millennium economics: private property, social sanction for self-centred individuals and human welfare measured by material consumption. Should the prerequisites of the last millennium be changed for the third millennium? If so, what to change?

Can we imagine private property rights protected for a single generation with restricted inheritance rights? Do we need to reexamine our assumption of self-centred individuals by expanding our concern to all human beings and assuring every human of a universal base standard of living? Should we use a multi-dimensional concept of human welfare to replace GDP? None of these questions have well-defined, implementable answers. But could they be the prime challenges that economics faces, going forward?

Endnotes

1   Rousseau, J., *The Social Contract and Discourse,* The Online Library of Liberty Collection, based on 1923 edition, p188

2   Ibid, p206

3   Childe, G., *What Happened in History,* Penguin Books, 1982, p55

4   Landes, D., *The Wealth and Poverty of Nations,* Abacus, 1998, p *xx*

5   Tam, H., *Against Power Inequalities, Reflections on the Struggle for Inclusive Communities,* Birkbeck Publicaiton, 2010, p6

6   Landes, D., *The Wealth and Poverty of Nations,* Abacus, 1998, p *xx*

7   Brunner, K., Economic Inequality and the Quest for Social Justice, *Cato Journal,* Vol.7, No.1 (Spring/ Summer 1987), p157

8   Ferreira, F., Inequality as Cholesterol, *Poverty in Focus,* International Poverty Center, June 2007, p20

9   Bowles, S., H. Gintis, *The Inheritance of Inequality,* www.unix.oit. unmass.edu/bowles, p12

10 Babbage, C., *The Economy of Machinery and Manufactures,* 1832, para 4

11 Ibid,

12 Wrangham, R., and N. Conklin-Britain, Cooking as a biological trait, *Comparative Biochemistry and Physiology,* Part A 136, (2003), p41

13 Ibid, p38

14 Watson, P., *Ideas, A History From Fire to Freud,* Weidenfeld & Nicolson, 2005, p23

15 Credit Suisse, *Global Wealth Report,* Research institute, October 2010, p4

16 Davies, J., S. Sandstrom, A. Shorrocks, and E. Wolff, The Global Distribution of Household Wealth, *Poverty in Focus,* International Poverty Center, June 2007, p4

17 Paine, T., *Agrarian Justice,* Digital Edition, 1999, www.grundsky.dk, pp 17-18

18 Ibid, p11

19 Carnegie, A, *The Gospel of Wealth,* p2

20 Ibid, p3

21 Paine, T., *Agrarian Justice,* Digital Edition, 1999, by www.grundskyld. dk, p15

22 King Committee on Governance, *Draft Code of Governance, Principles for South Africa, 2009,* p12

23 Bergh, A., The Universal Welfare State: Theory and the Case of Sweden, *Political Studies,*2004, vol.52, p748

24 Kokko, A., *The Swedish Model,* Working paper No.2010/88, UNU-WIDER, pp 23-5

25 Swedish Tax Authorities, *2010, Taxes In Sweden, An English Summary of Tax Statistical Yearbook of Sweden,* p8

26 Kokko, A., *The Swedish Model,* Working paper No.2010/88, UNU-WIDER, p20

27 Richardson, G., Torsten Rudenschold, *Prospects: the quarterly review of comparative education,* UNESCO, vol.XXIV, no.3/4, 1994, p440

28 Kokko, A., *The Swedish Model,* Working paper No.2010/88, UNU-WIDER, p21

29 Quoted in p 24 of *Sweden after the Swedish Model, From Tutorial State to Enabling State,* Mauricois Rojas, TIMBRO, 2004

30 Ibid,

31 Quoted in Marching to Bismarck's Drummer: The Origin of the Modern Welfare State, by Richard Ebeling, *The FREEMAN: Ideas on Liberty,* December 2007, p4

32 Sinha, D., Family Planning Perspective in Swedish Community, *The Journal of Family Welfare,* Vol.49, no.2, December 2003, p 23

33 Ibid, p23

34 Ibid, p24

35 Magnusson, L., The Swedish Model in Historical Context, *Kobe University Economic Review,* 52, 2006, p6

36 Ibid, p6

37 Stein, P., Sweden: From Capitalistic Success to Welfare State Sclerosis, *Cato Institute Policy Analysis No.160,* Sept, 1991, p6

38 Maddison, A., *The World Economy: A Millennial Perspective,* OECD, 2001, p 28, table 1-3

39 Marcuss, R. D. & R. E. Kane, US National Income and Product Statistics, Born of the Great Depression and World War II, *Survey of Current Business,* February 2007, p33

40 Ibid, p34

41 Quoted in *The Pardee Papers/ No.4/ January 2009,* Beyond GDP, The Need for New Measures of Progress, p8

42 Commission on Growth and Development, *The Growth Report: Strategies for Sustainable Growth and Inclusive Development,* 2008, pp 13-14

43 Stiglitz, J. A. Sen and J. Fitoussi, *The Measurement of Economic Performance and Social Progress Revisited —Reflections and Overview,* http://www.stiglitz-sen-fitoussi.fr/documents/overview-eng.pdf, p13

44 Malthus, T., *An Essay on the Principles of Population,* London, Printed for J Johnson, in St. Paul's Church-Yard, 1798, p96

45 Nordhaus, W. and J. Tobin, Is Growth Obsolete? Cowles Foundation Paper 398, p4

46 Marshall, A., *Principles of Economics,* The Online Library Of Liberty Collection, 8th Edition, p28

Postscript: Reflections and Conclusion

Religion which is understood by everyone is useful to none. Is it the same with Economics?

— Anonymous

Looking at this short history of economics, we can see that the dominant influence of economic factors on human life is of recent origin. Three critical ideas brought about this change. Chronologically, the first of the three was the concept of title to property in the absence of possession; a distinctly human innovation. The royal grant of monopolies to trading companies in England is the second of the ideas. Quite unintentionally, this grant gave a latent sanction to the pursuit of an economic agenda, unmindful of the social costs. The third concept is also from England, the philosophy of utilitarianism. Utilitarianism provided a mechanism for converting qualitative factors like happiness into quantitative units of utility, setting the stage for material prosperity to emerge as the primary economic goal.

Connected with these ideas, three basic questions were debated among economists. All the three questions arose at around the same time, i.e. when the Industrial Revolution was in full swing. The first question relates to the nature of economics. Is it like a physical science with an universal and unalterable human motive of self-centred behaviour driving human action or is it a social science which assumes that human motives are malleable? The second question poses the conundrum of whether social welfare is a summation of individual welfare or whether individual welfare is derived from the common social welfare. The third and the final question relates to the advantage derived from choosing between free markets and a more restrained, socially conscious system of exchange of goods and services. While there is no settled answer to these questions, the dominant view in the last two decades favoured treating economics as a science, focused on realizing individual welfare through free markets.

The increased importance accorded to economics did result in many benefits, the biggest being material prosperity as evidenced by the quantity, quality and range of goods and services available. A resultant byproduct is the increasing longevity of the average human life. Just for a movement if we ignore the negative impact and focus on the positives, the increased prominence of economic aspects in the last sixty years has ensured that peace prevailed for the most part, and wars, when they did surface, were short and brought to an end quickly by businessmen playing a key role, driven by the financial losses they incurred.

Turning to the negative front, economics added many new challenges in human life, the biggest being growing inequality in wealth and income. The division of society into the rich and the poor is a distinct human invention, absent in the animal kingdom where only the strong and the weak exist. The singular focus on economic growth has also invited the dangers of environmental calamity due to over-exploitation of natural resources. The subtle but growing danger of that wealth and income inequality poses to our peaceful existence has suddenly come into public view with the 'Occupy Wall Street' movement rapidly spreading across the world. It appears that in the twenty-first century, the challenge of colonization will not be a political issue as it was in the twentieth century. With corporate influence pervading personal lives, it is directly taking on an economic colour even in democratic countries bypassing the political route that was essential for it to survive in the previous century.

Looking back, the economic history of the last millennium was shaped by the Black Death of 1348-50 in Europe, the Great Depression of 1930 in US and the institution of the 'Nobel' Prize in Economics in 1969. Likewise, the influence of ideas first expounded in *The Wealth of Nations* by Adam Smith, *Treatise on Political Economy* by Jean Baptiste Say and *The General Theory of Employment, Money and Interest* by John Maynard Keynes are still visible even today.

Turning to the future, it is exciting and engaging to speculate about which events will be the trigger and what ideas will provide the solution to the three major challenges of today: the growing income and wealth disparity, environmental degradation and economic colonization. History tells us that solutions arise in the geography where problems are most acutely felt. Perhaps this indicates that we need to look for answers in Asia or Latin America. Could the answer be some form of tax on inheritance that dilutes the concept of private property which not only funds the creation of a universal social security system but also latently promotes the concept of universal human fraternity by diluting the social acceptance of self-centred behaviour. I believe that a favorable environment for inheritance tax and universal social security system will be in place only when a more comprehensive measure of human welfare replaces the current position occupied by GDP to measure economic progress. Being an optimist, I believe that we will find answers sooner than later, and to me Utopia has only one meaning, that of an ideal place. I hope its second meaning as an elusive place will soon be consigned to history and has no practical use.

Appendix

The Sveriges Riksbank Prize in Economic Sciences in Memory of Albert Nobel was awarded:

In 1969, to <u>Ragnar Frisch and Jan Tinbergen,</u> for having developed and applied dynamic models for the analysis of economic processes.

Traditionally, economics was a literary discipline. It listed causes based on simple observation of casual connections. These two laureates developed **mathematical models** to replace the vague subjective observations by identifying mutual relationships between economic variables based on mathematical relationships.

Frisch built a mathematical model that simulated economic cycles. In his models, variations in investment and consumption under certain monetary policy constraints produced wave-like movements. These wave movements had lengths of four to eight years. Tinbergen built an econometric model structured around some fifty equations and determined coefficients with leads and lags to explain how an economy performed.

Their work was implemented in Sweden and Holland. Frisch's work influenced the system of national accounting and budgeting in Sweden. Tinbergen developed for Holland an econometric model for forecasting and planning economic policy.

Their work was expected to 'assist the poor countries of the world' develop.

In 1970, to <u>Paul A. Samuelson</u>, for the scientific work through which he developed static and dynamic economic theory and actively contributed to raising the level of analysis in economic science.

The development of economics as an analytical science took two distinct paths. The first was econometric models used for estimation and empirical applications, as pioneered by Frisch and Tibergen. The second path used econometric models in theoretical research that did not have immediate empirical applications.

Samuelson was recognized for his contribution in **rewriting parts of economic theory**, where he aligned analytical techniques with problems. His four major contributions cited in the prize presentation ceremony were:

1. **Correspondence Principle**: This principle bridged the static and dynamic analytical techniques. Economic theory had traditionally focused on equilibrium positions. Samuelson focused on how the economic system moves to stability after a disturbance. Thus he linked dynamic analytical techniques of studying disturbances and factors leading to stability to static analysis of equilibrium positions. This is called the Correspondence Principle.

2. **Revealed Preferences**: Traditional consumption theory started with the assumption that households had well-defined preferences among different consumer goods baskets. Based on this assumption, the impact of

changes in incomes and prices were derived by deductive methods. Samuelson observed household behaviour in choosing amongst different consumer goods baskets subsequent to changes in income and prices. He used these observations to validate theoretical conclusions.

3. **Superiority of free trade**: Benefits from international trade were well-known. It was also recognized that income among different groups in the country was redistributed by free trade. Samuelson showed that even after this redistribution, the country as a whole gained, as the losses suffered by certain groups were more than compensated by the amount gained by other groups.

4. **Turnpike theory**: This is based on the analogy of gaining access to an expressway, which can slow down speed, but the lost speed is more than regained once on the expressway. Samuelson outlined that the best path to maximum growth can involve lower consumption levels compared to the consumption levels both at the beginning and at the end.

In 1971, to <u>Simon Kuznets,</u> for his empirically-founded interpretation of economic growth which has led to newer and deeper insight into economic and social structures and process of development.

Kuznets' contribution was in quantifying with precision the size and changes in national income. He also explained the impact of qualitative changes in consumption and production on national income. He built models to **explain economic growth** over centuries, which also incorporated non-economic factors like population growth, technology, industrial structure and market forms.

Some of the concrete observations from his empirical study are:

1. Presence of long growth cycles of twenty-year-long periods, influenced by rate of population growth
2. Over decades, the propensity of households to save is amazingly stable
3. In the short-run, propensity to save varies with cyclic fluctuations

Increasing productivity of real capital used in production is seen over time. Technological progress, raising the quality of manpower, and structural changes in industry and commerce contribute to this. His study showed that in Sweden productivity increase was 13 times as much as it used to be over a hundred years and in Japan six times as much in the two decades after World War II.

In 1972, to <u>John R. Hicks and Kenneth J. Arrow,</u> for their pioneering contribution to general economic equilibrium theory and welfare theory.

In 1874, Leon Walrus had created an abstract model of an economy by quantifying different goods, their prices, and quantities, as well as how income generated in that economy will be distributed among different groups. Presented in the form of mathematical equations, it highlighted the inter-relationship between the different components of an economy. This was a major contribution that led to the development of the General Equilibrium theory in Economics. However these were in general terms that were not amenable to further analytical studies. The contributions from the two laureates made analytical studies on General Equilibrium theory possible.

Hicks developed a systematic model based on the behaviour of consumers and producers. This enabled an analysis of impacts coming from outside the economic system. Changes in harvest yields, consumer tastes and price expectations of business and their impact on prices, production, employment and interest rates could be studied. His models used theories of consumption and of capital based on profit maximization.

Arrow's contribution was on two fronts. He developed an **abstract economic model based on Set theory** which made further analysis of the General Equilibrium theory possible. Proving this theory required two assumptions: that firms maximize profits, and that individuals maximize utility. The second contribution was in his doctoral thesis. Arrow had asked the question, is it possible for a society to find acceptable, democratic rules for making a collective ranking of different alternatives in order of desirability? His answer was no. This was contrary to the accepted prevailing belief of the Welfare theory. With it he formulated the Impossibility theorem, which states that Economics can explain only individual choices but not social choices.

In 1973, to <u>Wassily Leonteif</u>, for the development of the input-output method and for its application to important economic problems.

An economy is an interrelated network of multiple industries that produce thousands of products, where one or more product goes into the production of other products. Leonteif constructed a mathematically and statistically rigorous model to study the **input-output implications of various industries** in the economy. This model helped analyze the impact of changes in volume and costs in different products and its impact on the overall economy. The model was used to study the impact of the following:

1. Effect of disarmament in United States after the Second World War and its impact on the US economy,
2. Effect of rearmament in United States for the Korean war and its impact,
3. The model can also be used to study the impact of oil price changes and its cascading effect in the economy.

The model developed is helpful not only for centrally-planned economies but also for market-driven economies by anticipating market movements without waiting for the events to unfold.

In 1974, to <u>Gunnar Myrdal and Friedrich August Von Hayek</u>, for their pioneering work in the theory of money and economic fluctuations and of their penetrating analysis of the interdependence of economic, social and institutional phenomena.

The two winners of the year worked in areas beyond 'pure economics'. Both the economists studied problems beyond the scope of the narrow economic framework, using economic models and techniques of analysis.

Myrdal studied the factors that contributed to the **prevailing state of the black population** in the United States and the possibilities for their development. He used economic equilibrium models and dynamic analysis of the cumulative processes that flow from disturbances. He showed that a large number of economic and social factors like education, health, living conditions, job satisfaction, discriminatory attitudes on the part of employers and trade unions, result in a vicious circle, making it impossible to identify any particular factors as final causes. The utility of his research is relevant to developing countries in areas like:

1. Character and causes of unemployment,
2. Nature of the inefficiency of farming,
3. The diffusion effects from industrial development in a given country, based on its cultural, social and economic conditions,
4. Importance of social discipline in an economy.

Hayek evaluated different economic systems and identified problems in the socialist central planning system and the value of prices as essential information carriers on cost and demand conditions in a market economy. He based his results on the criteria of efficiency in use of the knowledge and information contained in great masses of individuals and businesses. His work triggered extensive research in the area of **comparative economic systems.**

In 1975, to <u>Leonid Vitaliyevich Kantorovich and Tjallling C. Koopsman,</u> for their contribution to the theory of optimal allocation of resources.

Limited resources are a feature in all types of economies. Hence, optimum resource allocation in an economy is relevant to both socialistic and capitalistic economies for policy formulation. Two individuals working separately in two different types of economies arrived at the same solution to resolve this challenge.

Kantorovich was confronted with the problem of resource allocation in a factory to maximize production in the Soviet Union. He invented the **technique of Linear Programming** to solve it. A byproduct of this technique is the shadow price, which was used as accounting price. He subsequently applied this technique to macroeconomic problems of resource allocation in order to formulate a Theory of Optimum Planning for socialistic economies. He concluded that rational decentralized planning could be achieved in a socialistic economy using shadow price as the basis for profitability calculations.

Kantorovich opened a new school of thought among the socialist economists who recommended decentralized decision-making using shadow prices and unique interest rates.

In the 1940s, Koopsman working in the British Merchant Shipping Mission, Washington was confronted with the problem of optimally routing empty ships. He solved this problem using Linear Programming and shadow prices. He also extended the application of Linear Programming to macroeconomic problems. He saw resource allocation in a competitive economy as the output of a Linear Programming solution. He saw this solution as a basis for formulating a General Equilibrium Theory. This he articulated as 'Activity Analysis Theory', which used price as the link between Theory of Resource Allocation and General Equilibrium Theory.

This theory is useful in making policy decisions about allocation between investment and consumption, a decision that involves the choice of welfare between generations.

In 1976, to <u>Milton Friedman</u>, for his achievements in the field of consumption analysis, monetary history theory and for his demonstration of the complexity of stabilization policy.
Freidman challenged the current knowledge and assumptions about economic theory and provided new insights. A strong belief in the free market system combined with his negative bias towards government intervention played a critical role in his contribution.

Friedman brought back the focus to money and monetary policies that had lost ground with the advent of Keynesian economics with its sharp focus on fiscal policies in dealing with business cycles and inflation. He was the first to identify the lag effect between decisions and reactions in the economy in obtaining correct timing in stabilization policies for correcting business cycles. Another distinct contribution by Freidman was in the effect of trade-offs between unemployment and inflation rates. He showed that the trade-off between unemployment and inflation rates was only a temporary effect. Over the long run, i.e. beyond five years, unemployment below a structural equilibrium level leads to a cumulative rate of wage and price increase, primarily due to the role that expectations play.

On the theoretical front, Friedman distinguished between current annual income and permanent income. He identified based on empirical study that a larger amount of temporary income is saved compared to the proportion of permanent income saved.

His work, *A Monetary History of the United States 1867-1960* is a comprehensive historical-statistical output covering a whole range of developmental phases, institutional changes, contributions made by leading politicians and bankers, all with a balanced analysis.

In 1977, to <u>Bertil Ohlin and James E. Meade</u>, for their path-breaking contribution to the theory of international trade and international capital movements.

Ohlin studied international trade, a 'basic issue in the science of economics'. He provided a new explanation to the factors contributing to trade between countries by developing a theory called Heckscher-Ohlin theory (as an article written by Eli Heckscher provided the inspiration for it). This theory states that a country would export goods that use a factor of production which is in ample supply compared to its domestic demand. Illustrating this with the example of Australia and England, he explained that Australia, which had large quantity of land, would export wool, while England would export labour-intensive textiles. Based on the theoretical construct of this theory, he drew two conclusions. One, such trade is a substitute for the lack of international mobility of the factors of production and helps normalize the price for the factors of production and second, tariffs on labour-intensive goods protect the high wages in that country and, likewise, tariffs on capital-intensive goods provide an income distribution in favor of capital owners.

Meade also studied international trade by looking at the balance of payment position of a country. He showed how a country could achieve the seemingly conflicting objectives of full employment by promoting its exports, while at the same time handling a surplus balance of payment position, under certain specific conditions.

In 1978, to <u>Herbert A. Simon,</u> for his pioneering research into the decision-making process within economic organizations. The initial assumption made in economic theory is of firms working in a competitive market to maximize their profits. This assumption was soon rendered invalid, as firms grew in size and spread their operations across multiple countries. This led Simon to study the **decision making system in large commercial organizations.**

In his book *Administrative Behavior* published in 1947, he questioned the concept of a rational decision maker pursuing profit maximization as the goal, which is at the centre of Economics. He found that decisions were made in large organizations based on acceptable solutions to the multiple stakeholders and not necessarily the profit-maximizing choice. His insights provided an excellent foundation for empirical research.

In 1979, to <u>Sir Arthur Lewis and Theodore W. Schultz</u>, for their pioneering research into economic development with particular consideration of the problems of developing countries.

Lewis developed the **Escalator theory of growth**, of why some countries get on the escalator and walk, while other stand still on the escalator and some don't get on to the escalator at all. His analysis led him to discover two distinct models of economies. One, an economy based on subsistence-oriented agriculture with low growth and the second a market-oriented high-growth industrial economy that generates savings leading to capital formation. His analysis showed that the shift in labour from agriculture to manufacturing accelerated growth. His second observation was that while both the economies produced food, it was their second product that determined the terms of trade. He used the example of coffee for the agricultural economy and steel for the industrial economy and showed that under certain circumstances the terms of trade were determined by labour productivity in agriculture.

Schultz studied the relationship between **poverty and underdevelopment in agriculture**. He found that in the USA, the return on human capital, i.e. education, is higher than the return obtained on physical capital. In addition he studied agricultural development from multiple human angles.

Both focused their work on poverty elimination and development in underdeveloped economies.

In 1980, to <u>Lawrence R. Klein,</u> for the creation of econometric models and the application to the analysis of economic fluctuations and economic policies.

The Great Depression of the 1930s influenced the first phase of building economic models that studied economic cycles.

It influenced governments to collate and share additional economic data on a periodic basis with the general public. The post-war years saw the economy booming, which resulted in a change in focus of the objectives for which economic models were built. The new need was to forecast growth rates over the next few quarters if not a couple of years.

Klein developed a **macroeconomic model to generate economic growth forecasts**, which included the organizational institutions that could be used for policy consultations and also was able to make adjustments for global economic changes. This model helped analyze the socio-economic effects of political decisions on economic front. This helped answer the questions normally raised by mass media, consultants, decision makers in corporations and organizations both in administration and politics. His contribution included the 'Wharton model' and Project Link, which connected macroeconomic models of different countries, including Third World and Communist countries. Project Link helped refine the forecasts of international trade, capital movements and other economic fluctuations.

In 1981, to <u>James Tobin,</u> for his analysis of financial markets and their relations to expenditure decisions, employment, production and prices.
Tobin formulated the **risk theory for asset allocation** by individuals and institutions amongst cash, bank deposits, bonds, shares and physical assets. The individuals are expected to make their decision based on yield and risk. By accumulating the decisions of individuals, the demand and supply for various assets e.g. bonds and shares, is arrived at, which then can be used to explain interest rates and equilibrium prices. An important contribution made by him was in arriving at 'q' ratio, which

expresses the relationship between the market price of an asset and its replacement cost. He showed that if this ratio is below 1, then firms will acquire existing companies rather than building new assets.

In 1982, to <u>George J. Stigler,</u> for his seminal studies of industrial structures, market functioning and the causes and effects of public regulation.

Stigler bridged the gap between the theory of Economics and the market reality by developing two new areas of study – **Economics of Information and Economics of Regulation**. In the Economics of Information, he questioned the assumption made in economic theory of all participants in the market having perfect information. He noted that the cost of searching for and disseminating information showed that buyers normally neither can nor want to be fully informed. Lack of information resulted in price rigidity, price and quality differences and waiting times. Extending this concept to labour markets led to new insights on unemployment and inflation. He also studied the adjustment lags that hamper rapid movement of capital and labour from low profit industries to high profit industries. Based on empirical evidence, he found a new insight that adaptability to technological and market changes are more critical than exploiting the economies of scale.

Stigler also studied the feasibility of price cartels in creating monopolistic situations. He found price cartels are not effective as the cost of enforcing these agreements far exceeded any gains that would accrue to the participants. During the course of this study he found that legislation often achieved what market participants could not. Economic legislation often protected the interests of certain firms, industries and occupations, rather than the interest of the general public. Special lobby groups influencing legislation could have been a factor. His analysis led to new research in this area and opened up a new field, the Economics of Regulations.

In 1983, to <u>Gerard Debreu,</u> for having incorporated new financial methods into economic theory and for his rigorous reformulation of the theory of General Equilibrium.

In the eighteenth century, Adam Smith explained how the invisible hand operating through the self-interest of individuals brought the economy to a stable state of equilibrium, by regulating the activities of the producers and consumers by equating demand and supply. In the nineteenth century, Leon Walrus created a mathematical model to show how different markets for goods, services and factors of production in an economy came to a state of equilibrium, thereby formulating the General Theory of Equilibrium. While it was an abstract model, its practical application was questionable.

Debreu, along with Kenneth Arrow, developed the **Arrow-Debreu model** which showed that in reality multiple markets can reach a state of equilibrium under certain assumptions: that the firms in the economy work to maximize profits, and the individuals in the economy maximize their utility. Initially this was a theory that applied only to an economy with private enterprises. Later, Debreu expanded this theory to cover economies with public sectors and taxes in states of uncertainties. The IMF has applied the Arrow-Debreu model to economic systems to find solutions for problems faced by them.

The Arrow-Debreu model reaches equilibrium under two assumptions: 1) Competitive equilibrium exists if each person in the economy possesses some quantity of every good available for sale in that market; 2) Labour resources exist which are capable of being used in the production of desired goods or services.

In 1984, to <u>Richard Stone</u>, for having made fundamental contributions to the development of system of national accounts and hence greatly improved the basis for empirical economic analysis.

Stone was an assistant to John Keynes in the Treasury department of Great Britain during the World War II. Stone developed a **double entry system of accounting for National Income** by matching every item of income/expenditure with its opposite effect. For instance, household income with expenditure of the enterprise sector, national savings and investment. Thereby he created a system of cross-checks to provide accuracy while summing up numerous types of transactions. Soon his work was expanded to the international arena by the United Nations. All the work to implement this system of accounting for international arena was led by Stone. The benefit of this system of national accounting has accrued to all international organizations like UN agencies, OECD and the World Bank by providing a base for further analysis.

In 1985, to <u>Franco Modigliani,</u> for his pioneering analysis of saving and of financial markets.

Keynes, in his General Theory of Employment, had formulated his theory of savings based on empirical observations. He noted the proportion of income saved increases as the level of income increases. But in United States, the aggregate data collected did not reflect an increase in savings percentage with increase in income. This paradox became an object of study.

Modigliani, along with his student Richard Brumberg, formulated his new theory of savings based on **Life-cycle**

Hypothesis. They noted that savings were related not just to income, but was also related to wealth, expected future income and the age of the individual. The reason was that individuals saved for their retirement. The Life-cycle hypothesis theory of saving was applied in formulating social-insurance systems and the impact of budgetary deficits on various generations.

The other significant contribution made by Modigliani was the **Modigliani-Miller theorems**. In a pioneering study of corporate valuations, they concluded that the enterprise value of a company, (i.e.: the sum total of market capitalization and debt) would not change with change in debt levels, in a perfectly functioning financial market. Any increase in the debt level increased the risk of equity and thereby correspondingly reduced its value. They later extended this theory to show that dividends declared by a firm too would not affect its market value.

In 1986, to <u>James M. Buchanan Jr.</u>, for his development of contractual and constitutional bases for the theory of economic and political decision-making.
Buchanan developed the **concept of public choice**, which extended the domain of rationality considered in economic decision-making to the political sphere.

Exchanges in modern society are based on the voluntary exchange of property titles. Self-interest is the primary driver for these economic exchanges. Buchanan examined whether this self-interest was contained only within the economic sphere or did it also prevail in the political sphere. The prevalence of large budgetary deficits that benefit the current generation at the cost of the future generations was an illustration of self-interest extending to the political domain. Here, the current generation increased their self-interest at the cost of future generations who do not have a voice. Likewise, he noted that in legislations governing business, producers, being better organized, would lobby for more favourable decisions in contrast to the diffuse and unorganized consumers.

A critical extension of the public choice theory is in looking at the trade-offs involved in making political decisions. Buchanan quantified the issues involved in the trade-offs by quantifying on the one hand the high cost of obtaining unanimity with the risk of coercing the dissenters on the other hand. This research has led to a deep understanding of the issues involved in the rules and norms of social systems. This theory also helps integrate the economic and political decision making system within the legal-rule framework.

In 1987, to <u>Robert M. Solow,</u> for his contribution to the theory of economic growth.

Solow developed **a new model for understanding the complex economic growth process.** With a given technology, he noted that in the long run, capital investment per worker will be constant. This by inference means productivity per worker and real wages will be constant. In the short run, in a perfectly functioning market for labour and capital, as the interest rates decrease, firms will opt for a more capital-intensive model and when the interest rates increase, they will switch to a less capital-intensive model. However, in reality, technology is not constant. Therefore by inference, he arrived at the fact that it is technology that drives growth. He also identified that technological progress is embedded in capital goods, which was another significant contribution.

In 1988, to <u>Maurice Allais</u>, for his pioneering contributions to the theory of markets and effective utilization of resources. Adam Smith had identified the merits of the free market, when he pointed out that there was no contradiction in both the consumers and producers acting in their self-interest. Through the mechanism of price, both their interests were reconciled. This descriptive idea was translated mathematically by Leon Walrus, but that model could stand up to more rigorous examination. Vilferdo Pareto took the logic of free markets further when he identified 'Pareto optimality': the most optimal situation in an economy arising from the free voluntary exchange of goods and services.

Allais created strong **mathematical models to evaluate conditions under which social efficiency, stability and equilibrium can be achieved** in an economy with decentralized decision makers, i.e. in economy of markets. He also incorporated the impact of returns to scale in this economy by studying the impact of investments made in infrastructure.

In 1989, to <u>Trygve Haavelmo,</u> for his clarification of the probability theory, foundations of econometrics and his analysis of simultaneous economic structures.
Haavelmo was recognized for his **pioneering contribution to econometrics**, i.e. methods used to estimate and test quantitative economic relations. Economic analysis was limited by two major constraints – the formulation of testable theories and individual decisions affected by numerous interdependent factors.

Haavelmo showed that economic theories stated in probabilistic terms could be tested. In addition, he formulated a new method by which the problem of interdependency could be resolved by use of mathematical statistics. He developed a model that avoided the bias which arises in attempts to make isolated estates of relations in large interdependent models. The means he used was the simultaneous estimation of the entire model structure.

In 1990, to <u>Harry M. Markowitz, Merton H. Miller and William H. Sharpe,</u> for their pioneering work in the theory of financial economics.

The three together developed a **new field of Financial Economics and Corporate Finance**. Their efforts are to be seen in the context of the growing importance of financial markets for a modern economy.

Markowitz recognized the value of the trade-off between expected returns and variance of returns in taking investment decisions. In this process he showed that the risk of an investment could not be viewed in isolation, but as a contribution of each asset that made up the investment. He developed a model to construct an optimum portfolio by using a quadric programme.

Sharpe developed the Capital Asset Pricing Model (CAPM). The CAPM shows that the optimum risk portfolio of a financial investor depends only on the portfolio manager's prediction about the prospects of different assets and not on his own risk preference. This model showed how risk can be bought and sold, and hence how risk can be spread using capital markets.

Miller was recognized for his contribution to the modern theory of corporate finance along with Modigliani. Their contribution had two elements – in a perfect market the capital structure of a firm does not impact the enterprise value of the firm, i.e. the sum of debt value and market capitalization. The second contribution was on the impact of dividend payments on the market capitalization of the company.

In 1991, to <u>Ronald H. Coase,</u> for his discovery and clarification of the significance of transaction costs and property rights for the institutional structure and functioning of the economy.

Coase developed a framework to **explain the institutional structure in an economy.** He answered the question, why do firms exist? What purpose do they serve that individuals themselves cannot fulfill in an economy? He identified the transaction cost of contracting as a major factor that contributes to institutional structure. If the transaction cost of contracting is zero there would be no firms. Firms, or the institutional structure in an economy, are the result of a trade-off between the transaction cost of contracting and the disadvantages of administered prices. This new view provided tremendous insights into the study of markets.

Coase's second contribution was in viewing exchanges as changes in the ownership rights over goods and services. He examined judicial decisions in legal systems and concluded that it has implications only due to transaction costs. If there were no transaction costs, it would really not matter which way the court decided, as the party who benefits the most from the property will acquire it from the other, for a price, in the event the court does not grant them the right over it.

In 1992, to <u>Garry S. Becker,</u> for having extended the domain of microeconomic analysis to a wide range of human behaviour and interaction, including non-market behaviour.

Becker expanded the concept of rational behaviour in matters of economic choice to a **purposeful behaviour in wider spheres of human activity.** Using this new concept, he identified its application in multiple areas, including:

1. Investment in human capital: The impact of on the job training and education levels on the wage structure in society.

2. Change in the role of family: Viewing family as a 'small factory' producing services for its members, he explained the rise of special support institutions like schools and day-care centres to rising wages. As the wage level grew, there was a larger incentive for family members to work outside the household. This explanation provided an answer to the falling fertility rates in the advanced economies and the higher fertility rates in rural areas in comparison with urban centres.

3. In the area of crime and punishments he noted that more than the harshness of punishment it was the certainty of conviction that deterred crimes.

Turning his attention to the issue of discrimination on the grounds of gender and race in a society, he identified that the price was paid not just by the individual who faced the discrimination, but also by the discriminator in economic terms.

In 1993, to <u>Robert W. Fogel and Douglass C. North</u>, for having renewed research in economic history by applying economic theory and quantitative methods in order to explain economic and institutional change.

Both of them used new counterfactual alternatives to **analyze economic history in understanding profound changes** in the economy. They attempted to answer questions like what contributes to economic growth, and why some countries are rich while others are poor etc.

Fogel's study displaced the importance given to railways for economic growth in USA. This study later led to the questioning of many more economic growth stories linked to a 'great innovation'. In another important and controversial study he showed that slavery, despite its moral taint, was an efficient market solution. It did not collapse on its own. Ineffectiveness, unprofitability and the pre-capitalistic nature of the institution were the popular reasons attributed to its abolition. He disproved these by showing that only a political decision abolished it and it did not fall on its own inefficiencies.

North studied the period prior to the civil war in USA and the long periods of superior growth in Europe. He too concluded that technological innovation was overrated as a contributor to growth. Institutions played a more critical role in economic growth, he noted. He found that though inefficient, they were significant contributors to growth as they reduced uncertainty. He noted that institutions can be both an accelerator and an inhibitor to economic growth. To illustrate this he compared the relative performance of England with its free markets and property rights with France which had a more rigid institutional framework. This resulted in England growing ahead of France during the period immediately following the Industrial Revolution. Today, the same principle explains why countries outside North America and Western Europe have had a poorer growth record.

In 1994, to <u>John C. Harsanyi, John F. Nash Jr. and Reinhard Selten</u>, for their pioneering analysis of equilibria in the theory of non-cooperative games.

The world provides various situations of non-cooperative games, where the gain for one depends not just on their own decision but is equally dependent on the reactions of the counterparts. The three laureates, each individually contributing a part, provided a **framework for arriving at the optimal decision in non-cooperative game situations**.

Nash Jr. developed the concept of the Nash equilibrium, more popularly known as Game Theory. Harsanyi extended the concept further by looking at more realistic situations where the different decision makers had varying levels of information, i.e. situations of information asymmetry, as in markets. This situation prior to Harsanyi's contribution was considered an insurmountable problem, which he resolved. Selten further refined the range of solutions in these situations by eliminating the improbable though possible solutions with his concept of perfect equilibria.

In 1995, to <u>Robert E. Lucas Jr.</u>, for having developed and applied the hypothesis of rational expectations, and thereby having transformed microeconomic analysis and deepened our understanding of economic policy.
Lucas Jr. highlighted the dangers of using a statistical relationship uncritically to draw economic-policy conclusions. In his critique of this inference, he showed that individuals and firms were rational in behaviour and would adjust for this statistical expectation.

In the 1960s, the Philips curve was considered sacrosanct, backed by empirical proofs. It plotted the relationship between unemployment and inflation. One inference was that an increase in the inflation rate would promote employment and thereby reduce unemployment levels in an economy. As some countries in 1970s allowed inflation levels to rise, to their shock they found that the employment levels did not correspondingly increase. This was considered as proof of Lucas Jr.'s hypothesis of rational expectation. From this he showed that high inflation levels had no economic benefit, only large costs. With it the monetary authorities stopped stoking inflation to higher levels and started targeting low inflation rates.

In addition, Lucas Jr. highlighted that monetary and fiscal policies cannot be used to generate employment. Employment could be generated only by effecting structural changes to make labour markets and wage formation function more effectively.

In 1996, to <u>James A. Mirrlees and William Vickrey,</u> for their fundamental contributions to the economic theory of incentives under asymmetric information.

The laureates studied optimum decision-making under systems where there is asymmetric information among the different parties. In markets like insurance, credit and labour, and in income tax matters, one party has substantially more information than another. For instance, in insurance, the buyer of insurance is better informed about his or her condition or the condition of the assets, likewise the borrower in the credit market and the wage earner in the labour market. In income tax the reaction of the taxpayer to additional tax on income is similarly known only to the tax payer.

Vickrey found a methodology to identify the social opportunity cost of decisions in sealed bids auctions. As opposed to the highest bidder winning at their bid price, Vickrey proposed a new system of awarding the bid to the highest bidder, but at the second highest bid price. In this process, the real value of the bid to the participants would be known, as they would bid what it was worth to them, even as they only paid an amount lower than that, giving them an incentive to win. This method of bidding has relevance in auctions for government securities, air traffic concessions and band spectrum licenses in telecom. He also started working on a new model to determine income tax structure such that the tax system does not distort individual economic behaviour. Here the objective was to factor in the individual's choice, considering their productivity. While he made good progress he could not mathematically solve this complex model.

Twenty-six years later Mirrlees in 1970s solved this problem thereby identifying true individual preferences. He showed how contracts can be designed in a way that the principal's interests are taken into account by the agent. This contribution has important applications in many different areas where information asymmetry prevails.

In 1997, to <u>Robert C. Merton and Myron S. Scholes</u>, for a new method to determine the value of derivatives.

For the development of a new method to value one type of derivatives – the options. Options provide the holder with a right but not the obligation to either buy or sell a good at some point of time in future. Though this instrument was in existence for more than two millennia, a rationally-acceptable pricing model was not in place. The two laureates along with Fischer Black developed a method for valuing options, popularly called the 'Black-Scholes option pricing model'. In this model they overcame the challenge of measuring risk by using the volatility of asset prices. This pricing model led to an explosive growth in the use of derivatives in the last two decades.

In 1998, to <u>Amartya Sen,</u> for his contribution to welfare economics.

Changes in welfare in a country over time and comparison of welfare among different countries were not feasible under the utilitarian principle, which considered each individual with the ability to make a choice for the better. But comparisons of a society over time and point comparisons across different societies required common measures of welfare. In the absence of equality between individuals and similar conditions among countries this comparison was not feasible.

Studying the origin of famine, Sen found that considering the poor as one group was not meaningful as the imbalance between the needs and resources were evened out. Hunger is a sign of extreme poverty, and is most visible during a period of famine. Studying the famine in the Sahel region of Sahara in 1970s, he found the impact on nomadic herds was much more acute compare to that on non-nomadic farmers. As resources dwindled for both, the bargaining position of the herds reduced drastically compared to that of the farmers, leading to many deaths. Sen proposed new measures as indicators of welfare, income inequality and poverty, which have found extended use.

In 1999, to Robert A. Mundell, for his analysis of monetary and fiscal policy under different exchange rate regimes and his analysis of optimum currency areas.
Mundell developed a model for understanding the short term impact of changes in fiscal and monetary policies on domestic currency value with respect to foreign currencies. He, along with Fleming, developed a model, popularly known as the Mundell-Flemming model, in the 1960s when the fixed exchange rate scheme of the Bretton Woods system was in existence. Anticipating future developments, the model explains how the domestic currency value changes with changes in monetary and fiscal policy under both the fixed rate regime that was prevailing then and the floating rate regimes that came into existence following the collapse of Bretton Woods Agreement in 1971.

In 2000, to <u>James J. Heckman</u> for his development of the theory and methods for analyzing selective samples, and to <u>Daniel L. McFadden,</u> for his development of the theory and methods for analyzing discreet choice.

Both laureates worked on the analysis of micro data, which is involved in the study of individual decisions like number of hours worked, choice of occupation, place of residence, travel mode and choice of marital status and number of children.

Heckman developed models for handing selective samples in a statistically satisfactory way. McFadden developed a model for studying discreet choice. Both their contributions together created a new field of study – the New Economic theory of discreet choice. McFadden's work found application in the design of the Bay Area Rapid Transport System and in valuing the cost of oil spills.

In 2001, to <u>George A. Akerlof, A. Michael Spence and Joseph E. Stiglitz,</u> for their analysis of markets with asymmetric information.

The three laureates studied information asymmetry in markets and its impact on human welfare.

Akerlof studied the transactions between better informed players and the poorer informed ones. He found that sellers in many markets had better information than buyers. At any given price, a seller of high quality goods is less inclined to sell than a seller of low quality goods. Rational buyers anticipating this, suspect that the goods they are being offered are of inferior quality. This suspicion keeps the buyer away, pushing the prices further lower, which in turn further discourages the seller of high quality goods. This results in a situation of downward quality bias in markets, an adverse selection bias. In these situations, free markets do not work. Akerlof suggested that many market institutions had come up to prevent this process of adverse selection.

Spence studied the issue of how agents with superior information could credibly 'signal' their better information to the less informed. He noted that for the credibility to be retained, high quality sellers should adopt 'signals' that would be too expensive for low quality sellers to mimic. Some examples of high cost signaling he identified were expensive advertisement, guarantees and highly taxed dividends paid by companies.

Stiglitz and Michael Rothschild studied how the less informed agents can improve their position. They found that 'screening by self-selection' a good tool for less informed agents communicating their preference. In the example of insurance contracts with a menu of policies –low premium with high deductible and high premium with low deductible, – clients divided themselves into low risk clients and high risk clients by their choice of policies. High risk clients prefer the high premium low deductible, leaving the other choice to the low risk clients. Stiglitz studied the impact of asymmetric information in many other markets like credit, finance and labour markets.

In 2002, to <u>Daniel Kahneman,</u> for having integrated insights from psychological research into economic science, especially concerning human judgment and decision-making under uncertainty and to <u>Veron L. Smith,</u> for having established laboratory experiments as a tool in empirical economic analysis, especially in the study of alternate market mechanisms.

Economic theory assumes a rational, self-centred individual. This assumption has often been questioned, but without any empirical proof. The two laureates by their specially designed experiments provided that this assumption under uncertainty does not hold good.

Kahneman enriched economics with fundamental insights from cognitive psychology. One of the major observations he made were that individuals give equal credence to mean values from both large sample and small samples, while the theory of sampling shows that means derived from large samples are more probable. In the second observation, which is called the 'Prospect theory', he pointed out that individuals compare outcomes to a referenced level rather than to an absolute scale. This insight shows an individual's response can be biased with a judicious selection of reference level.

Smith examined the interactions among individuals in a market, in contrast to decision making by individuals studied by Kahenman. For the first time, Smith created models where experiments could be conducted to determine outcomes and compare them with alternatives available.

Both Kahneman and Smith contributed to expanding economics by introducing a new domain, Behavioural Economics.

In 2003, to <u>Robert F. Engle III,</u> for methods of analyzing economic time series with time varying volatility (ARCH) and to <u>Clive W.J. Granger,</u> for methods of analyzing economic time services with common trends (cointegration).

Engle III developed new methods for analyzing economic time series with varying volatility using ARCH. He noted that turbulent periods with high volatility in markets are followed by calmer periods. Prior to the advent of the ARCH method, forecasting based on these volatility patterns was not possible. With ARCH he created a new field called 'Financial

Econometrics'. This helps in computing volatility that measures risks and is used in solving hedging problems.

Granger studied the analysis of macroeconomic variables with complex interplay among them over time. For instance in the study of wealth, income and their impact on consumption, wealth fluctuates in short periods due to changes in share price and property values, while income fluctuations are over longer periods. Traditional statistical methods provide meaningful insights. Granger developed a model to separate the dynamics in an economic system into forces that generate adjustments to long-run equilibrium and forces that lead to short-run fluctuations using the concept of 'cointegration'.

In 2004, to <u>Finn E. Kydland and Edward C. Prescott,</u> for their contribution to dynamic microeconomics, the time consistency of economic policy and the driving forces behind business cycles.

The laureates working together provided **fresh insights into business cycles.** In the 1970s the prevailing explanation for business cycles was variations in demand. This concept was expounded by Keynes in the aftermath of the Great Depression. The prevailing explanation also held that government action could prevent business downturns.

These two laureates examined the 1970s situation of stagflation, i.e. high inflation coexisting with unemployment. According to the Keynesian theory such a situation could not exist. The government action to counter this situation was not met with the desired result. They found the reason for ineffective response was in the low credibility of government action, which they called 'time consistency problem'. The ability of the government to change their response was the inhibitor. Instead they advanced a new insight that effectiveness is enhanced by announcing a prior commitment to economic policy, which is credible and politically feasible. This led to a change from isolated policy responses to policy making institutions.

In addition, in 1982, Kydland and Prescott worked together to advance the view that it is the supply side that contributes to the business cycle – giving the example of crude oil supplies in 1970s and the slow down in the growth rate of technology. Their view was further reinforced in the 1990s, when the technology-based IT boom led the economic revival.

In 2005, to <u>Robert J. Aumann and Thomas C. Schelling</u>, for having enhanced our understanding of conflict and cooperation through game-theory analysis.

Both the laureates studied the conditions under which conflict and cooperation thrive in an economy. Aumann used a mathematical approach, while Schelling adopted an economic approach. Both studied the cooperation vs. conflict situation against the backdrop of the Cold War, when the threat of nuclear weapon usage was a real possibility.

Schelling found that under certain circumstances, by limiting their options one party can strengthen their position. His analysis showed that reducing the capability to defend would strengthen their position rather than limiting their capacity to attack. Likewise, uncertain and gradual retaliation is more credible than certain and immediate retaliation. These principles have application beyond defense, in analyzing competitive marketplaces. By investing in a large plant that increases the average cost of production, a player in the market could deter new competitors from entering, as they would be intimidated by the potential power to retaliate.

With his mathematical analysis, Aumann showed that Game Theory applied in long-running relationships with frequent interaction promoted cooperation. He was the first to conduct a full-fledged and formal analysis of long run relationships, also called Repeated Games, a facet of Game Theory.

In 2006, to <u>Edmund S. Phelps,</u> for his analysis of intertemporal tradeoffs in macroeconomic policy.

Phelps advanced knowledge on the trade-offs between unemployment and inflation. The prevailing view held that low unemployment and low inflation rates were incompatible. The Philips curve depicted the potential choices available based on the combination of the two factors. Phelps challenged this view when he introduced the element of inflation expectation. He introduced the view that individuals and firms decide based on the future expectation of prices and brought in the third element of inflation expectations into the two-factor analysis of unemployment and inflation. He held that in the long run, when the inflation expectation becomes inflation, the relationship between inflation and unemployment is ended. In such a situation, unemployment in the long run is determined by how the labour market and other markets function. Thus, any stabilization policy can only influence short-run unemployment and not long-run unemployment.

High inflation coexisting with high unemployment in the 1970s proved his hypothesis. A corollary of his hypothesis was how short-run economic trade-off decisions can influence the future possibilities of unemployment and inflation. This new insight prompted better understanding of the capital formation process in the areas of decisions to save and invest by parents and their influence on the next generation. Phelps extended this concept from physical capital to human capital when he studied investments made in education and research. His analysis showed that economic growth was influenced not just by the growth in educational level but was also dependent on the actual level of education at any point of time.

In 2007, to <u>Leonid Hurwicz, Eric S. Maskin and Roger B. Myerson,</u> for having laid the foundations of mechanism design theory.

In an economy, multiple transactions take place outside the markets. This is especially true where the buyers and sellers do not reach a conclusion on the price, i.e. how to share the cost or benefits of that transaction. This typically happens when information on the benefits and costs are not known to the other party.

Mechanism design theory outlines the process by which non-market transactions can be regulated to the optimal benefit. It consists of three elements

1. First, predict the behaviour of both the buyer and seller under a given set of rules
2. Using Game theory, evaluate the consumption, production and environmental stress as per the predicted behaviour
3. Develop a mechanism considering the behavioural implications that best meet the goal.

Hurwitz viewed the economy as an information system that allocates resources based on messages transmitted between agents. This view enabled the notion of 'incentive compatibility.'

Maskin evolved the Implementation theory that separated inferior equilibria from the desired ones.

Myerson developed the mechanism design theory to games of incomplete information, i.e. where an agent does not know the cost of other agents.

In 2008, to <u>Paul Krugman</u>, for his analysis of trade patterns and location of economic activity.

Krugman identified a set of two principles that had applications in two distinct fields – international trade and economic geography – to explain the two critical emerging trends, of growth in international trade as a percentage of GDP and increasing urbanization.

Krugman in 1979 explained why trade among countries with identical characteristics in similar products occurred. For instance, why does Sweden export Volvo and Saab cars to Germany while at the same time it imports Mercedes and Volkswagen cars from Germany? He noted that the producers were driven by economies of scale to set up large plants, while the consumer wanted variety. This for the first time explained the prevailing international trade flows of similar goods exchanged. The prevailing trade theories had only explained trade in different categories of goods among countries.

Twelve years later, Krugman expanded his research to explain the growing attraction for urbanization and the rural decline. Using the same two principles of economies of scale and customer preference for variety, he noted that cities optimized transportation costs, thereby becoming an attractive point for both producers and consumers to converge, explaining the economic rationale for urbanization.

In 2009, to <u>Elinor Ostrom</u>, for her analysis of economic governance especially the commons and to <u>Oliver E. Williamson</u>, for his analysis of economic governance especially the boundaries of the firm.

The two laureates were recognized for their contribution to **understanding institutional innovations** essential for realizing human welfare from technological innovations.

Ostrom studied the system of managing common properties like lakes, woods, pastures and groundwater. Conventional wisdom held that private ownership or government regulations were the best management solution. She instead discovered that rational usage was only a part of the solution. The more important part was user participation in creating, monitoring and enforcing the rules of usage.

Williamson studied why some transactions take place within an organization, while other similar transactions take place between firms in the marketplace. He discovered that it was not efficiency, as was commonly believed, which regulated this process, but the more human aspect of conflict of interest. His study provided deep insights into what types of decisions should be centralized and what others should be left to be decided by voluntary agreements.

In 2010, to <u>Peter A. Diamond</u>, for his contribution to the fundamental theory of markets by focusing on the impact of search costs and to <u>Dale T. Mortensen and Christopher A. Pissarides</u>, for developing the DMP Model based on search costs to explain the relationship between unemployment and vacancies in labour markets.

The Classical view holds that in perfect markets buyers and sellers find each other without incurring additional costs. However in reality this is not the case, as buyers and sellers incur search costs. The search cost is the highest in markets for employment and housing.

In 1971 Diamond published a paper in which he quantified the impact of markets with search costs. He concluded that in markets with search costs equilibrium prices are equal to the prices which a monopolist would fix in a market without search costs. Subsequent research in this area threw up an interesting finding. In unregulated markets with search costs the outcome may not be efficient. This is due to the fact that multiple outcomes are possible in these markets of which only one is efficient. This research provided a basis for government intervention in markets to promote efficient outcomes.

Mortensen and Pissarides developed a model called the Diamond-Mortensen-Pissarides Model to analyze the impact of search costs in labour markets. The model takes into account the activities of the unemployed, recruitment behaviour of firms and wage formation. The model can be used to analyze the average duration of unemployment spells, number of vacancies and real wages. It provides an explanation for the Beveridge Curve, which traces the relationship between labour market fluctuation from high unemployment and few vacancies to low unemployment and many vacancies. When vacancies and unemployment move in tandem, it provides insights into the efficiency of labour markets and structural changes in the economy.

In 2011, to <u>Thomas J. Sargent,</u> for studying how the effects of *systemic policy shifts* spread through the economy using macroeconomic models and to <u>Christopher A. Sims</u>, for studying how *economic shocks* affect the working of an economy using macroeconomic models.

The work of the two economists is complementary. Both relied on the fact that private and public agents look ahead and are influenced by expectations. Both used historical macroeconomic data to analyze the relationship between different macroeconomic variables. While Sargent analyzed the impact of systemic policy shifts like changes in interest rate or tax rate, Sims analyzed the impacts of economic shocks like oil price changes.

Sargent constructed a mathematical model of the economy using known relationships between macroeconomic parameters. He then solved this model for known changes to validate it. Historical data was used in the model to identify fundamental parameters that do not change due to systemic policy shifts.

Sims, on the other hand, constructed a mathematical model of the economy using Vector Auto-Regression. Using this model he developed a method to identify economic shocks as distinct from policy induced changes. He then used the impulse-response analysis to identify the impact of the economic shocks on other macroeconomic variables.

Their combined contribution forms the basic foundation for modern macroeconomic analysis.

Annexure

			Classification of the Winners of the Sveriges Riksbank Prize in Economic Sciences in Memory of Albert Nobel		
Sl no	Year	Winner	For	Subject	Classification
1	1969	Ragnar Frisch	Mathematical Modeling of an economy	Macroeconomic modelling	New Models
2	1969	Jan Tinbergen	Mathematical Modeling of an economy	Macroeconomic modelling	New Models
3	1970	Paul A. Samuelson	Lifetime contribution	Economic Theory	Lifetime
4	1971	Simon Kuznets	Model to explain economic growth	Macroeconomic modelling	New Models
5	1972	John R. Hicks	Model to link real economy with monetary economy	Macroeconomic modelling	New Models
6	1972	Kenneth J. Arrow	Economic model for analyzing General Equilibrium theory	Macroeconomic modelling	New Models
7	1973	Wassily Leonteif	Input-output implications of various industries	Macroeconomic modelling	New Models
8	1974	Friedrich August von Hayek	Comparative Economics	Market / Property Rights	New Insights

Classification of the Winners of the Sveriges Riksbank Prize in Economic Sciences in Memory of Albert Nobel					
Sl no	Year	Winner	For	Subject	Classification
9	1974	Gunnar Myrdal	Poverty & discrimination among Negros	Poverty & Human Welfare	New Insights
10	1975	Leonid Vitaliyevich Kantorovich	Linear Programming for resource optimization	New Techniques / Tools	New Models
11	1975	Tjailling C. Koopsman	Linear Programming for resource optimization	New Techniques / Tools	New Models
12	1976	Milton Friedman	Lifetime contribution	Market / Property Rights	Lifetime
13	1977	Bertil Ohlin	Factor intensity theory for international trade	International trade	New Hypothesis
14	1977	James E. Meade	Conditions for achieving full employment & surplus balance of payment	International trade	New Hypothesis
15	1978	Herbert A. Simons	Decision making in large firms not for optimizing profits	Market / Property Rights	New Hypothesis

Classification of the Winners of the Sveriges Riksbank Prize in Economic Sciences in Memory of Albert Nobel

Sl no	Year	Winner	For	Subject	Classification
16	1979	Sir Arthur Lewis	Escalator Theory of Growth	Economic Growth	New Hypothesis
17	1979	Theodore W. Schultz	Return on investment in education & agriculture	Poverty & Human Welfare	New Hypothesis
18	1980	Lawrence R. Klein	First model to forecast growth instead of analyzing growth	Macroeconomic modelling	New Models
19	1981	James Tobin	Risk theory for Asset Allocation	Financial Markets	New Hypothesis
20	1982	George J. Stigler	Study of Industrial structure & Markets	Market / Property Rights	New Hypothesis
21	1983	Gerard Debreu	Economic model for analyzing General Equilibrium theory	Macroeconomic modelling	New Models
22	1984	Richard Stone	Double entry system for National Accounting	Macroeconomic modelling	New Models
23	1985	Franco Modigliani	Corporate Valuation and impact of debt financing	Financial Markets	New Hypothesis

Classification of the Winners of the Sveriges Riksbank Prize in Economic Sciences in Memory of Albert Nobel					
Sl no	Year	Winner	For	Subject	Classification
24	1986	James M. Buchanan	Public Choice theory	Economic Theory	New Hypothesis
25	1987	Robert M. Solow	Understanding Growth Models	Economic Growth	New Models
26	1988	Maurice Allais	Mathematical model to show superiority of market economy	Market / Property Rights	New Models
27	1989	Trygve Haavelmo	Contribution to Econometrics	New Techniques / Tools	New Models
28	1990	Harry M. Markowitz	Portfolio Theory	Financial Markets	New Hypothesis
29	1990	Merton H. Miller	Corporate Valuation and impact of debt financing	Financial Markets	New Hypothesis
30	1990	William H. Sharpe	CAPM Model	Financial Markets	New Models
31	1991	Ronald H. Coase	Institutional Structure & Property rights	Market / Property Rights	New Hypothesis

Classification of the Winners of the Sveriges Riksbank Prize in Economic Sciences in Memory of Albert Nobel					
Sl no	Year	Winner	For	Subject	Classification
32	1992	Garry S. Becker	Analyzing purposeful behavior in human activity	Market / Property Rights	New Hypothesis
33	1993	Robert W. Fogel	New insights into Economic History	Economic Growth	New Insights
34	1993	Douglass C. North	New insights into Economic History	Economic Growth	New Insights
35	1994	John C. Harsanyi	Game Theory with information asymmetry	New Techniques / Tools	New Models
36	1994	John F. Nash Jr.	Nash equilibrium in Game Theory	New Techniques / Tools	New Models
37	1994	Reinhard Selten	Eliminating improbable outcomes in Game Theory	New Techniques / Tools	New Models
38	1995	Robert E. Lucas Jr.	Extending Rational expectation to macro economics	Macroeconomic modelling	New Insights

Classification of the Winners of the Sveriges Riksbank Prize in Economic Sciences in Memory of Albert Nobel

Sl no	Year	Winner	For	Subject	Classification
39	1996	James A. Mirrlees	Mathematical model to compute social opportunity cost of decisions	Financial Markets	New Insights
40	1996	William Vickrey	Methodology to identify social opportunity cost of decisions	Financial Markets	New Insights
41	1997	Robert C. Merton	Valuing derivatives	Financial Markets	New Models
42	1997	Myron S. Scholes	Valuing derivatives	Financial Markets	New Models
43	1998	Amatya Sen	Contribution to Welfare economics	Poverty & Human Welfare	New Insights
44	1999	Robert A. Mundell	Model to analyze impact of fiscal and monetary policy changes in an economy	Macroeconomic modelling	New Models
45	2000	James J. Heckman	Analysis of Microdata analysis	Economic Theory	New Models
46	2000	Daniel L. McFadden	Analysis of Microdata analysis	Economic Theory	New Models

Classification of the Winners of the Sveriges Riksbank Prize in Economic Sciences in Memory of Albert Nobel					
Sl no	Year	Winner	For	Subject	Classification
47	2001	George A. Akerlof	Evolution of market institutions as an answer to asymmetric information	Market / Property Rights	New Hypothesis
48	2001	A. Michael Spenser	How agents with superior information can signal in markets	Market / Property Rights	New Hypothesis
49	2001	Joseph E. Stiglitz	How less informed agents can improve their position	Market / Property Rights	New Hypothesis
50	2002	Daniel Kahneman	Assumption of rational behaviour under uncertainity invalid	Economic Theory	New Insights
51	2002	Veron L. Smith	Created models to study human behaviour	Economic Theory	New Insights
52	2003	Robert F. Engle III	Create a new field of financial econometrics with ARCH	Financial Markets	New Models
53	2003	Clive W. J. Granger	Cointegration for analyzing forces that influence different time periods	Macroeconomic modelling	New Models

Classification of the Winners of the Sveriges Riksbank Prize in Economic Sciences in Memory of Albert Nobel					
Sl no	Year	Winner	For	Subject	Classification
54	2004	Finn E. Kydland	New insights into Business cycle analysis & identified the time consistency problem	Macroeconomic modelling	New Insights
55	2004	Edward C. Prescott	New insights into Business cycle analysis & identified the time consistency problem	Macroeconomic modelling	New Insights
56	2005	Robert J. Aumann	Understanding of conflict and cooperation through game theory analysis	Economic Theory	New Insights
57	2005	Thomas C. Shelling	Understanding of conflict and cooperation through game theory analysis	Economic Theory	New Insights
58	2006	Edmund S Phelps	Analysis of Intertemporal tradeoffs in macroeconomic policy	Macroeconomic modelling	New Insights
59	2007	Leonid Hurwicz	Mechanism Design Theory to regulate non market transactions	Market / Property Rights	New Hypothesis

<table>
<tr><td colspan="6">Classification of the Winners of the Sveriges Riksbank Prize in Economic Sciences in Memory of Albert Nobel</td></tr>
<tr><th>Sl no</th><th>Year</th><th>Winner</th><th>For</th><th>Subject</th><th>Classification</th></tr>
<tr><td>60</td><td>2007</td><td>Eric S. Maskin</td><td>Mechanism Design Theory to regulate non market transactions</td><td>Market / Property Rights</td><td>New Hypothesis</td></tr>
<tr><td>61</td><td>2007</td><td>Roger B. Myerson</td><td>Mechanism Design Theory to regulate non market transactions</td><td>Market / Property Rights</td><td>New Hypothesis</td></tr>
<tr><td>62</td><td>2008</td><td>Paul Krugman</td><td>New insights into the reasons for growing International trade & Urbanization</td><td>International trade</td><td>New Insights</td></tr>
<tr><td>63</td><td>2009</td><td>Oliver E. Williamson</td><td>Rational for Intra-firm and inter-firm transactions</td><td>Market / Property Rights</td><td>New Insights</td></tr>
<tr><td>64</td><td>2009</td><td>Elinor Ostrom</td><td>Improved governance system for managing Common goods</td><td>Poverty & Human Welfare</td><td>New Insights</td></tr>
<tr><td>65</td><td>2010</td><td>Peter A. Diamond</td><td>Contribution to the fundamental theory of markets by focusing on impact of search cost</td><td>Markets/ Property Rights</td><td>New Insights</td></tr>
</table>

Classification of the Winners of the Sveriges Riksbank Prize in Economic Sciences in Memory of Albert Nobel					
Sl no	Year	Winner	For	Subject	Classification
66	2010	Dale T. Mortensen	Developed DMP Model based on search costs to explain relationships in labour markets	Market / Property Rights	New Model
67	2010	Christopher A. Pissarides		Market/ Property Rights	New Model
68	2011	Thomas J. Sargent	Studied how the effects of systemic policy shifts spread through the economy using macroeconomic systems	Macroeconomic Modeling	New Insights
69	2011	Christopher A. Sims	Studied how economic shocks affect the working of an economy using macroeconomic models	Macroeconomic Modeling	New Insights

Acknowledgements

I have often heard the saying 'ignorance is bliss'. Till recently I did not realize its implications. Had I known four years back what I know today, I would not have picked the history of Economics as a topic to write about. With hindsight I can see that the vast terrain, multiple contours and different perspectives would deter the wise, but not the ignorant or the passionate with time to explore.

Without the time to explore, this book would not even have begun. My extreme gratitude goes to Mr Azim Premji and Mr Suresh Senapaty of Wipro for providing me with a flexible work arrangement that gave me the time to explore my passion. In addition, I would like to offer my special thanks to Mr Premji for writing the Foreword to the book. Our most distinguished Josephite colleague Rahul Dravid readily agreed to endorse this book. My special thanks go to him for supporting a fellow Josephite.

I am blessed to have a circle of friends who are voracious readers and spared time from their busy schedules to read the manuscript chapter by chapter as it was written and refined over four years. My heartfelt thanks go to Anurag Behar, Joseph George, Kumar Alok, Lakshminarayana, Narayan P.S., Pavan Rao, Ravi Menon, Sreekanth Sreedharan and Veena Padmanabhan for sparing their valuable time and providing me with their incisive comments.

As the manuscript reached the halfway mark, I reached out to subject matter experts to seek their guidance. Their immediate response and proactive support was, to say the least, encouraging and it impelled me to push ahead with vigour. Prof. Vijay Shankar

Vyas, Prof. Narayana and Prof. Mahadevan in particular went through the manuscript and provided me valuable guidance, while Prof. Desphande of the Institute of Social and Economic Change and Prof. Rupa Chanda of the Indian Institute of Management, Bangalore provided me with an opportunity to present my nascent ideas to their knowledgeable team for critique. With humility I wish to acknowledge their generosity in providing me with an audience and encouragement.

Authors know the gap between a manuscript and a book is wide, and for many too wide to cross. My friend, Radha Radhakrishnan, put me in touch with Mr Chapal Mehra of Westland who, to my good fortune, liked the topic and commissioned the book. In his hands the manuscript underwent rigorous scrutiny from multiple angles, educating me in the process of writing a book like no school can. In Ms. Shalini Krishan, the editor of the book, I found a refined communicator picking words like a jeweller selects gems and illuminating arguments by cutting the flab and sharpening the focus. But for these three, there would be no book, only a manuscript.

Four years is a long gestation time. The support I received from my close friends and family members was unwavering even as the scheduled due date was deferred multiple times. Moods swing with the pace of progress, and bearing the brunt of this was my wife, Rajeswari, and our son, Manu Jagan, who patiently put up with my quirky ways, even as they prodded, pushed and encouraged me to complete the book. Words are inadequate to express my true feelings for their support.

Only my name is on the cover, which reflects the limitations of this book. Credit for much of what is good in the book goes to those named here and all the shortcomings, to yours faithfully.

9 789360 456702